W9-DEL-407

Your

Career

Planner

Eighth Edition

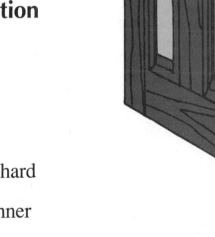

David Borchard

Cheryl Bonner

Susan Musich

 KENDALL/HUNT PUBLISHING COMPANY
4050 Westmark Drive   Dubuque, Iowa 52002

Book Team
Chairman and Chief Executive Officer   Mark C. Falb
Vice President, Director of National Book Program   Alfred C. Grisanti
Editorial Development Supervisor   Georgia Botsford
Developmental Editor   Tina Bower
Vice President, Production Editorial   Ruth A. Burlage
PrePress Manager   Kathy Hanson
Production Editor   Carrie Maro
Permissions Editor   Colleen Zelinsky
Cover Design Manager   Jodi Splinter
Cover Designer   Deb Howes
Senior Vice President, College Division   Thomas W. Gantz
Vice President and National Field Manager   Brian Johnson
Managing Editor, College Field   Paul Gormley

Previously entitled *Your Career: Choices and Changes*

Copyright © 1980, 1982, 1984, 1988, 1992, 1995, 1999, 2002 by Kendall/Hunt Publishing Company

ISBN 0-7872-8189-1

All rights reserved. No part of this publication may be reproduced,
stored in a retrieval system, or transmitted, in any form or by any
means, electronic, mechanical, photocopying, recording, or otherwise,
without the prior written permission of the copyright owner.

Printed in the United States of America
10   9   8   7   6   5   4   3   2   1

CONTENTS

ABOUT THE AUTHORS

David Borchard, Ed.D., NCC is a professional counselor/educator with over 25 years of experience in career/life planning as a career service center manager, a college educator, a career counselor, a writer, and an organizational career management consultant. Dr. Borchard specializes in career development, leadership assessment, and designing careers and lifestyles for the 21st century. He has taught graduate-level career development courses at The Johns Hopkins University and consulted with organizations such as the U.S. Department of Education, Social Security Administration, Office of Personnel Management, the Veterans Administration, several Maryland Government agencies, AARP, AT&T, the International Monetary Fund, the Public Broadcasting System, and Fairfax County Government. Over the past several years, he has been working with World Bank staff helping them redirect their careers for employment in 21st century's knowledge era. He has written high-visibility articles on leading-edge issues in career/life development and created career assessment resources such as Life Directions Profiler and the Internet-based Career Passion Revealer. Dave, a Myers Briggs INFP, spends leisure time rock gardening, canoeing on the Potomac River, and walking his dogs in the "almost heaven" countryside of West Virginia.

Cheryl Bonner, M.Ed., NCC has been in higher education for almost 20 years, with the majority of that time spent in career development. For the past eleven years she has been the Coordinator of Career Development at Bucks County Community College where she has taught career decision making courses and recently developed the course to be taught "campus free" to distance learners. As past president of the Middle Atlantic Career Counseling Association, she has had the opportunity of being a part of a team of career experts who have developed conferences to provide counselors in education, government and industry with state of the art career skills. Originally trained to be a special education teacher through her undergraduate education, she never left her first love of teaching. She is a frequent speaker at conferences and training events on the topics of career, life planning, mission, and calling. She is also an adjunct professor at both the undergraduate and graduate levels.

Cheryl is an ENFP who loves to be involved in many things and projects at once. She happily enjoys dabbling in many things, not needing to be proficient in all of them. Realizing that life cannot be satisfied just in the worker role, she is an adult education facilitator at her church, an advisor to a student club on campus, a photographer and a learner of new things. During her rare free time, she can be found with husband Bill working on their home and garden, strolling along the nearest beach, wandering through a park or exploring a new town.

Susan Musich, M.Ed., GCDF, is an international career consultant and a certified Global Career Development Facilitator. Susan's career has focused on both electronic career planning and job searches and the career transitions of professionals relocating to a different country. Susan coaches individuals and consults with international organizations, including the World Bank Group, the International Monetary Fund, the Inter-American Development Bank and the U.S. State Department. She is co-author of a book on the electronic job search process, *SAMS Teach Yourself Today e-Job Hunting*, published by Macmillan USA, 2000. Previously, she worked for the Peace Corps as the director of their career and transition services. There she authored several career and transition books for returning Peace Corps volunteers. Susan is the owner and managing editor of **www.CareerKiosk.org** Susan is an ENFP who enjoys creative brainstorming, training and writing. She continually strives to develop the I, S, T, and J in her to create balance and harmony in her life—both personal and professional.

LIST OF FIGURES

LIST OF TABLES

ACKNOWLEDGMENTS

This book is built upon the foundation of decades of groundbreaking work from countless numbers of professionals laboring in the field of what has come to be called career and life planning. It's a relatively new field, which came into existence early in the twentieth century with the pioneering work of Frank Parsons. As far as we know, he was the first to emphasize the need in career planning of knowing yourself, knowing the job requirements, and exercising "true reasoning" in fitting the two together. Career and life planning has been greatly enriched since then theoretically and experientially by the scholarly work of a great many people, but especially by Donald Super, who realized the relationship that exists between occupational choice and stages of self-concept development. John L. Holland's theory of personality-related interest patterns has had a powerful influence upon the field in relating self-assessment and occupational environments. We are especially grateful for the groundbreaking work of the following individuals and acknowledge their contributions to the self-understanding, career life planning, and cogent decision making that forms the context and content of this book:

- ☑ Drs. E. K. Strong and John L. Holland for their work in personality style assessment and linking motivational interests to appropriate occupational environments.

- ☑ Dr. Carl Jung for his innovations in psychological type and to Katharine Briggs and Isabel Briggs Myers for translating Jung's work into a useful assessment inventory in the form of the very popular Myers-Briggs Type Indicator (MBTI).

- ☑ Dr. Abraham Maslow for his work in motivation and personality and in helping us understand the hierarchical nature of human needs.

- ☑ John Crystal for his work in transferable skills assessment and Richard N. Bolles for popularizing Crystal's work. We also acknowledge Bolles for bringing career and life planning to the general public. His book, *What Color Is Your Parachute,* has become an enduring classic in the field, that along with his other writings and teachings has helped achieve a visible identity for the career/life planning field. We are also indebted to Dick for his generous permission to use his ideas and his transferable skills assessment in the chapter on identifying your skills.

- ☑ Ned Herrmann for his work in translating the insights of recent brain research into the Herrmann Brain Dominance Inventory. We are especially indebted to Mr. Herrmann for consent in the use of his ideas and concepts in the thinking style materials found in Chapter 4 of this book.

- ☑ Drs. Frederick Hudson and William Bridges for their work and insights on understanding and coping with life and career transitions. This is especially important knowledge in today's fast-changing workplace where career, job, and life change have become an ongoing process.

- ☑ Dr. Sidney Simon for his work, writings, and teachings in values clarification.

In this 8th edition of the book we are sad to say goodbye to two career counseling colleagues and authors who have been instrumental in the development and evolution of this book over the past twenty-some years of its history. Thank you John Kelly and Nancy Pat Weaver for the many hundreds of hours of work, experience, love, and devotion that you have contributed to this project in years past. We shall miss you and shan't forget your efforts and your nurturing support in bringing this publication to its current stage of evolution.

We are also delighted to welcome onboard two new authors to the newest manifestation of this book. Welcome to Susan Musich and Cheryl Bonner. Your professional career development expertise and extensive experience are welcome contributions to this work in progress. We also must acknowledge the contributions from dozens of colleagues and hundreds of students and adults whose input to this book has kept us on our toes and pressed up tight against the learning curve. We especially want to acknowledge Mary Multer Green for her exceptional editorial input in years past and to Fontelle Gilbert, a long-time colleague who has supplied ideas galore and input aplenty, and been a source of extraordinary support in all aspects of the book's progress over the years. Without the contributions of those we have acknowledged here and so many more too numerous to name, this book would be nothing more than a good idea whose time had yet to arrive.

INTRODUCTION

Success in the knowledge economy comes to those who know themselves—
their strengths, their values, and how they best perform."
—Peter F. Drucker, "Managing Oneself"
The Harvard Business Review, March–April 1999

CAREER/LIFE PLANNING IN THE KNOWLEDGE ERA

Searching for a satisfying career is a complex and difficult undertaking whether you're doing it for the first time or in the process of seeking a career change. The task is challenging even for the savviest of decision makers. There are at least three reasons why this is so. The first is that you are attempting to make objective choices about outer world options from the subjective domain of "the self." It is unlikely that any but the very lucky can find a satisfying career without first knowing him/herself. And since, at the self level, you are one vast realm of psychological subjectivity, understanding yourself does not come easily. Of course, you can become aware of your behavior through the mirror of those who know you and are forthright enough to report on your observable behavior. While such knowledge is extremely useful in effective self-management, how much help is it in making career-relevant decisions? It's not your behavior that makes your career and life choices—it's what's behind the behavior. And what's behind, under and, around your behavior is the self, the mysterious inner realm of emotions, cognition, needs, values, and inclinations. Just try to put your finger on the "self" or even to see it in a mirror.

The second dimension of complexity that you must contend with in career choice is discovering your available options. Options exist in what is euphemistically referred to as the "world of work." What is the world of work? Where is it? And how do you know where you might fit in nicely (and, we might add, get paid well financially and psychologically, in the process)? The truth is that careers are carried out in the workplace, and these tend to be places like businesses, organizations, hospitals, governments, the corner bar, and that little dotcom down the street (which probably recently went out of business). The workplace is immense, it is amorphous, and it's changing rapidly.

Change is the third element of complexity in today's career-choice challenge. The workplace is changing at a depth and breadth that is unprecedented in human history. Futurists have been telling us things like:

- ☑ all of the technological and scientific knowledge at our command today will be but a small fraction of what is known just five years from this current moment.

- ☑ most of the jobs of today will be either extinct or completely transformed within ten years or less.

- ☑ you can expect to change jobs many times and careers two, three or more times during the course of your twenty-first century working life.

So then, how can anybody realistically expect to make an intelligent decision about what kind of career is best for them (i.e., will prove fulfilling and satisfying to the self in the workplace of today, tomorrow, and ten years hence)?

HOW THIS BOOK CAN HELP

This book can serve as a career-planning guide to help you deal with the complexities we have enumerated above. The book features a decision-making model that takes you through the process of self-assessment, "knowing yourself," and then of directing you to occupations likely to satisfy the demands of that inner "self" to which we have been referring. While progressing through the book you will have plenty of opportunity to know yourself better through activities that include: clarifying your personality style; understanding your brain-dominance orientation; defining your natural talent preferences; and clarifying your values. The book's content, process, and references have all been carefully selected to help you make better decisions in those life and career matters that will shape and create your future. We must confess that the workplace is just too big and complex for us to tell you exactly where you might get a job capable of satisfying your career needs. The last chapter offers a process designed to help you become a more effective job seeker, and find a good place to start or restructure your career.

One thing to keep in mind as you progress through the book is that there is no easy way to make an intelligent career choice. There are of course easy ways to make stupid career choices, but we shan't waste your time with those. We should add that this is a "workbook" and that means you will have to work diligently, and without pay, to achieve the outcomes this book is intended to provide. The outcomes are:

- ☑ gaining familiarity and practice with the skills essential in career and life decision making.
- ☑ discovering your preferred natural talents (those you want to feature in your future) and understanding how they might be transferable within the workplace.
- ☑ identifying what it might take for you to experience personal satisfaction and fulfillment in your career.
- ☑ assessing, in general terms, where you would most like to contribute your unique natural talents and develop your skills.
- ☑ becoming familiar with the primary sources of occupational information and knowing how to use them effectively in your career and life decision making.
- ☑ developing personal goals as a reference for guiding your career and learning plans.
- ☑ learning how to develop action plans for achieving your career objectives.
- ☑ becoming a more perceptive and skillful problem solver in matters affecting your career over your life span.

WHO THE BOOK IS FOR

This workbook is not intended for people under pressure to make an immediate job or career change. It takes reflection, concentration, self-assessment, research, exploration, and communications to do this process well. All of this takes time in a relatively stress-free state-of-mind.

You are likely to find this process helpful if you are:

- ☑ a student entering college and needing to clarify your career objective before choosing your academic program.
- ☑ a college student who has become disenchanted with your academic program and career objective.
- ☑ a college student about to graduate and needing to define your career purpose and get a career-related job.

- ☑ anyone preparing for a first career.

- ☑ anyone seeking self-understanding and better life-choice decision-making skills.

- ☑ an adult seeking a career change for more satisfaction in your work.

- ☑ an adult realizing that changing circumstance will make your current career situation unsustainable and feeling uncertain where to go next with your career.

- ☑ an employed worker needing to find a new direction for your career and to define and market your transferable skills.

HOW TO USE THE BOOK

We have selected a workbook format to provide more opportunity to interact personally with the content. Please <u>DO</u> make notes anywhere and everywhere in the book and keep your book as a reference for future years. That, incidentally, comes as advice from a number of individuals who have informed us they have found the book and their notes and responses to the process to be a valuable reference for career management.

We have found that it generally works best to do a small amount of work at any one sitting and then give yourself time to think and reflect. Read some, do some exercises, put it down for a while and then come back to it later.

This workbook has been used by individuals working alone, by groups working together, and in college courses all across the country. From our experiences with the thousands of individuals who have used this book over the years we believe that the greatest benefit will be obtained by discussing the processes and your responses to them with others. Doing so provides opportunity to expand your ideas through giving and getting feedback. If you are unable to join a course, consider starting your own group. Of course, doing the workbook on your own is much more beneficial than doing nothing at all. Motivation is the key to a successful outcome.

Complete the materials in this workbook with the knowledge that doing so can get you where you want to be in self-understanding, career decision making, and job-hunting savvy. We can make this assertion with confidence since the contents have evolved over twenty-some years of research and experience-based learning, through eight editions with input from hundreds of readers and dozens of career counseling professionals. While searching for a satisfying career is complex and difficult, we know the process can be highly enjoyable, because after all—the primary subject matter is "you." What could be more fascinating than that?

Similar to small businesses that open and close, Web sites come and go. This means that some of the Web sites listed in this book will probably change during the time you are reading this material. Therefore, we have created a page on the Web where you can go to ensure you have the most up-to-date links for each of the chapters. To find these links, go to **www.CareerKiosk.org** and click on "Updated links for *Your Career*." These links will ensure that you have accurate links and access to great sites on the Web!

Making Career Decisions in a Changing World

Before you can put together your new career plan, you are going to have to understand two things: first, what is really happening in the workplace and second, how to assess your own resources for dealing with it.
– William Bridges
You & Co.: Learn to Think Like the CEO of Your Own Career

Do you know people who—

☑ Unwittingly avoid or consciously refuse to make decisions?
☑ Make small decisions easily, but panic about making decisions that will impact their future?
☑ Have gotten into their career more by accident than by planning and preparation?
☑ Hang onto jobs they hate for security rather than risk seeking their real passion?

If so, you know people who have settled for less freedom and a lesser quality of life because they didn't know how to make decisions or because they were unwilling to make difficult choices.

How Seymore's father saw him   How Seymore's mother saw him   Seymore's mother and father

| How Would You Enhance Your Life If You Became a Big-time Lottery Winner? |

- Buy a dude ranch in Montana?
- Study psychology in Zurich?
- Create an Outward Bound course for disadvantaged kids?
- Become a Zen master?
- Study acting and go for the big time?

- Start your own furniture making shop?
- Create your own bed and breakfast lodge?
- Study foreign languages and explore the world's cultures?
- Become a computer guru and live on a mountaintop?

WORK, LIFE, AND THE LOTTERY

Have you noticed how many people dream of winning the lottery, assuming that doing so would instantly and automatically improve the quality of their lives? What would you do if you won the lottery? Let's say that you won enough money to support yourself (and your family, if that's in your picture) in grand style for the rest of your life.

Would you, as a wealthy person, include work in your future? If so, you just might be one of those few who have discovered a rather well-kept secret, but we're getting ahead of ourselves here! (You will have to read on to discover what that is.) If you're sure that you would never work if you didn't have to—why is that? Could it be that you view work as a drudge, an unpleasant activity made necessary perhaps because of original sin, a family or cultural work ethic, or just the basic need to keep bread on the table? Do you see work as a necessary evil that keeps you from what you would rather be doing?

It probably comes as no surprise that most people report that they would quit their jobs without a moment's hesitation should they hit the lottery big time. Why would anyone freely elect to work, for that matter? There's only one reason, say most people—"to make a buck!" Actually, there are some very good reasons for working, even if you don't have to. Psychological research suggests there are at least five basic motivations for working:[1]

- ☑ income
- ☑ having something to do with our time and energy
- ☑ a way to achieve identity and status
- ☑ a way of having personal and professional relationships
- ☑ a source of meaning in life.

Regardless of the motivations for work, most people still think their lives would be better if they didn't have to work. But consider a group of retirees known to one of the authors of this text. They all retired relatively young, in good health and were financially secure with lots of disposable income. After a few years of travel, visiting, and leisure activities they all began to get restless. One by one, they got part-time jobs, began volunteering and took up new hobbies. Conversations with them revealed that they missed the sense of structure, the camaraderie and the sense of purpose and identity that work had given them. The one thing they did have that many of us lack was the choice regarding what to do with their time. Pretend that you were able to "retire" at your current age or that you won the lottery. How would you spend your time?

Imagining what you might do if you won the lottery is actually a productive way to expand your thinking on how to have a more interesting life. Common responses to that question are things like travel, pay off bills, permanently inhabit the beach, do absolutely nothing, buy a new car/house/wardrobe. If traveling is your answer, think about this: Where would you go? What does traveling really mean to you? How long would you want to do it? And, what would you do when the "bloom" eventually wears off traveling? Or, if your vision involves paying off bills, rushing off to the shopping malls, or simply doing nothing—consider how those things would enhance the total quality of your life?

---

[1] Abraham Maslow, *Motivation and Personality*, 2nd ed. (New York: Harper & Row, 1970).

Money, in itself, doesn't automatically produce a meaningful life (nor does a life of ease). While we're not advocating poverty here, we are aware that people whose lives have been full and interesting used their time, talents, and energies for work they cared passionately about. This may be what British playwright George Bernard Shaw (1856–1950) had in mind in reporting that he wanted to be totally used up when he died. He wanted to have no unused talents nor unfulfilled life/work desires left in reserve on his last day here. Perhaps Shaw, who needed almost 100 years of vigorous living to achieve his stated desire, was advocating for a fundamental principle of life vitality. Most of us really want to be engaged in things that are interesting and worthwhile!

DEFINING CAREER

There are many ways to be engaged in things that are interesting and worthwhile. Paid work is just one of them. We spend a lot of time at work. Ideally work shouldn't be a means to an end. We shouldn't just work so we have the money to live outside of work. Work, when it engages our unique combination of talents, interests, personality, and values, is wonderful. In fact, we believe that it is such an important of our existence that this entire book is written to help you find that type of work that is the best fit for you. However, work is just one of the many life roles that we play that make up career. Donald Super, a person who studied career development in America in the last half of the twentieth century, proposed the idea that career is really made up of many different life roles.[2] People who are happy in their "careers" are those who are able to integrate those roles together. Let's look at some of those roles that Super says we play:

Child—Beginning at birth, this role is played until the death of our parents. Throughout childhood, this role is a major one. As we reach adulthood, we may play this role less or more depending upon our family structure. Many people find themselves playing this role as their parents age and they need to become more involved in helping them with health care and financial decisions.

Student—Most of us play this role through formal education until the 12th grade. After that, this role is played on and off while we pursue advanced degrees, take noncredit courses related to work or other life areas or interests or any other way in which we are involved in learning.

Worker—This refers to the paid work role. It could be a part-time job delivering papers or the full time job of newspaper reporter. This is the role that we will concentrate on throughout this book.

Homemaker—At some point, most people will be responsible for a home, be that the house with the white picket fence, the downtown penthouse, or the college apartment that is shared with three roommates. Beginning when a person establishes a residence separate from one's parents, this role addresses the various responsibilities of home operation including decorating, bill paying, food preparation, and maintenance.

Spouse/Partner—This role centers on the building and maintaining of a satisfying long-term relationship with another person. Some people never play this role, others play it until death, while others play it intermittently.

Parent—Like many of the other roles, not everyone will choose to play this role. This role involves the activities of raising children. It is a role that is played with the most effort during the child's early years. It begins to taper off as the child becomes more and more independent.

Citizen—Many people give back to their communities in some way. This role addresses the ways in which we participate in our communities. Some people are involved on school boards or other volunteer political offices, others belong to civic groups or seek involvement in the local educational or religious communities.

Leisurite—Leisure time seems to be a rarity in today's society, but how we spend our leisure time can provide balance to the other roles we play. A person who spends a lot of time with other people in the other roles may elect to spend leisure time alone in activities such as running or hiking. Leisure time also allows for the pursuit of other things that may not be found in the other roles such as physical activity for a person with a sedentary job or gardening for a person who enjoys physical and aesthetic activities but has no way of integrating them into other life roles.

---

[2] Donald Super, "A Life-Span, Life-Space Approach to Career Development," *Career Choice and Development*. D. Brown and L. Brooks ed. (San Francisco: Jossey-Bass, 1990).

Super noted that we play these roles throughout our lifetimes. At some points, we may be playing all eight. The concept of life-role theory can be exciting. It tells us that career does not just have to be relegated to the 9–5 workday, but that career, like the strands of a rope, is the integration of all the roles we play.

When we talk about career, we mean all of it. Not just the paid worker role but the volunteer experiences, our families, and our free-time activities. Like the pieces of a puzzle, when they all fit together, they work to make a complete picture. Most of us do not play all of the roles at once, and some of us do not even play all of the roles during our lifetimes. You may choose not to enter into a serious long-term relationship with another person, or you may choose not to have children. You may decide that you don't want to spend time in the citizen role. Perhaps you know some people who have chosen not to play the paid worker role. They spend their time taking care of children and a house and in volunteer activities. Those people who are happy in the combination of life roles they have selected, according to Super, are those that have found a satisfying career.

This concept is incredibly freeing. People suddenly don't have to get all of their interests, abilities, values met in one single occupation—translated that means the pressure is off to make one choice that is going to be the perfect decision for the rest of their lives. One person was considering two occupational choices but was torn because one paid a lot of money while the other allowed a greater contribution to society. Since these two values seemed to carry equal weight and the student couldn't find a career that met both of them, there appeared to be no best answer. Based upon Super's life-role theory, the student decided to pursue the job that paid more money (the worker role), but began volunteering in the community (the citizen role) to meet the need to help people.

When you have a vision for the life you really want, ask yourself, Is there any way I might possibly achieve that without the aid of a big lottery win? Many of us use money, or the lack of it, as an excuse to avoid going after what we truly want in life. In truth, you already have something more powerful than money. It's your natural endowments, including your mind, your creativity, life energy (maybe even your good looks). Our world could greatly benefit from the cumulative effect of a lot more people pursuing what they care deeply about. Why not be one of them? The next time you're inclined to buy a lottery ticket in hopes of becoming rich, consider instead meditating upon a vision of what a fully engaged and challenging life might be.

A PERSONAL GUIDE

But how do I discover what a deeply fulfilling life and career would consist of? How can I know what my unique interests and best potentials really are? How do I find a meaningful career? Clearly these are

---

Table 1.1
A Few Things Your Career Will Dictate or Influence

- Esteem and self-worth
- Talents used and developed
- Interests that are expressed and energized
- Financial resources
- The nature of organizations with which you will associate
- Where you will live
- Lifestyle
- Health and vitality
- Longevity
- Activities you will perform
- Type of knowledge you will acquire

- Kinds of people with whom you will associate
- Time, energy and resources for:
  leisure
  family
  personal growth
  professional growth
- Kinds and levels of responsibilities you will have
- What you will be learning
- Employment contract
- Your friends and associates
- The contributions you make

perplexing questions for everyone. But don't give up; there is hope. A willingness to seriously address questions such as the above is an important step in getting answers. Remember that career in terms of paid work may not be singularly satisfying. Use this book to guide you in your quest for greater self-understanding so that you can make a career choice that is best for you, but be aware that some of the deeper questions of life and meaning and purpose may not be found in getting a better job. There are other books written on these topics of spirituality, love, and personal acceptance. Dick Bolles writes that most of us move from "I need to find a job that I like" to "I need to find my purpose in life." He offers that these are deeper questions of the heart that are unique to each of us and probably won't be answered through a book such as this.

As we consider our lives, we are often quick to run to our families or friends to find the answers. We forget that we may actually be able to find the answers within ourselves. We come to this life equipped with a wise inner guide. Unfortunately, far too few of us ever consult with or pay attention to our own inner counsel. We're just too busy and preoccupied with the sights, sounds, and activities of the outer world. Devoting quiet time for self-reflection directed to important life and career questions can lead to "discernment." Discernment comes from the Latin word *discernere*, which means 'to separate,' 'to distinguish,' 'to determine,' 'to sort out.'[3] Intuition is a human capacity, a form of intelligence accessible only in the vast reaches of our quiet minds. Accessing it involves asking the hard and specific questions of ourselves, tuning out the loud music and other outer worldly distractions vying for our attention, and tuning into the quiet consultation of our inner guidance system.

CAREER AND LIFE CHAPTERS

Many people think of career choice as a simple act governed by the single-minded logic of getting a good job. If you're a college student or a re-careering adult, your career selection logic might be to complete an academic program that leads to a top-paying job, regardless of what the job might be. Such a motivation involves this potentially dangerous as-

sumption: When I get a job with a high salary my life will fall into place.

There is far more to life than a high salaried job. We have seen too many people whose single-minded focus on job has brought them to the sobering realization that their jobs have come to control their lives. That might be OK if you love your job, but what if you don't? What if you find it doesn't utilize and develop your talents and/or engage your interests? What if it conflicts with your core values? What if you become a fast track manager and then one day are stunned to realize that your kids are being brought up by their nanny because you've been too engaged in work? For reasons such as these we urge you, regardless of your life stage, to give the process of creating your future serious attention.

Career/life decision making is an ongoing and lifelong process because we're going to be faced with important life and work choices for as long as we're around. In a way, our lives are like books of many chapters. Your book of life has some past chapters and many more, we hope, in the future. Your career and life book probably has some overall general direction (a story line) to it with major and minor themes emerging and fading. We write our books one chapter at a time. Here we are concerned about your future chapters, especially the next one.

Career and life decision making involves work in two realms—the inner universe of self and the outer world of possibilities (see Figure 1.1). Exploring the inner realm involves assessment and self-discovery, particularly in identifying and defining those interests, values, and skills you identify as important to your future. The outer universe of work requires that you learn about possibilities and options available and suited to your unique talents and attributes—now and in the future.

As you become involved in this process of writing the next career chapter of your life you may feel restricted by any number of circumstances and conditions that appear to be limiting your options. If so, please bear this in mind—the work world is huge, multi-dimensional, and ever changing. We'll have more to say about overcoming your barriers later on, but for now keep this simple truth in mind. There are always more opportunities than any single individual, on his/her own, can possibly be aware of. So, whether you are currently more motivated by mate-

3. Gill Farnham, Ward McLean, *Listening Hearts: Discerning Call in Community* (Harrisburg, PA: Morehouse Publishing, 1991).

Figure 1.1
The Two Universes of Career and Life Decision Making

Inner World	Outer World

Skills	Options
Potentials	Possibilities
Interests	Evolving Trends
Personality Style	Future Developments
Attributes	Alternatives
Values	Choices

---

rial success than inner values, here is your best strategy: find a career direction that you could really enjoy and which would capitalize on your top strengths and personal assets.

JOBS AND CAREERS

The term *career* is often misunderstood. Often you hear the terms *career* and *job* used interchangeably. We think of *job* as employment. It's what somebody is paying you to do. Jobs have traditionally been viewed as long-term positions for which we were hired, given titles, and provided an annual salary along with some associated benefits. Traditionally jobs came with job descriptions. These defined what kinds of tasks and responsibilities you did and did not do (That's my job! That's not my job!). If we are to believe futurist thinkers such as William Bridges, *Job Shift*,[4] and Jeremy Rifkin, *The End of Work*,[5] jobs are disappearing! The concept of *job* came in with, and now may be going out with, the industrial era. We may need, therefore, to begin thinking of employment in a very different way. William Bridges advocates thinking of ourselves as con-

tracting agents with expertise suited to particular kinds of work for hire.[6]

A *career* implies that you have prepared for and are building expertise and experience in a particular field, trade, or business endeavor. Career defines the general nature of work that you see yourself prepared (or preparing yourself) to perform. Career serves as a frame of reference for the kinds of work you will seek, qualify for, and accept. It is also the context in which you will continue to develop new skills and insights. Ben Affleck's career is acting;

Web Connect

If you'd like to read an excerpt from Jeremy Rifkin's "The End of Work," you can do so by going to **www.eff.org/Publications/E-journals/CyRev/Cyrev3.html** and clicking on Creating Jobs in the Third Sector: The Alternative to Welfare.

---

4. William Bridges, *Job Shift: How to Prosper in a Workplace Without Jobs* (Reading, MA: Addison-Wesley, 1994).

5. Jeremy Rifkin, *The End of Work* (New York: A Jeremy P. Tarcher, 1995).

6. William Bridges, *You & Co.: Learn to Think Like the CEO of Your Own Career* (Reading, MA: Addison-Wesley, 1997).

he's had a number of jobs making specific movies. An airline mechanic may master her trade (career) through a combination of training and supervised work experiences and obtain employment (jobs) with various airlines throughout her career.

CAREER AND SELF-CONCEPT

From our earliest days, we get personality programming and career-image shaping messages from our families, cultures, and social environments. As we develop, we acquire an image of ourselves, a self-concept. Most of us are not even consciously aware that we possess one, but it's there and it is very likely to be reflected in our behaviors and actions. The important point here is that we unconsciously seek jobs and pursue careers to match our inner self-image. For example, people who acquire self-images that are neat, well-organized, and good with numbers may seek careers as accountants or actuaries (these are the folks possessing statistical skills who do things like compute insurance rates and analyze how likely we are to have an accident if we own a small red sports car with a great big engine). Those who develop an intellectual's self-concept may pursue professions featuring rigorous mental concentration such as law, physics, or literary scholarship. Those who acquire a nurturer's "self-view" may track themselves towards career roles as social worker, nurse, or vocational rehabilitation therapist.

Unwitting career selection works well for some, but not for all. The problem is that our self-concept may evolve from an inaccurate understanding of our true nature. Some of us acquire self-limiting and handicapping concepts in the form of lack in self-confidence. From an early age, self-concepts begin developing in response to what we hear our parents and elders say about us, such as "Isn't she just the perfect little mother," or "He's just like his father" (when Father is a lawyer, or stone mason), or "He's going to be a super athlete," or "She's a mental wizard." When others make biased observations, either negative or positive, they influence the shaping of our youthful self-image.

A poor self-concept undermines your career development as well as your life satisfaction. Fortunately, we can change our self-concept over time and through conscious attention. By taking a more deliberate and systematic approach to determining your skills, personal traits, preferences, needs, and values, you can bring your self-image into line with your true abilities and desires. You can also greatly enhance your self-confidence by knowing what you are particularly good at and what you can achieve with your talents and abilities. The payoff for generating an accurate self-concept can be tremendously gratifying. This kind of self-knowledge can guide you through appropriate employment and career changes, make you more resilient in dealing with life's challenges, and guide you in finding a sense of security within yourself, even in difficult times.

Change and Transitions

Difficult times are unavoidable. Nancy Schlossberg is a researcher and professor who studied adults in transition. She discovered that the people who were able to maintain a positive attitude regarding the transition and were able to gain control over the transition were those that came out the healthiest. She defines transitions: an event or non-event that alters our lives.[7] Transitions can be things like going to college, changing jobs, getting a promotion or moving to a new city. They can be negative things like the loss of a parent or a job. We can't avoid transitions no matter how much we'd like to. But the secret to dealing with the natural transitions in life is how much control we have over them. If we decide to take a job in a new city because it is a good professional opportunity, we have a lot of control over the transition. If, however, our company moves to a new city and we can either go or lose our jobs, then we may feel that we don't have a lot of control over the transition.

When you think about your career, how much control do you believe you have over the factors that will impact your career decisions? If you are in school or are thinking of going back to school, who will determine what your major will be? Do you believe that it is your choice, or are there family members or employers who are insisting that you select a specific career path? The more you own the decision and keep control over it, the better able you will be to select a path that is best for you.

[7.] Nancy Schlossberg, *Overwhelmed. Coping with Life's Ups and Downs* (Lexington, MA: Lexington Books, 1989).

POSITIVE MENTAL IMAGING

Negative thinking undermines decision-making ability. Could you conceive of anyone performing successfully as a decision maker if their view of the world allowed them to see only mediocre and/or un-inviting options? People able to see a future filled with interesting opportunities willingly invest in effective decision making.

As you begin this decision-making process, we offer you a challenge. See if you can entertain a viewpoint that the future presents you with limitless possibility and that your opportunities now are greater than at any time in history. Try out the assumption that the future will present you with continual opportunities for such things as:

☑ discovering just how excellent you are capable of becoming

☑ growing and developing in ways you've barely dared to dream about

☑ making satisfying contributions

☑ creating and operating your own business

☑ working from your high-tech cottage on a mountaintop

☑ becoming a cyberspace citizen of the world

It may be worth noting here that there are many kinds of work that you would dislike and/or not perform very successfully. There are also many types of work that you would fully enjoy and in which you could thrive. The kind of work that fits us depends upon our uniqueness. We have different fingerprints and different interests. We are also uniquely talented. Fortunately, there are many different kinds of work available now, and there will be even more in the future.

CAREER DECISION MAKING

In spite of the critically important role that career plays in life, most people slip into careers and their associated lifestyles with very little forethought or preparation. In fact, most of us spend more time selecting new clothes or a new car than we do in deciding upon our careers. Based on years of experience in assisting career seekers and job hunters, career planning specialist Richard Bolles concludes that most people choose their occupation absent-mindedly, and make career decisions in haphazard fashion—without awareness that there are real alternatives from which to choose.[8]

Making a decision is required whenever we are faced with more than one alternative or confronted with unsettling circumstances. Whether we rationally or intuitively settle these questions or reach our conclusions consciously or unconsciously, we have made our decision. Many of us are afraid of decision making. Actually, we're probably afraid of making a wrong choice or even one that's less than perfect. For these reasons, too many of us look for others to tell us what to do, while others of us master procrastination, and some of us even put off coming to a decision indefinitely.

Unfortunately, avoiding decisions does not result in eliminating risks or unwanted outcomes. At best, not making a decision results in keeping things the way they are, and at worst, we miss a window of opportunity to avoid an unpleasant result or set the stage for a good outcome. This is true even with everyday decisions. For example, if you stay at home on a Saturday evening because you can't decide whether to go to the movies, see a play, go bowling, or visit a friend, the result is the same as deciding to stay at home. Incidentally, staying at home by choice feels much better than staying at home out of default because you couldn't make up your mind.

In a more serious vein, what are the consequences to people in jobs they hate (or an academic program that does not suit them) when they do nothing to change? The result of indecision is predictable. They are, in effect, deciding to stay with an unsatisfactory situation. By not deciding, you forfeit the opportunity of achieving a better outcome.[9] In a sense, you give up your control of the situation. Your performance, self-confidence, and attitude could suffer as a result.

[8.] John C. Crystal and Richard N. Bolles, *Where Do I Go From Here With My Life?* (Berkeley, CA: Ten Speed Press, 1978).

[9.] Gordon Porter Miller, *Life Choices* (New York: Thomas Y. Crowell, 1978) 4.

Figure 1.2
Reminders on Career and Life Decision Making

*to have personal freedom—
take control of your decision-making*

The key to life/career choice is
- *self-understanding*

Decision making is:
- *a developed skill*
- *not a genetic endowment*

Want a fulfilling life?
- *choose your career*

STEPS TO CAREER-PLANNING SUCCESS

Separating career/life planning into smaller steps makes the choice process less daunting. In this book, we use six steps. Each step of the way, you will be gaining knowledge to help you make decisions about your next life chapter and insight for goal setting. Chapter 2 discusses how to use online tools and resources to gain an overview of all the steps in the career planning process.

Step 1. Identifying skills is accomplished by examining talents and competencies. Chapter 3 shows how your skills are revealed through everyday activities you have performed well at home, in school, and in voluntary and paid jobs. You will also determine which of your strengths will best enable your career success.

Step 2. Clarifying personal preferences is accomplished by discovering your natural traits and interests to see which careers best match your style. Chapter 4 helps you to do this by exploring your thinking style—the way you prefer to access information and use your mental gifts. Chapter 5 explores your personality-related interest patterns. Chapter 7 helps clarify your true needs and values—your "deep-core" motivators.

Step 3. Finding interesting options draws upon the self-knowledge acquired in the earlier steps to identify careers of potential interest. At this point, you will be compiling a master list of your better options. Chapters 6 and 8 show you how to discover and explore your occupational alternatives.

Step 4. Making a choice helps narrow down your alternatives and identify your best career selection. Chapter 8 helps you evaluate these career alternatives in terms of your skills, preferences, and occupational outlook. *You may want to revisit this chapter several times in the years ahead as you are faced with critical new life and career choices.*

Step 5. Setting goals and making plans involves developing the specific goals and plans needed to translate your career decision into action steps. Chapter 9 shows how to design meaningful goals and plans for a career that will fit into the life you want to have.

Step 6. Implementing your career helps you turn goals and plans into reality. Chapter 10 shows how to overcome barriers that can disrupt your best-laid plans. Chapter 11 shows you how to develop an effective strategy for obtaining work related to your career goals.

After you have completed the steps (and even along the way) it is important that you review your decision. For the most part, this will occur after you have completed this book. As you go along, you will probably take small steps towards your career. Perhaps you decide to become a veterinarian. You start on the road to this career by taking a science class, you get a part-time job at a veterinarian's office so you can be exposed to the occupation, and you volunteer at the SPCA. After a few months, it is important to think about things. Use your discernment and listen to the inner voice. Honestly look at your new experiences and the information you have gathered about yourself. This will help you know if you want to continue on or if you need to adjust your goals based upon your new knowledge of work and of yourself. If you decide that this wasn't the best choice after all, then go back through the first six steps and determine a better choice. Most people are afraid of making the wrong decision so they either pick something and force themselves to live with the result (like it or not), or they don't pick anything and stay in their current situation. By reviewing the choices as we go, we allow ourselves the freedom to make slight adjustments or even major changes before too much time has been invested in the decision. The original veterinarian decision can be adjusted to a veterinary technician if we realize we could be just as satisfied in this similar occupation with less time and money invested. Reviewing our decisions along the way helps us to have more control of the outcomes.

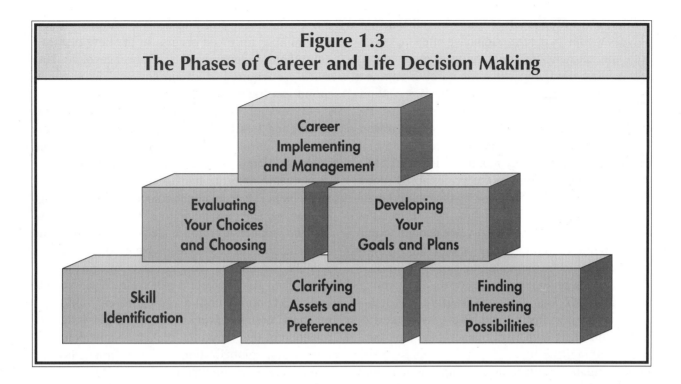

Figure 1.3
The Phases of Career and Life Decision Making

Career Implementing and Management

Evaluating Your Choices and Choosing

Developing Your Goals and Plans

Skill Identification

Clarifying Assets and Preferences

Finding Interesting Possibilities

CAREER DEVELOPMENT OF THE PAST

The bureaucratic career became the principal mode of career life over the past century—thanks primarily to the growth of giant industries. This mode is characterized by all aspects of career identity and opportunity being closely tied to rank in an organization. Individuals, in this mode, willingly abdicate their personal identity in favor of identity offered by organizationally defined job titles, rank levels, and employment status. Motivation is associated with the ability to move upwards in the hierarchy, i.e., achieving the next higher level along with additional perks, such as parking spaces, more impressive titles, increased salary, and offices with windows.

The conventional wisdom reflected by the bureaucratic mode was that it was unrealistic to assume that common people (i.e., middle-class) could exercise much personal autonomy over their careers. In fact, the conditions of the industrial era actually provided rather limited opportunities for most individuals to manage their own careers. The primary career objective was to get a job with a Fortune 500 company. Thereafter, one's career development was determined almost exclusively by the individual's gen-

der, educational preparation (blue- or white-collar tracks), the employing organization, and on-the-job performance.

People (meaning men from an industrial-era perspective) were expected to get a job and provide for their families without particular regard to their interests, skills, or potential. Work was not supposed to be fun, and the organization called the shots. A primary employment goal was to work your way up the corporate ladder and hang in there until retirement. Only in the retirement phase of life could people expect to exercise control over their lives. But even that newly available freedom was often overshadowed by a self-limiting viewpoint: I've worked hard for the right to never have to work again, and I don't intend to.

Rosabeth Moss Kanter, Harvard professor and consultant to leading organizations worldwide, notes that a much smaller number of individuals opted for very different career modes—professional and entrepreneur.[10] In marked contrast to the bureaucratic careerist, professionals define themselves more by the field they are in than the organization that employed them. Their allegiance is to their profession and their motivation is to develop within their field rather than to move up the organizational career lad-

10. The Peter Drucker Foundation, *The Organization of the Future*, "Restoring People to the Heart of the Organization of the Future," Rosabeth Moss Kanter, (San Francisco: Jossey-Bass, 1997) 139–150.

der. In fact, professionals working as full-time employees within an organization have often had to decline the "moving-up" orientation in order to stay within their field, e.g., remaining a civil engineer rather than moving to general manager, or continuing in the field of macroeconomics rather than becoming a bureau chief. The premier career reward for those in the professional mode comes through establishing a noteworthy reputation in their field.

In contrast to those in the professional mode, the career motivation for those on the entrepreneurial track was in creating products or services that people or organizations would value enough to purchase. While entrepreneuring is generally thought of in regards to formulating one's own business, it also involves producing value within an organization through one's own creative efforts—entrepreneuring. Entrepreneurs are motivated by controlling their own work, generating something out of nothing, and sharing in the monetary rewards directly related to personal accomplishment (such as pay for commissions, managers growing their own territory and reaping the associated rewards, and innovative employees receiving payment for creating new revenue-producing or cost-saving programs or services). Rosabeth Moss Kanter points out that women and minorities have generally been more successful in professional and entrepreneurial careers than in bureaucratic careers.[11]

The Death of Bureaucratic Careers

It is obvious that the workplace has seen a dramatic shift in the last ten years. As we have moved from an industrial society we have seen a shift in the picture of work. Where work was once a triangle shape that was characterized by top-down thinking and control, the new model suggests that we are more of a diamond with the decision making being spread throughout the organization. In the original triangle, an estimated 15% of the workforce was responsible for setting the direction of the organization, making the rules and handling all problem solving. In terms of skills, this translates to 85% of the workforce not needing to have advanced skills—they simply followed orders. In the new diamond configuration, supervisory and higher-level thinking skills are required of all employees. The new diamond has traded security, clear lines of advancement, and job entitlement for freedom, independence, and flexibility.[12] There is little room in the new configuration for the unskilled workers that made up a large percentage of the triangle model.

Organizations are transforming themselves from large, hierarchical structures composed of many rungs of management, administrative support, and assembly-line productions into smaller, less structured, and more flexible entities that can change and reorganize quickly. Downsizing, reorganization, merging and re-engineering have become a part of organizational life and will continue until a very different workplace emerges. Jeremy Rifkin refers to all of this as the culmination of the "Third Revolution"—in which computerization, globalization, and work re-engineering completely restructure the workplace.

In the last 30 years, the idea of work has changed as the long-term security that came with a job has evaporated. The concept that one stays with a company from birth to death no longer exists. But in its place is the existing notion that you can go anywhere and do anything. No longer are we confined to gender, race, or socioeconomic stereotyping. We no longer follow our parent's career paths. My father was a farmer so I am a farmer is simply no longer the case. With this newfound freedom has come a newfound stress. We are hired at a company because we have a skill that they want. But when that skill is no longer needed, we are also no longer needed. The other stress that exists is from the very nature of the multitude of options to select from. "My father was a farmer . . ." mentality, while not necessarily offering excitement, did offer a kind of stability and an odd sense of freedom. We were freed from having to make a decision about our futures, therefore freeing us from making wrong decisions. In the triangle configuration, once we made the decision to work for company X, no matter how miserable we were, at least we knew we had the security and predictability of a weekly paycheck.

11. Rosabeth Moss Kanter, "Careers and the Wealth of Nations: A Macro-perspective on the Structure and Implications of Career Forms," *Handbook of Career Theory*. M. B. Arthur, D. T. Hall, and B. S. Lawrence, eds. (Cambridge: Cambridge University Press, 1989) 506–521.

12. Rich Feller and Gary Walz, *Career Transitions in Turbulent Times* (Greensboro, NC: ERIC Counseling and Student Services Clearinghouse, 1996).

The new diamond tells us that we need to keep up with the times. There is little room for those that lag behind. Whether we are contingent or temporary workers as Rifkin and Bridges propose most of us will become or we are a part of the core staff, we still need to use the skills required of the organization or our services will no longer be needed and we'll be asked to "move on." Many two-year and technical schools are seeing a great number of people coming back to school to build on their bachelor and masters degrees. They need to keep the skills portfolio current or they'll find themselves missing out on opportunities.

The restructuring of corporate structures is not the only change that is occurring. Almost anywhere we look we see the impact of change in areas such as: a global economy impacting work locally, accelerating technology that continually makes some work obsolete and generates other work; a shift in the nature of work from primarily manufacturing based to service and information oriented. Add to this picture a changing population with increasing numbers of older Americans and greater numbers of females and minorities (many of whom are entering the workplace and moving into positions formerly dominated by white males). The results have produced massive restructuring within those organizations that were the mainstay of the industrial-age job market. These were also the places where most people pursued their careers.

Most of what we have believed about careers, in fact, comes from the culture of these industrial giants and the corporate world. But since the late 1970s, we have seen these organizations transform their nature as they struggle to remain afloat in an era of massive change. Jeremy Rifkin (*The End of Work*) reported that U.S. corporations were eliminating two million jobs annually in the mid '90s. And these trends are not restricted to the U.S. Germany, Japan, Sweden and others have seen major changes and layoffs.

Corporations all over the industrial world have found it necessary to reinvent themselves to keep from being bowled over by relentless global competition. Not even the federal government, that traditional bastion of twentieth century secure employment, is immune from the forces of change. This massive bureaucracy is being forced to change from imperatives to: consume less of the nation's limited budgetary resources, become more productive, and to shrink to more manageable proportions.

Web Connect

Reading about the constant changes affecting careers and development enhance your ability to plan your career and maintain your employability. The article briefs provided by *New Work News* <www.newwork.com> can help you stay on top of business news that impacts career mobility. *Fast Company's* site has a great career article entitled **New Economy 101** at <www.fastcompany.com/launch/neweconomy101.html> is a crash course in the new world of work.

If you'd like to read more about the changes affecting career decision making, check out the Population Reference Bureau's "Report on America: The Career Quandry" at www.prb.org: by clicking on the topic "Employment" and then clicking on the article title.

The employment mode most impacted by the restructuring is the bureaucratic career. The once-proud bureaucratic career is ignominiously coming to an end in a blizzard of corporate layoffs, downsizings, mergers, and restructuring. New modes of work are now emerging—and we need to face that unsettling reality. With the decline of the bureaucratic career goes the once-prized values of corporate loyalty and promotion motivation. Corporate ladders, those career advancement hallmarks of the mass-production heydays, are disappearing. The last vestiges of corporate commitment to guaranteed career-long employment may have vanished in 1993 when IBM publicly conceded it could no longer honor that decades-old legacy. One of the authors, who had been assisting IBM's disposed workers at that time, will always remember an ex-manager breaking into uncontrollable sobbing in his counseling office. She was overcome with emotion in part because of her job loss, but even more in grief that this great institution had lost a valued heritage and would never again be the same.

The Career Shift	
Fading Paradigm	**Evolving Paradigm**
• Job security and one company careers responsibility	• Career management an individual
• Career ladders and promotion for seniority professional	• From invisible bureaucrat to visible
• Job specialties and pay for position	• Matching core assets to work activities

DEATH AND REBIRTH

An unwelcome job dissolution announcement can be to a career what an unexpected terminal medical diagnosis is to a life—a devastating shock. But both kinds of notices can also serve as wake-up calls. In either case, denial tends to be the first predictable reaction, followed by anger and grief. A growing body of literature on this subject suggests that those who are able to move through these emotional stages and accept death's inevitability are able to let go of their attachments to the past and then move through life's final transition—often in an apparent state of bliss. In a similar manner, the death and dying of a lifestyle or career can awaken us to the inevitability of life-affirming change and transition.

While impending physical death signals an ending to the reality we have known in this dimension, career death can actually awaken us to intriguing new possibilities and a rebirth experience in the here and now. Many who have gone through major career transitions report that their job loss was actually a blessing in disguise, as is suggested by this quote from one of our career-changing clients: "It forced me to reassess myself and discover new interests which have led me to work I like much better."

WORK IN THE POSTBUREAUCRATIC CAREER

Where does all the change occurring in the workplace leave us careerwise? One thing is certain—no longer can we assume that working hard, performing assigned job functions, and being a loyal employee assure our employment security. Nor can we look to a secure career path with a single employer. What this means for people choosing their careers for the first time or needing to make career changes is that just about everything we took for granted about our careers in the past is now outdated.

We need new perspectives and new approaches to twenty-first century career development.

Like it or not, our personal futures and our career development have become our personal responsibility. Because today's job market reality is increasingly amorphous, unstable, non-hierarchical, nontraditional, and uncertain, we can expect to be changing jobs and making career transitions frequently. This leads to one inescapable conclusion—we had better become proficient career self-developers and life transition managers.

The good news is that while the bureaucratic career is ending, employment is not. We'll just need to get used to working differently, and thinking about and preparing for our work futures differently. For one thing, we all face a future of numerous and frequent work transitions, probably with a number of different employers.

In the new workplace, a variety of working modes are evolving and the demand for professionals and entrepreneurs is growing. Now you could become a consultant operating either independently, in a flexible networking group, or with a consulting agency. You might elect to create a home-based job or opt to work in one or more part-time options, either under the employment of one or more organizations or through temporary agencies. The possibilities, heightened by Internet capabilities, are limited only by our imagination and resources.

PACKAGING OURSELVES FOR INTERESTING WORK

How do we prepare ourselves for a viable career in the new work world? Futurists, such as career transition expert William Bridges, are now advocating that we begin thinking about ourselves careerwise as a personal business in which we offer specific prod-

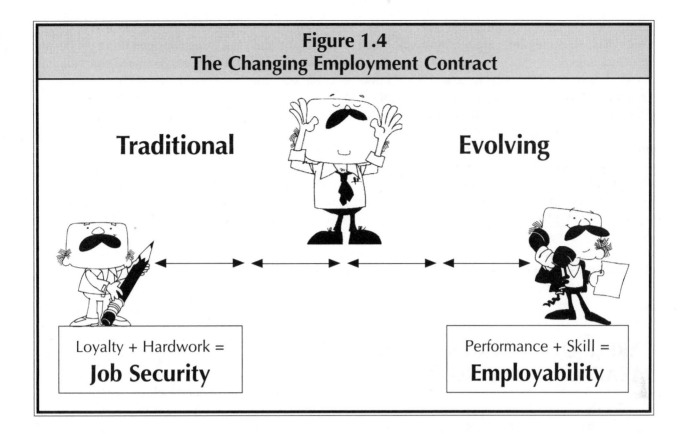

Figure 1.4
The Changing Employment Contract

Traditional

Evolving

Loyalty + Hardwork =
Job Security

Performance + Skill =
Employability

ucts to those customers needing what we have to offer. Our product is the skills, knowledge, and personal assets that we possess.

No matter which work mode we choose to pursue in our work and career, we are going to need to undertake a number of career management tasks in order to maintain our employability. We need to stop thinking about ourselves and presenting ourselves by bureaucratic job labels. We will need to be able to clearly and comfortably define ourselves via our marketable attributes—our expertise, personal assets, knowledge, and viable experiences. We'll also need to be able to define ourselves in terms of the value we can add to potential employers. Value added can best be translated from our achievements from the past that demonstrate our transferable skills and point to our future potentials and capabilities.

We'll need to master the skill of presenting ourselves via the service we can offer, and/or the knowledge and skills we have acquired and can demonstrate. We'll need to market ourselves on the basis of specific contributions we have made. We'll need to show how these have translated into some kinds of important and definable results, such as how we generated revenue, brought in new customers or retained old ones, enhanced quality of service, motivated

people to work together more effectively, trained employees to use new technology, creatively solved significant problems, or produced new opportunities.

Many have called this our "skills portfolio." We need to show what we can do, not just the label of where we have worked.

CAREER RESPONSIBILITY AND RESOURCES

Traditional career development of the bureaucratic variety has long been viewed as primarily an organizational responsibility. Organizations laid out clearly defined occupational tracks, provided whatever training they felt was needed for individuals in these tracks, evaluated individual performance, and promoted based on the evaluations of supervisors. The individual's career development responsibility involved initial educational preparation in order to achieve entrance eligibility into an occupational series and thereafter to perform dependably. In the new workplace, however, career development is becoming a very different proposition. Organizations are moving towards flatter, leaner, less hierarchical structures. They are hiring far fewer full-time employees and more contracted services and employees. And they are employing much, much more technology.

We live in a world in which technological information is doubling every five years and its applications are being rapidly incorporated into every conceivable aspect of organizational life and work. In order, therefore, to remain technologically and educationally resilient we need to view our learning as a high priority and an ongoing personal responsibility. Professional growth is far too important to leave to chance or in the hands of an organization for whom we currently happen to be working. Having a forward-looking educational/professional development plan enables us to maintain our knowledge and skills at a level appropriate to the kind of career future we desire.

CAREER DEVELOPMENT IN PARADIGM SHIFTING TIMES

We can't always avoid unexpected shocks like losing a job, but we can be better prepared for change by viewing career decision making as a continuing, lifelong process rather than as an occasional event. We can do this by integrating the two separate but intimately related universes: the evolving inner world of self and the rapidly changing outer world. The following career development model diagram shows a relationship between the separate worlds. These two worlds have a simultaneous impact on our lives.

Figure 1.5 suggests that there are always a variety of dynamic forces acting upon us as we pursue our careers. These forces are generated both from the outer and inner worlds. A major change in either realm upsets a pre-existing equilibrium and initiates an inner drive to regain a personal comfort zone. This process works much as thermostats regulate room temperature. We all possess a thermostatic-like regulating mechanism that operates to keep our systems at a self-determined, albeit unconscious, comfort zone. When anything upsets this idiosyncratic setting, our system reacts by attempting to return things to normal.

For example, a great many of those who lost tenured track positions, such as middle managers with General Motors, aeronautical engineers with Lockheed, and blue-collar workers with Bethlehem Steel, suffered serious psychological consequences. Emotional trauma is experienced not only from the actual loss of salary and benefits but even more so from the perceived loss of status and sense of self-worth related to intangible factors such as job status, title, position, or organizational association. The reaction to such a traumatic event can rob us of hope and leave us not only frightened and reeling, but unsure of who we are or the meaning of our life and work. Concentrating our problem solving and decision making solely on getting another job won't necessarily reestablish homeostasis, that is, return us to our old personal comfort zone. In terms of the career process model, such effort would make no more sense than merely repairing the body of a car dam-

---

Table 1.2
Ten Keys to Career Opportunity and Employability in the New Workplace
• Know yourself—your marketable talents, motivations and assets
• Define yourself in value-added terms
• Marketplace awareness—where can your assets and energies contribute
• Be future intelligent
• Clarify your career field and become a visible performer
• Actively participate in a professional association
• Develop and maintain an active network in your field
• Have a professional development plan—invest in your future employability
• Become a career change and transition master
• Take responsibility for your career future through your daily decision making

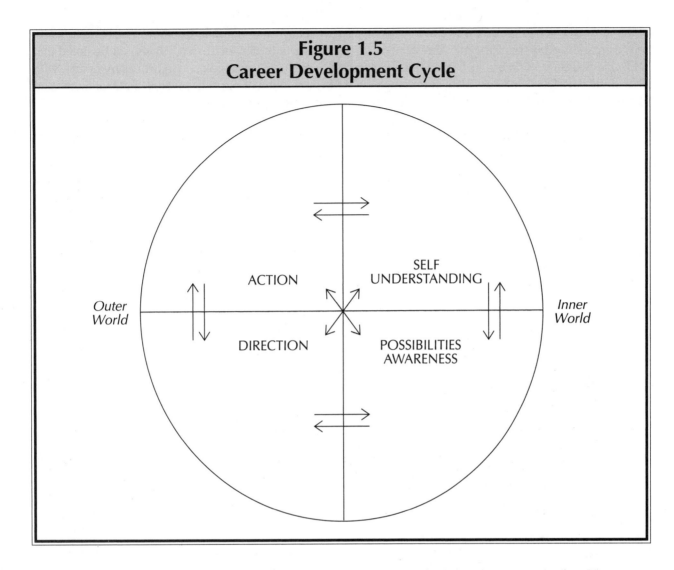

Figure 1.5
Career Development Cycle

Outer World

ACTION

SELF UNDERSTANDING

DIRECTION

POSSIBILITIES AWARENESS

Inner World

aged in a head-on collision without attending to the engine. When the world dramatically changes around us, we need to change ourselves in appropriate ways. An important aspect of this change must address the human engine—the self.

A major change within the inner realm of the self (physical, psychological, spiritual) can also upset the psyche's equilibrium and produce career ramifications. Dramatic and unforeseen changes, such as the loss of a dearly loved one or a traumatic deterioration in one's own health, are sure to disrupt an established sense of personal order. But there are other and less apparent dynamics that generate perplexities for the inner world—confrontations with one's aging, emotional burn out, personal meaning crises, personal values shifts, spiritual awakening, and existential angst. Even those just beginning their careers struggle with understanding themselves, be-

coming independent from parents, and establishing themselves as adults.

The model shows that our attention continually moves from a focus in one quadrant to another as we respond to the dynamics of inner and outer forces. There is no sequential order to this process; we just

Web Connect

Managing transitions is key to self-development. For additional articles on transitions, such as "How You Can Handle Change Better," check out William Bridges and Associates at **www.wmbridges.com**

might jump from any quadrant to another at any time. Expanding personal insight may lead us to ACTION, and some actions may force unpredictable SELF-UNDERSTANDING or create interesting new DIRECTIONS. New POSSIBILITIES may occur to us at any time—even in the shower, driving to work, or over a beer with a friend. It should be noted that we begin this cycle in our early formative years, with the evolution of our self-concept, and that there is no end to this process.

CASE STUDY
PAULA

At the midpoint of what seemed to have been a secure career track, Paula's position as an accountant with a Washington, D.C., commercial real estate firm abruptly ended with a job-termination notice. Like thousands of others in the finance industry, Paula was the victim of a tidal wave of mergers, consolidations, and "right-sizings." Even though she had been successful as an accountant, she had never fully enjoyed this kind of work. However, since she was unsure what else might be better and because she was fully supporting herself with a nice salary and benefits, she had stayed with the job, giving little consideration to her future. But then, in her forties, the job termination convinced her that the time had come for a major career change. She concluded that since seeking job security would be a blind alley anyway, she might as well invest the time and energy to discover what she really wanted to do.

Before receiving her job termination Paula had been preoccupied with the outer-world dynamics of her career. Now, shocked by the unexpected job loss, she was forced into reassessing what to do next. In terms of the career development cycle, she was catapulted from the ACTION quadrant into the SELF-UNDERSTANDING quadrant. She could not go back to what she had; those kinds of positions were melting like old snow in warm spring showers. But after long tenure in one industry, she felt unprepared to deal with her major predicament—what did she want and what was available?

Paula decided to engage the services of both a professional therapist and a career counselor to obtain deeper self-awareness and to help clarify her personal interests and career possibilities. Her self-inquiry focused around questions such as Who am I now?, What do I truly value?, What are my core personal assets?, What do I really want?, and What new possibilities are available or could I create?

With new insights into these kinds of questions, she moved on to the POSSIBILITIES AWARENESS quadrant of the model. She began developing a lengthy list of options that would capitalize on her top talents and engage her strongest interests. We often encourage clients in this phase to develop 40 or more possibilities without being too concerned about their practicalities. The most important thing here is to tap creative ideas, particularly those that connect with personal potentials and passions. The emphasis is on quantity rather than quality. The rationale for this is that you can't get to real quality without first generating powerful ideas. Such ideas tend to originate intuitively and creatively rather than deductively and analytically. Analysis is called for later in the decision-making process when the wheat (brilliant ideas) must be separated from the chaff (unworkable ideas).

Paula was able to choose a new career direction after exploring those she believed to be her best bets. Self-assessment helped uncover a creative bent (new awareness after concentrating on her analytical skills for so many years) in the form of love for art and aesthetic appreciation of old buildings. Through information interviews with people in the arts, architecture, and related fields, she discovered the historic preservation field and learned which colleges offer degrees in that specialty. She went on to obtain a bachelor of science degree at one of these colleges, doing so well that she opted then to continue on for a master's. When last heard from she was preparing to work with an architectural firm in the business of restoring and regenerating deteriorated downtown centers of historical communities.

Paula recognized that this transition would probably not be her last. Yet in spite of the temporary nature of today's career situation, she has a sense of security that comes from preparation for the reality of the changing world in which she lives. She has a much clearer knowledge of who she is, what she wants in her life and career, and how to market her strengths. Although she doesn't know how long her current employment situation will last, she feels confident in her ability to market herself, get jobs, and create income-generating work as a consultant. She no longer intends to find job security with a Fortune 500 corporation but is much more content to work in smaller organizations where she can make a difference and have some fun in the process.

CRITICAL ISSUES AND NEW REALITIES

Change in today's workplace is of such magnitude that the reality we knew is undergoing radical alteration. Futurists refer to change of such magnitude as paradigm shifts. Paradigm shifts bring both negative and positive outcomes. The bad news is that little remains of our once relatively stable and predictable occupational world. The good news is that the new era has opened up unprecedented opportunities for just about everyone willing to take advantage of them. Doing so, however, necessitates creative decision making and assertive transition management.

The emergence of a new era forces us to examine old assumptions and to formulate new concepts about life, work, and career. One such concept has to do with the role of fun and personal passion in work. Neither fun nor passion were considered to be legitimate career objectives in the past. But that is changing! That's because there are far more choices available to more individuals than ever before. There has never been a better time for discovering ways to find our passions in work.

Assessing personal and deeply felt interests is a career consideration for many reasons. One of these has to do with an employer's perspective on hiring. In today's market reality, what employers in their right minds would hire people whose only objective was to get a job? Especially if they were able to acquire the skills and commitments of people who

have a real passion for the work? Additionally, in a world filled with a great variety of choices and rapidly expanding possibilities, why would anyone elect to spend their time in work they disliked?

Figure 1.6
The Relationship: Passion and the New Workplace

minus passion for your future you'll feel more stress and have less energy

– Passion

+ Passion

transcend the fear of change with a compelling vision

Stress is another reason to change our perspectives about career decision making. The uncertainties of these times provoke anxiety. The current stress levels are undoubtedly elevated by decades of conditioning to seek job security and avoid risk. Pursuing a personal passion may well be the best antidote to "new-age" stress.

In this regard, passion is directly related to energy and inversely related to stress. Unremitting stress robs us of energy, enthusiasm, and hope. These, conversely, are just the ingredients that our personal passions generate. Both stress and passion involve the imagination in anticipation of the future. Personal energy becomes directed, concentrated, and action-focused when we visualize ourselves achieving interesting goals. We motivate ourselves from the inside out—a highly self-empowering process.

Stress, on the other hand, involves preoccupation with frightening possibilities, draining away energy into deceptive fantasies—a self-victimizing activity.

For those who fail to take advantage of the opportunities for self-development and self-direction that the newly evolving knowledge-service era increasingly provides, the future may look dismal. Their best hope may be to hit the lottery big or to squeak into a cushy retirement. For those recognizing the opportunities available in the new era and willing to take full advantage of them, the future has never been brighter. It is a perceptual difference! Viewing the future through the eyes of fear results in becoming victims of our feelings. Seeing the promise of the future generates hope, energy, and enthusiasm. It's your choice!

 ## EXERCISE 1-A. CAREER ROLE MODELS

Does the idea of "having a career" bring a role model to mind for you? Perhaps your career role model is a parent, a spouse, or someone you greatly admire. One of the authors of this text thinks of Swiss psychiatrist Dr. Carl Jung as an ideal career role model while another thinks of scientist Albert Einstein, and the third identifies with Peanuts creator Charles Schultz.

a) What individuals come to mind whose careers might serve as ideal role models for you?

b) In what ways do you identify with the individuals you have listed above?

EXERCISE 1-B. YOUR LIFE AND WORK _____

1. If you were to write a novel of the story of your life to date:

   a) What titles would you give to your major chapter headings? List several of them:

   b) What do you see as the primary themes of your life story to date?

   c) What title would you give to the novel of your life story to date?

   d) What might the jacket cover of your life story novel look like? What are some of the things that might be on the jacket cover? Draw one, let your imagination run freely!

2. If you were to continue your life story into the future:

a) What are some themes you might elect to write into the continuation?

b) What are some possible titles you might elect for the next chapter of your life story?

c) What are some titles you might consider for Part II of your life story?

EXERCISE 1-C. YOUR CAREER/LIFE ROLES

Think of the life roles you are currently playing (child, student, worker, parent, partner, homemaker, citizen, leisurite). What do you enjoy about each role?

Think about the life roles you anticipate playing (child, student, worker, parent, partner, homemaker, citizen, leisurite). How do you think these roles will blend together to help you create a satisfying career/life?

EXERCISE 1-D. YOUR CAREER/LIFE DECISIONS OF THE PAST _____

A career/life decision is one that has had a significant effect on your career and your life. In the spaces provided below, list several of the most significant career/life choices you have made so far in your life. Examples: early childhood memories (changing training wheels on bike, joining a youth choir, etc.), first work experience, summer job, selection of high school courses, decision to attend college, first job, job change, getting married, having children, leaving home, moving, joining the service.

Start by listing the earliest decision you can recall and then record each subsequent major career/life choice in chronological order to the present time. Enter your decisions to the right of the numbers below, leaving the line to the left blank for now.

My Career/Life-Shaping Decisions of the Past and How I Made Them

___ 1. _____

___ 2. _____

___ 3. _____

___ 4. _____

___ 5. _____

___ 6. _____

___ 7. _____

___ 8. _____

___ 9. _____

___ 10. _____

_____

EXERCISE 1-E. ASSESSING YOUR DECISION-MAKING STYLE _____

From the list below, select the best description(s) of how you made your choices in Exercise 1-D above. Fill in the lines to the left of each decision in 1-D with the appropriate letter(s) from the following list:

A. Took the safest way.

B. Took the easiest way.

C. Let someone else decide for me.

D. Did what I thought others expected me to do.

E. Did what I had been taught that I should do.

F. Did the first thing that came to my mind.

G. Did nothing.

H. Chose what I felt was intuitively right.

I. Consciously weighed all of the alternatives available and then chose the best one.

J. Used some other approach. _____

_____

ASSIGNMENTS

1. From the exercises above, what did you learn about the way you have made your career/life decisions in the past?

2. What effects have your past career/life choices had on your life? How do the outcomes of these decisions affect you now?

3. Based on what you learned about your past career/life decision-making style and the effect of these choices on your life, what changes would you like to make?

 Similar to small businesses that open and close, Web sites come and go. This means that some of the Web sites listed in this book will probably change during the time you are reading this material. Therefore, we have created a page on the Web where you can go to ensure you have the most up-to-date links for each of the chapters. To find these links, go to **www.CareerKiosk.org** and click on "Updated links for *Your Career*." These links will ensure that you have accurate links and access to great sites on the Web!

REFERENCES

ARTICLES

"Managing Your Career/Special Report." *Fortune* 15 January 1996:33–79.

Barner, Robert. "The New Career Strategist: Career Management for the Year 2000 and Beyond." *The Futurist* Sept.–Oct. 1995.

Borchard, David. "Planning for Career & Life: Job Surfing on the Tidal Waves of Change." *The Futurist* Jan.–Feb. 1995.

Butts, Dan. "Joblessness, Pain, Power, Pathology and Promise." *Journal of Organizational Change Management* 10 (1997):111–129.

BOOKS

Bird, Caroline. *Second Careers, New Ways to Work After 50*. New York: Little Brown & Co., 1992.

Bolles, Richard N. *What Color Is Your Parachute?* Berkeley, CA: Ten Speed Press, Revised annually.

Bridges, William. *Creating You & Co.: Learn to Think Like the CEO of Your Own Career*. Reading, MA: Addison-Wesley, 1997.

Bridges, William. *Job Shift: How to Prosper in a Workplace Without Jobs*. Reading, MA: Addison-Wesley, 1994.

Hudson, Frederick. *The Adult Years: Mastering the Art of Self-Renewal*. San Francisco: Jossey-Bass, 1991.

Leider, Richard & David Shapiro. *Repackaging Your Bags: Lighten Your Load for the Rest of Your Life*. San Francisco: Berrett-Koehler, 1995.

Handy, Charles. *Beyond Certainty: The Changing Worlds of Organizations*. Boston: Harvard Business School Press, 1996.

Rifkin, Jeremy. *The End of Work: The Decline of the Global Labor Force and the Dawn of the Post-Market Era*. Putnam Books, 1995.

Virtual Career Planning

Changing the world means not just the latest technology or gadget or business plan that Wall Street falls in love with. Creating a revolution also requires contemplation, introspection, even some skepticism.
—Mark Gimein, Writer, Newsweek
"How to Use the Internet to Choose or Change Careers"

Do you know people who—

☑ Turn on their computer to find career information before going to a library?
☑ Can find the career information they want on the Internet within a few minutes of searching?
☑ Can rattle off the names of the biggest career planning and job search web sites?
☑ Access online career information in order to plan their career and launch their job search?

If so, you know people who have learned how to tap the virtual wealth of career planning information and services available through the Internet.

At last Kim realized what had gone wrong with her Internet job search. She had made a terrible mistake by leaving the first "r" out of driver.

TRADITIONAL METHODS OF CAREER PLANNING: LIBRARIES AND CAREER CENTERS UNPLUGGED

Until the 1990s, the public library was the most coveted research destination for those embarking on a career search. Most libraries were packed with countless occupational reference materials, volumes of employer descriptions and annual reports, the leading career books with the latest advice on how to plan a career and search for a job, and periodicals brimming with employment trends. The typical person would need to spend weeks combing these voluminous publications to find the most up-to-date information on an industry or career field.

"Searchable" text meant using your index finger to glance at the text in search of self-identified "key words," hoping, of course, not to skip critical information. Frequently, one would copy pages of employment articles from texts, newspapers, magazines, and trade journals only to spread them out on the living room floor and try to make some sense of the information and data presented.

Overall it was a time-consuming yet critical process for effective career planning. One could expect to spend many days and evenings with nickels in hand and folders to haul home a heavy load of photocopied materials.

Before the computer became a standard tool in the late twentieth century, the luckiest of all career planners was the campus-based college student. Campus libraries were a few steps away from dorms and parking lots, but even better than that was the career center library—a pre-Internet version of the one-stop career shop. A career planner's dream: All the materials you could hope for to plan a career and conduct a thorough job search. Replete with formal and informal assessments, this campus career center included all the career, industry and employer reference materials and files you could possibly imagine, videos to help you at different stages of the process, and real live career counselors to counsel, advise and coach you through the process. Yes, those were the days.

As public libraries and career centers catapulted their business into the Information Age to serve their clients, the libraries and centers no longer existed as we once knew them. From paper references to virtual references, the Internet—within one decade—forever changed libraries and centers large and small, public and private, career and conventional. By the new millennium, the research resource of choice for career planning was—and remains—the Internet.

The medium for research and career planning changed—but did the process for career planning change as well? This critical issue we'll explore in this chapter.

THE INFLUENCES OF TECHNOLOGY ON CAREER PLANNING

Career centers got a real boost in the late 1980s and early 1990s when computers started working their way into career center designs. Soon career planning software was developed by several companies and resumes and cover letters could be produced quickly. Public demand for more computers in public and educational institutions helped launch the age of technology—the Information Age—as we know it today. Computers quickly became a staple for students to write papers and reports. As the Internet made an appearance on campuses nationwide in the early 1990s, students' demand for virtual services pushed career centers to quickly become technology centers and conduits of virtual information—albeit very minimal career information to start. Sooner than most e-services, career planning information and assistance crossed the digital threshold and glided gracefully into the Internet era (see Figure 2.1).

The Internet has revolutionized career planning. Never has there been a time of so much opportunity to explore careers and plan for your future while ac-

Words of Wisdom

In all this, it's useful to bear in mind that cyberspace is a tool, for both companies and job hunters—an immensely useful one, but not yet a substitute for the office behind the door marked PERSONNEL.
Mark Lange, VP, Business Development/ HireSystems

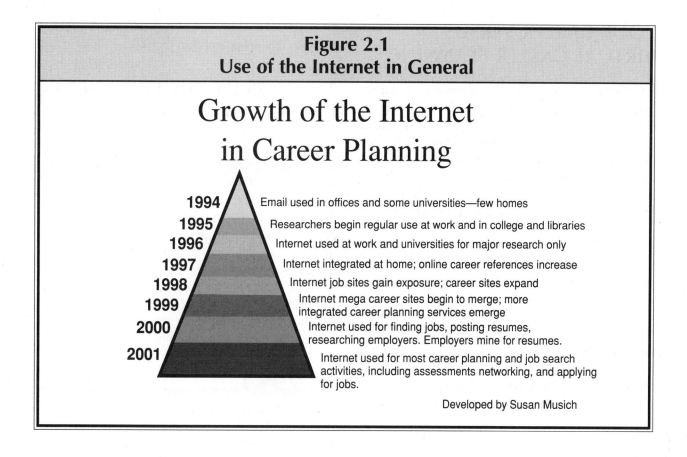

Figure 2.1
Use of the Internet in General

Growth of the Internet in Career Planning

1994 — Email used in offices and some universities—few homes

1995 — Researchers begin regular use at work and in college and libraries

1996 — Internet used at work and universities for major research only

1997 — Internet integrated at home; online career references increase

1998 — Internet job sites gain exposure; career sites expand

1999 — Internet mega career sites begin to merge; more integrated career planning services emerge

2000 — Internet used for finding jobs, posting resumes, researching employers. Employers mine for resumes.

2001 — Internet used for most career planning and job search activities, including assessments networking, and applying for jobs.

Developed by Susan Musich

commodating the need for identifying up-to-date and relevant information with minimal research time—relatively speaking, of course.

In the mid-1990s, you could access basic information about many companies—particularly those that had joined the Internet revolution early on and established web sites that included simple company profiles. Previously, you needed to call a company and ask them to mail a copy of their annual report, or you would spend hours in the library pouring through the many business reference materials and periodicals to learn more about the organization. The Internet was a research tool to access information and explore some career opportunities.

By the late 1990s, however, the virtual landscape changed dramatically. From a basic resource to an integrated career planning tool, the Internet began showing signs of its true potential with regard to career development. Interactivity was the name of the e-game. Web sites now allowed for applying to colleges, taking courses online, assessing different dimensions of yourself and receiving the results, cross-referencing career and industry research, matching interests to career fields, finding specific data on lo-

cal jobs, networking and communicating with people around the world, being advised and coached by career counselors, and conducting a job search by posting resumes online and searching multiple job banks from only one site.

Career counselors around the country have worked at an amazingly fast pace to stay on top of the ever-changing career-related web sites. Universities and colleges have led the way in the career development field by creating their own web sites to host career information and resources. Now many even offer web-based advising, assessments, and other services.

Web Connect

If you're interested in reading more about the influence of technology on careers, recruitment and other areas, take a look at the wealth of information available on NUA Internet Surveys at **www.nua.com/ surveys**.

YOUR CAREER VERSUS VIRTUAL CAREER PLANNING

If the Internet is truly the super career source that we purport, then you must be wondering why we encourage you to use this book in planning your career. The answer is simple: Because the Internet provides the information, but does not evaluate it; and because the Internet is a medium that relies heavily on an intuitive approach by the end-user, the Internet presents information in a way that can derail a guided approach designed to ensure a thorough career planning process. Therefore, this book is a tool to help you go through an effective and purposeful process that will keep you focused and moving forward to meet your career planning goals.

We strongly believe, however, that the vast resources available online are valuable and can augment the information and exercises contained in this book. Therefore, we have added web resources to introduce you to relevant and quality online resources that may be helpful now or at some point in the future.

We have made an attempt to demystify the process of using the Internet in conjunction with your career planning and your job searching by identifying useful web sites that are noted throughout this book to help you. There are many excellent career sites, but just as you do not need five different hammers to build a solid house, our intention is not to provide a comprehensive selection of the career sites—you don't need all of them. You only need what will help you complete the task to achieve your goal. This book stands alone on that account, but the sites will, in some cases, provide additional information on a topic, or provide additional resources to help you complete a task.

The career planning information online has exploded in the last few years and will most likely continue to grow even more in the years to come. You have probably already used the Internet for some career planning and job hunting tasks, such as searching for courses to take, exploring internship or employment possibilities, and perhaps even taking some online career assessments or "quizzes." What you may not be familiar with, however, are some of the lesser-known—yet high-quality—career planning resources online that can help you as you read the chapters and work through the exercises in this

book. In each chapter, we have presented a few of the sites that are relevant to the task at hand.

TEN USES OF THE INTERNET IN CAREER PLANNING

Most people think of the Internet as a resource for the job search, such as finding jobs, posting resumes, and preparing for interviews. Most people, however, use online resources and services that have minimal value when they could be accessing resources that provide maximum impact (see Figure 2.2). Savvy individuals are learning to tap the wealth of career planning resources that have developed and matured in recent years. By the end of this chapter, we hope, the "Methods" pyramid in Figure 2.2 will invert to reflect your knowledge of the value in using the Internet for career planning purposes.

Career planning information and services that are wrapped in Internet clothing often create endless discussions and debates among career development professionals with regard to information quality, career counselor preparation for and competence with technology, and myriad ethical issues surrounding technology-driven services. But the bottom line is that these services and resources are in demand—and in the e-world, where there is demand, there is immediate supply.

Thus, as more and more people have flocked to their computers, the e-world has wittingly taken command and responded to the demand with overwhelming quantity, but questionable quality. More evaluation of such e-services is needed to ensure the end-users receive what they need and expect. This issue is not unique to the online career planning resources, but pervasive throughout the e-service world. However, consulting with a web-savvy career development expert (your career planning professor, a career counselor or other such expert) can help shape your e-journey and help you surf the web for value—not volume. Figure 2.3 displays the best overall areas of content and services now online to help with career planning and job searching.

SELF-ASSESSMENT

With thousands of career sites competing for online attention, assessments and quizzes have served as an attraction for people who seek some direction with their career planning and job search-

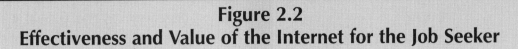

Figure 2.2
Effectiveness and Value of the Internet for the Job Seeker

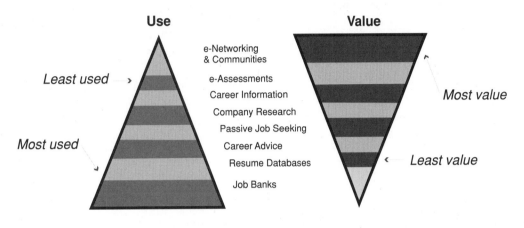

Effectiveness & Value of Web for Career Planning

Use

Least used →

Most used →

e-Networking & Communities
e-Assessments
Career Information
Company Research
Passive Job Seeking
Career Advice
Resume Databases
Job Banks

Value

Most value →

← Least value

Developed by Susan Musich

Effectiveness and Value of the Internet for the Job Seeker (adapted from Richard N. Bolles' model "How Job Seekers Find Work")

ing. These assessments and quizzes can provide insight and additional information to help you learn more about yourself and how you fit in the world of work. We have found some valuable sites—several are noted in the following chapters—but we caution you in taking such assessments without professional assistance to review and interpret the results. Keep in mind that career assessments are *not* prescriptive—they cannot tell you what you *should* do or *could* do. Instead, they only offer additional information that must be factored into the larger career planning equation.

A growing trend is that employers are beginning to offer assessments on their own sites. Usually these assessments are offered on the pages where they post jobs and discuss work opportunities with their company. These assessments are designed to determine whether or not you are the "right fit" for the company. In other words, you may be the best qualified applicant, but might not fit in with the organization's culture.

EXPLORING CAREERS AND INDUSTRIES

The strength of the Internet lies in the ability to research and cross-reference information easily and quickly. Exploring ordinary possibilities is where your research skills can be tested to produce extraordinary information. Whereas once this aspect of career planning took weeks to uncover the best information, you now have golden nuggets of career and industry information at your fingertips within seconds. Professional associations, government organizations, and specialized career sites offer up-to-date information and data that can help you explore and find information that can help you gauge your interest in pursuing such a career or field.

RESEARCHING EMPLOYERS

Not only are volumes of employer profiles available at numerous web sites, but employers themselves offer information about their organization on their own web site. Available online are annual re-

Figure 2.3
Ten Best Uses of the Internet in Career Planning

1. Self-assessment
2. Exploring careers and industries
3. Researching employers
4. Finding career and job information
5. e-Networking and e-communities
6. Career guidance and coaching
7. Practicing for interviews
8. Developing and posting resumes
9. Searching and applying for jobs
10. Continuing education and training

ports, company profiles, salary scales, company culture, company-specific discussion groups, project information, and a whole lot more to help you examine different employers and what they can offer your career (as well as what you can offer them).

FINDING CAREER AND JOB INFORMATION

From labor statistics to job search logistics, you can find information on just about every stage of career planning and the job search. However, you will be treading into territory that varies from site to site in appropriateness and quality. One site may offer information on the ten best-paying careers or the best way to write a resume, but the site may be geared toward those living in a particular region, or those with a particular level of education. Most university and college career centers' web sites offer links to information that should be appropriate for you. We suggest you start there. If you're looking for other sites, check with a career web expert or consult the resources listed at the end of this chapter.

E-NETWORKING AND E-COMMUNITIES

Once it was considered taboo to develop networking relationships with others if not done in a face-to-face setting, but the Internet has changed the way we communicate and the way we interact with society. In fact, it has expanded our opportunities to connect with others whom we may never see. Most 20-something students know this already, as they grew up with a mouse in hand and an e-mail address

for close friends. This communication style probably comes to them naturally. Older students, students who didn't grow up with computers, and many students from other countries, however, may not think of e-communication as a natural interaction. If you're comfortable with e-mail, listservs, bulletin boards and chat rooms and are already connected to this medium, then you're ready for the next step: to explore opportunities through online communities to enhance your career planning efforts. If you're not comfortable with e-communication, then we suggest that you read *Networking on the Internet* at http://dlis.gseis.ucla.edu/people/pagre/network.html by Phil Agre. This 70-plus-page article is, in our opinion, the best guidance for online networking. It is geared toward doctoral students, but the guidance, overall, is applicable to all students. It is updated regularly and provides details on how to network effectively online.

CAREER GUIDANCE AND COACHING

While the Internet can serve as a communication tool, it cannot always replace the face-to-face interaction and synergy that comes from working directly with a career counselor or advisor. Nonverbal communication is a large part of the career counseling process and without advanced video capabilities, e-career counseling can become a virtual mishap. We are seeing an increase in online coaching and advising services, but we hesitate to support this approach without evaluating each individualized service. On the other hand, there are some online guidance sites that can be helpful, such as *The Washington Post's* online career advice at www.washingtonpost.com (click on *Washington Jobs* on the home page and then click on *Advice* on the career pages). This site—and other similar sites—tend to write more generally about career planning topics. They allow you to post questions to career experts, and also allow you to go through the other questions and responses.

PRACTICING FOR INTERVIEWS

There are numerous online articles offering tips and tricks for mastering the interview. Practicing how to interview and then evaluating yourself and practicing again seems to make a whole lot of sense. University and college career counselors have been helping students for years to practice interviews through mock or video-taped interview practice. Now you can go to a few sites to actually read the questions, select or type in your best response, and then see how well you handled the question. Read more about this in Chapter 11, *Searching for a Job to Fit Your Talents*.

DEVELOPING AND POSTING RESUMES

Resume styles have always changed with time, and with the emergence of the Internet, they have changed once again. In some cases, such as with scannable resumes, traditional resume rules don't apply. You can find cyberwide guidance on how to develop a resume in varied formats. The quality of the information on doing so varies significantly. Resumes can be tricky, so it's best to make sure you get your guidance from a reputable source. We offer some suggestions in Chapter 11, *Searching for a Job to Fit Your Talents*.

In addition to developing your resume, many career sites allow you to post your resume for employers. Depending on the statistics you read, you will note that anywhere from two to 40 percent of online resumes reap contacts by employers. These varied statistics indicate the fact that nobody really knows how well this is working for job seekers overall. Success of this probably depends on your career field (high-tech folks *should* post online) and your preference for employers. Larger employers can afford the high fees that accompany resume bank searches for hard-to-fill positions, while smaller and midsized companies may forgo the high fees for more traditional paper resumes or applications.

SEARCHING AND APPLYING FOR JOBS

The foremost reason career planners and job seekers wade through the Internet is to find jobs. With millions of jobs listed and instant access and sorting capabilities that narrow an extensive search down to ten or so dream jobs, job listings lead many to believe that they have exclusive access to this information. Such an attitude traps thousands of people daily into endlessly searching and applying for jobs found in these databases—only to wait and wait and wait for a response that usually never arrives.

So, why bother with these job banks? In fact, there is good reason to bother with them. These job banks can greatly enhance your career planning effort. By identifying the skills, knowledge, and abilities that are required for different jobs, you can get a sense of what it will take to land the career you think you would enjoy. We encourage you to back this up with other career research, but a quick trip across the job banks can give you a sense of a career field that you might be considering.

CONTINUING EDUCATION AND TRAINING

It used to be that a nice high school graduation gift was a set of luggage for college—or for the more fortunate, a car. Both were needed to get started in college. Now, however, a nice gift is a desktop or laptop computer—you can't do without it, or if you do, it's not easy. The computer has replaced the luggage just as distance learning is replacing the need for transportation. Now you can take courses online, supplement your education online, and even get an entire degree online. In a world where lifelong learning is becoming ever more important to a successful and developing career, it is good to know that learning can be done in a time and format that is convenient to you.

Words of Wisdom

"Call it the colonizing of cyberspace. Forget surfing: Today, people of like minds and interests are establishing Internet communities faster than any construction company in the brick-and-mortar world. According to a new Business Week/Harris Poll, 57% of those hopping on to the Net today go to the same sites repeatedly instead of wandering like nomads from one to the next. And of the 89% of Netizens who use E-mail, nearly one-third consider themselves part of an online community. 'We're at the beginning of an explosion,' says Andrew Busey, chairman and chief technology officer of ichat Inc., an Internet startup in Austin, Tex., that makes software for online chats. 'Community and communications is the next big wave on the Internet'."
Robert D. Hof, Internet Communities, Business Week, May 5, 1997
www.businessweek.com/1997/18/b35251.htm

EXERCISE 2-A. FINDING ONLINE INFORMATION

Just about every university, community college and technical school that has a career planning and placement office provides career-related information online. Go to your school's web site and find the career information provided for students. If your school does not offer this information, find the web site of an institution close in proximity to your school.

a) What kind of career information is offered to students? (such as career and job search services offered to students, informal assessments, career planning information, job search guidance, etc.)

b) Review the *Table of Contents* at the beginning of this book. List the type of career information on your school's career web pages that may be helpful to you as supplemental reading as you work through the chapters in this book?

c) Are there links to external web sites? What, in general, makes up the content of these external sites?

Words of Wisdom

"Like the PC, the Internet is a tidal wave. It will wash over the computer industry and many others, drowning those who don't learn to swim in its waves."
Bill Gates, Never Underestimate the Power of the Internet, article distributed by The New York Times Syndicate, August 1995.

THE INTERNET'S JOB, CAREER, AND BUSINESS BOON

Across the country and around the world, the Internet has done more than create an easier and faster forum for research and planning. In fact, it has resulted in the creation of millions of jobs and career opportunities. From low-tech content devel-opers to high-tech program designers, the Internet has created an industry that has transformed the modern world. The sudden emergence of jobs and opportunities has created an urgency for "e-talent." People of all ages are rushing to develop the mini-mal technological know-how in hope of being re-cruited by e-businesses.

As investors laid out cash to create virtual stores and e-services, thousands of newly declared entre-preneurs launched e-businesses in hopes of cashing in on the American dream within months, as opposed to years or a lifetime. Never has there been a time when so many millionaires were under the age of 30.

Because of its success, the high-tech world no longer carries the stigma of "geek," but instead wears the badge of envy. The career possibilities of-fered by the Internet continually change and new jobs continue to evolve. There is a glut of profession-als to fill the thousands of jobs that continue to open. Still, those who roll the high-tech dice take a risk in working in a field of constant change and no guaran-tees—as we saw when many of the dotcoms went bust in 2000 and 2001 and many lost their jobs.

These kids we hire off the Internet just keep getting younger and younger.

Web Connect

To read more about the impact of technology on jobs, careers, and business, check out *On the Edge of the Digital Age* at **www.startribune.com/stonline/html/digage/logfx.htm** This article series provides a fascinating look at how the author believes the "Digital Age" is evolving and what it will be like, based on numerous interviews with key experts and more than 50 books on the subject.

The Internet continues to redefine the demand and e-needs of society. As these needs are continually defined and refined, e-careers will continue to evolve, change, and expand.

SUMMARY

With the Internet's continual expansion of career information and services, it is important to note what it can and cannot do. The Internet is a rich resource to supplement your career planning, but it cannot replace the guided process that will help you in reaching your career planning goals.

Similar to small businesses that open and close, Web sites come and go. This means that some of the Web sites listed in this book will probably change during the time you are reading this material. Therefore, we have created a page on the Web where you can go to ensure you have the most up-to-date links for each of the chapters. To find these links, go to **www.CareerKiosk.org** and click on "Updated links for *Your Career*." These links will ensure that you have accurate links and access to great sites on the Web!

REFERENCES

Bloom, John and Garry R. Walz. *Cybercounseling and Cyberlearning: Strategies and Resources for the Millennium* American Counseling Association and CAPS Inc. In association with ERIC Counseling and Student Services Clearinghouse, 2000.

Gates, Bill, "Never Underestimate the Power of the Internet." Article distributed by *The New York Times Syndicate*, August 1995.

Harris-Bowlsbey, Joann, Margaret Riley Dikel, and James P. Sampson, Jr. *The Internet: A Tool for Career Planning* National Career Development Association, 1998.

Hof, Robert D. "Internet Communities." *Business Week*, 5 May 1997. www.businessweek.com/1997/18/b35251.htm

Keyy, Kevin. "Wealth Is Overrated." *Wired* March 1998:161.

Schlesinger, Eric S. and Susan Musich. *SAMs Teach Yourself Today e-Job Hunting*. Macmillan, 2000.

Your Skills in Action

"But I don't have many skills . . ."
"I've just been a housewife all my adult life."
"I've only had unskilled jobs."
"I just graduated from high school."
—anonymous students

Do you know people who—

☑ Believe that they don't have skills?

☑ Aren't aware of whether they prefer working with data, people, or things?

☑ Feel that they have skills but don't realize how these can transfer from one job or career to another?

☑ Are reluctant to change careers because they feel they don't have the right skills for the new career?

☑ Have highly developed talents but have difficulty finding and keeping jobs?

If so, then you know people who share common misconceptions about their personal skills. The truth is that all of us have a great many skills, and we are all highly talented in our own ways.

ABUNDANT SKILLS

Although almost everyone is uniquely talented, most of us have only a vague awareness of what our skills really are. It's unlikely that we will realize our unique potentials unless we are clear about what skills we possess. Understanding our unique skills can help us choose a career or see how our skills might transfer from one field, occupation, or job to another.

The word *skills,* as used here, refers to competencies or developed abilities needed to achieve a desired outcome or to make something happen. Skills are the foundation of all human achievement. Your skills continuously come into play in all your activities, from leisure to learning to work-related tasks, from routine actions to complex projects. It takes some blending of skills to do anything, even routine functions like talking, writing, walking the dog, taking out the garbage, or teaching your canary to talk.

As you study this chapter and perform the various exercises, we encourage you to keep two important ideas in mind. The first is that you can acquire skills in almost any area you choose. The second is that because each of us possesses unique genetic endowments and life programming, some types of skills will be easier and much more enjoyable to develop than others. Therefore, we encourage you not to underestimate your ability to acquire whatever skills are needed for your career and education. We do recommend, however, that you pay special attention to your natural endowments or your preferred skills. These are the skills that are the most likely to be the keys to your success—the skills that you will be motivated to use and to develop. Take your preferred skills into account as you make your career and life goals. Look for ways to capitalize on them; they are your unique gifts. The assessment activities of Chapters 3 through 7 are designed to help you clarify just what your unique gifts are. Exercises contained in Chapters 8 through 11 will assist you in setting goals to capitalize on your particular interests and potential.

TYPES OF SKILLS

Three types of skills are discussed in this chapter: functional, self-management, and special knowledge. Functional skills are abilities or talents that are inherited at birth and developed through experience and learning. They are aptitude related and determine your proficiency with data, people, and things. Self-management skills are the behaviors you have developed in learning to cope with your environment and the people and conditions in it. Special knowledge skills are those having to do with mastering a specific body of information related to a particular type of work, profession, occupation, educational or leisure activity. Special knowledge skills are what you have learned and committed to memory. The following table provides examples of the three different types of skills.

Web Connect

The list of skills on the following pages is quite extensive. However, if you wish to identify additional skills or think that the list of skills don't fully represent your abilities, you may add skills to the lists by going to **Creative Job Search's Online Guide** at **http://www.amby.com/worksite/cjs/cjsbook2/skill6d.htm** This site also helps you identify the adaptive skills that characterize you. We suggest that you carefully write in the additional skills selected under the appropriate heading. The skill labels on the web site are slightly different than the ones we've listed here, so here is some guidance: The job skills listed at the beginning fall under "J. Functional Skills" heading. The self-management skills in the second section fall under "JJ. Self Management Skills." The remaining skills listed under the transferable skills section all fall under " J. Functional Skills" category. For the purpose of this exercise, you only need to be concerned about placing these skills under one of the two headings—you needn't be concerned as to whether or not you have them in the correct subcategory.

An extensive list of transferable interpersonal and technical skills for "J. Functional Skills" can be found on the web site **Skills Zone** at **www.pch.gc.ca/Cyberstation/html/szone2_e.htm**

Table 3.1
Three Types of Skills

Functional	Self-Management	Special Knowledge
Starting new ventures	Energetic	Financial planning
Negotiating contracts	Determined	Real estate brokering
Creating new services	Resourceful	Catering
Diagnosing interpersonal problems	Insightful	Group dynamics
Repairing machines	Dependable	Brake systems (on cars)
Calculating taxes	Ethical	Accounting
Coaching athletes	Enthusiastic	Basketball strategy
Making decisions	Responsible	Career planning
Analyzing samples	Methodical	Chemical laboratory
Advising clients	Tactful	Divorce law

Functional Skills

Functional skills are natural abilities or talents that are acquired through heredity. Actually you acquire the potential for certain types of abilities genetically. These potentials are then either developed through your life experiences or remain dormant. If, for example, you inherited an aptitude for analytical problem solving, writing poetry, or persuading others, you may have developed this functional skill through school course work and/or practical application. Then again, you may possess a real potential for these skills but just never developed them for one reason or another. Perhaps you neglected to exercise these potentials because your life circumstances hindered their development, or perhaps you accepted a prevailing myth that people like you (of your sex, race, nationality, etc.) aren't good at this kind of thing—for example, women aren't good at solving math problems or men aren't good at nursing or nurturing others. There is also the possibility that you may have inherited a limited potential for these specific aptitudes and are unlikely to develop them into highly proficient functional skills no matter how diligently you apply yourself. The following relationships summarize these principles:

$$\text{Potential plus development} = \text{Functional skill}$$

+

$$\text{Potential plus nondevelopment} = \text{Latent functional skill}$$

+

$$\text{Potential life barrier} = \text{Erroneous conclusion that you have no skill in this area}$$

+

$$\text{Lack of potential plus effort} = \text{Frustration (and perhaps a modest skill development)}$$

Having a functional skill means that you are able to perform some specific type of activity, action, or operation with a good deal of proficiency. Simply put, it means that you can do a specific thing well. To have a functional skill one must first begin with the potential to develop a certain ability such as selling, shooting baskets, singing, solving complex mathematical problems, or envisioning how an object would look from many different perspectives. This potential must then be developed through experience, education, practice, play, and work.

Incidentally, functional skills are as likely to be developed in everyday activities as they are in the classroom. For example, do you remember the kid on your block who could sell anything, including his rusty old roller skates, to anyone, or the kid who could make the whole gang laugh anytime she wanted? These are examples of well-developed functional skills in the early formative stages of life. These people today still retain these abilities. The first kid may now be a very successful salesperson and the second a comedian (if they were astute enough to capitalize on their natural endowments). On the other hand, if they didn't, you might find them languishing around in a job and a lifestyle they hate. They may even think that they don't have much to offer and that life's not a whole lot of fun. If you were good at drawing as a child, you undoubtedly retain that potential today regardless of whether you have developed it into a well-used functional skill. If you were the leader of your neighborhood gang as an adolescent, you have that same potential to lead today, whether you are currently practicing leadership or are even aware of that potential.

Value of Functional Skills

Your functional skills are perhaps the most valuable assets you have in life. Youthful good looks are great, but they fade with age, while functional skills stay with you over a lifetime. Well-developed functional skills are truly more valuable than money. While money spent unwisely disappears quickly, functional skills actually increase through expenditure. And, even better, your functional skills represent the resources you need to earn money whenever you want. Beyond that, productively using your functional skills feels good. Both financial and psychological reward are attainable to those who intelligently use their functional skills. One of life's greatest satisfactions comes from fully utilizing your talents towards personally meaningful ends. And, conversely, one of the greatest causes of dissatisfaction in life is the realization that one's best talents are not being fully used and developed.

In today's world there is a particularly compelling reason for knowing what our best functional skills are. The world around us is changing at a rapid pace. Technology brings new advances daily. Unskilled jobs are decreasing while more demanding and technologically advanced jobs are increasing. Most career specialists predict that in our rapidly changing world, younger workers may need or want to change jobs as often as every three to five years and undergo significant career changes every decade or so. In our unstable world, older workers also are not spared from the need to make job and career changes.

In today's world there is a natural tendency to search for a constant, stabilizing factor, the "for-certain" element in life. The only real constant, however, lies within us, in the form of our personal attributes and talents. Your skills remain with you regardless of the job, occupation, or field in which you might be involved. As long as you know what your functional skills are, rapid change does not have to be a serious threat to you occupationally. If your job is phased out or taken over by a computer, you have the resources needed to make a successful job or career change because your functional skills are transferable. Your transferable skills allow you to move easily from one job to another where similar aptitudes are required. If you have been feeling trapped in a job that no longer

energizes you, it may well be time to transport your transferable skills into a more challenging situation. In fact, when you know exactly what your functional skills are, it is even possible to make changes without extensive retraining.

Skill identification can help you clarify what you have to contribute to a particular type of work and provide clues for suggesting where to go with your career. If, for example, you realize that you are talented at communicating, establishing rapport, and advising others, you may want to explore people-oriented occupations like teaching, counseling, nursing, or selling. Or let's say you know that you prefer hands-on activities with equipment, tools, or machines: you might consider a job in computer repair, medical technology, auto mechanics, robotic technology, electronic engineering, industrial arts, or aeronautics/astronautics.

Everyone Has Functional Skills

Perhaps you've said to yourself, "Well, I don't have many skills." If so, you are not alone in this misconception. People often visit career counselors feeling depressed and lamenting their lack of skills. These blues quickly vanish when they discover how traits or accomplishments they have taken for granted point to valuable skills. Experienced career planning specialists like Richard Bolles and the late John Crystal, through years of experience, have observed that people completing a thorough skills identification process discover 200 to 500 or more skills.[1]

The problem is not that you lack skills. Instead, you have so many individual skills that it's probably hard to recognize them. You also might not recognize them because you have used them so long and so well that they have become automatic and unconscious. Or you might discount your skills, erroneously assuming that anyone can perform those things that you can do well. Functional skills are a bit like icebergs in that the greater portion of them lie hidden below the surface of our everyday awareness. Even people who recognize their basic skills are often amazed to discover just how many specific skills the functional skills identification process can reveal.

Because people usually enjoy activities that they perform well, your first exercise involves recalling activities that gave you positive feelings. These feelings may come from within and/or may come from other people's favorable responses.

[1.] John C. Crystal and Richard N. Bolles, *Where Do I Go from Here with My Life?* (Berkeley, CA: Ten Speed Press, 1978) 70.

EXERCISE 3-A. REFLECTIONS ON THE PAST AND PRESENT _____

Reflect on the following questions, writing your responses in the spaces provided. Write whatever comes to your mind instead of trying to narrow your responses.

1. What compliments or other positive feedback have you received for particular activities? (Example: praise for organizing your art club's successful fundraising activity, compliments on the wood cabinet you designed and built.) Positive feedback may be as simple as a smile or as significant as a meritorious pay increase. Write down at least five different compliments, briefly explaining the situation.

2. When have you felt the most alive and energetic? List at least five specific situations. (Examples: jogging two miles daily, planning and preparing food and decorations for a dinner party, building a model airplane, thinking of ways to improve store displays at your first job.)

3. When have you felt the most confident and capable? List at least five situations. (Examples: giving a presentation and getting rave reviews, getting an "A" on a major exam in your toughest subject, having someone ask for your ideas/advice about carpentry work.)

4. What are you discovering about yourself? Are there any similarities in your responses? Make some notes here to help you remember your thoughts.

5. Review your responses to 1 through 4 above. What skills do you think you used in these various examples? List at least 10 of them in the space provided. You may want to ask a friend or family member to listen as you describe some of the things you have listed and see if they can help you find skills or abilities that you used.

Here is another chance to look at skills. This exercise involves describing successful experiences you have had in order to identify the skills you were using in the process. This is one of the best ways to become aware of and clarify your top skills. Once you know what skills you have used successfully in the past, you can make plans to capitalize on these same skills in the future.

Make a list of 15 achievements, large or small, from your past. These should be descriptive phrases of memorable activities or events where *you* contributed to a satisfying, but not necessarily perfect, outcome. The satisfaction may have come from improvement in a particular activity. Try to list particular events rather than general situations. For example, if getting good grades is one of your achievements, list the most satisfying "A" you've ever obtained, or if traveling is one of your achievements, indicate one particularly significant travel experience you had. The following is a list of some sample achievements to help you start thinking about your own achievements.

Cooking a gourmet meal (cordon bleu, for example)

Training a horse

Playing basketball (learning to play, or a particular game)

Enforcing regulations in a particular situation

Creating a report with complex tables

Playing a computer game well

Persuading someone to buy something

Managing people to reach a fundraising goal

Playing guitar for an audience

Writing a feature story for a community newspaper

Teaching a child to read

Helping a neighbor cope with her husband's death

Figuring out a new approach for an office project

Decorating the community center for Christmas

Writing song lyrics

Structuring a research project

Analyzing people's needs for improved computer equipment

Classifying information for a biology experiment

Repairing an auto engine

Refinishing a valuable old piece of furniture

Designing a prize-winning Halloween costume

Writing a piece of poetry

Your List of Achievements: (Keep in mind that achievements can be simple everyday things, but the requirement is that you had to put forth effort or work to make them happen.)

1.

2.

3.

4.

5.

6.

7.

8.

9.

10.

11.

12.

13.

14.

15.

From your list of 15, select the five achievements that made you feel the happiest, most satisfied, or most energetic. You may want to choose achievements that resulted in positive reactions from someone else, although this is not essential. Copy each of these descriptive phrases at the top of a blank sheet of paper. Next, write a paragraph or two describing each achievement. Start at the beginning and say it simply. Don't worry about grammar, organization, or any fine points of writing. Just tell what happened, describing exactly what you did to contribute to the satisfying outcome. Choose action words to tell what you did and include as much relevant detail as you can recall. The following examples show how a satisfying achievement can be elaborated upon in preparation for identifying skills.

Example 1: Doing a Bass Fish Mounting

Because I enjoy fishing a lot, I decided that I wanted to learn how to do fish mounting. The first step I took to achieve my goal was going to the library and checking out books about fish mounting. There I got some pretty good ideas of the types of mounts and procedures involved. Then I got in touch with a taxidermist who agreed to train me. I went to the taxidermist once a week for about three months. I would always bring a fish I had just caught to practice with. He showed me, step-by-step, how to clean and skin the fish and how to dry and preserve it. He also taught me how to put the finishing touches on a fish and then how to mount it in the desired position. I worked with him for about three months until he felt the work I was doing was of professional quality.

Shortly after I finished my training, I caught a large bass and decided to try out my skills. I cleaned the fish carefully, not leaving any meat behind that would spoil. Then I salted the skin and braced the fins in the positions that I wanted them in. Next I put a filler in the bass to give it its original shape back. I mounted the fish in an open-mouthed position in order to give it a fierce look as if it were feeding. After a few weeks of drying, my bass was ready to paint. I selected colors to bring back the original look and then gave it a coat of shellac to seal the paint and give the fish a wet look and the lifelike appearance. I think my final product is very professional; it's hanging on a wall in my house.

Example 2: Buying a Townhouse

I decided that I wanted to buy a nice place to live after my husband and I divorced. I dreamed of a place that would be attractive and located in a pleasant neighborhood where I could go to bed in the evening and hear the sounds of the wind in the trees and awake in the morning to the music of birds singing. I also envisioned a place that would not require much yard work and would be within a half-hour commute to work.

First I analyzed how much I could afford for a place and what my monthly payments ought to be. In considering the options within my price range, I figured out that a townhouse would be my best buy. Next, I began exploring the area to see what was available. Initially I thought I would like to buy in the Crofton area and found a realtor to work with. I looked at several places there but didn't find exactly what I wanted within my price range. Then I learned that there were some nice townhouses being built along the golf course in Upper Marlboro, so I drove out and took a look. I loved the location and the models.

It didn't require much consideration to decide that this was where I wanted to live. I selected the lot and the model I wanted and signed a contract. I was concerned that my monthly payments would be more than I could afford, but trusted that it would be possible to rent out the spare bedroom for about $400.00 per month.

I am now in my new townhouse and decorating it with a modest budget to make it feel like home. I was able to rent out the space by placing an ad in the *Post*. With this additional income I have been able to make my monthly payments by sticking closely to a budget. While things are currently a bit tight financially, I am confident that I will be able to make it.

WHAT KINDS OF SKILLS DO YOU HAVE?

As you were writing down responses for Exercise 3-A and B, did you notice that various action words described your skills? If these words reveal your involvement in accomplishing something or making something happen, they are directly describing a functional skill you possess. Maybe you *organized* a team, *composed* correspondence, *operated* equipment, *balanced* a ledger, *prepared* a speech, *repaired* a radio. These kinds of skills are called functional skills because you can apply them (make them function in) to various situations.

Your paragraphs may also contain words that suggest other types of skills, those that describe your behavioral traits. Descriptive words like *neat, punctual, curious, easygoing, good judgment, honest, resourceful, self-confident, reliable,* and *decisive* reveal your self-management skills.

EXERCISE 3-C. IDENTIFYING SKILLS FROM YOUR ACCOMPLISHMENTS _____

Skill Assessment Survey

This survey is designed to assist you in assessing your functional and self-management skills and deciding what specific skills you prefer to use in your career.

Directions

1. First, copy the title from each of your five achievement paragraphs above into the five spaces provided for that purpose at the top of the Skill Assessment Grid.

2. Next, determine to what extent you used certain skills in each of your five achievements. To do that, use the following scale to evaluate how much a skill was engaged for a particular achievement. Place an appropriate number in the grid for every skill listed. Do this for all five of your achievements. When you have completed this exercise, there should be a number in every box formed by the intersections of the five skills you are evaluating and the skills listed on the grid. Please note that there is a place to add additional skills, if you believe that you used a particular skill in one of your achievements that is not listed on the grid. Use column 6, *Catch-All,* to assign ratings to any skills that you know you have used but have not revealed in your paragraphs.

To What Extent Did You Use a Skill in This Achievement?

0 = Did not use this skill at all

1 = Used this skill minimally

2 = Used this skill moderately

3 = Used this skill to a considerable extent

4 = Used this skill very extensively

3. After determining the degree to which you have used these skills in your favorite achievements, determine your level of enjoyment in using these skills and how important it will be for you to use and develop each skill in your new career. Assign a number in the "preference" column of the grid using the following rating scale:

Your Preference for Using This Skill in Your Career

0 = *Dislike,* don't want to use or develop this skill

1 = *Indifferent,* don't care if I use or develop this skill

2 = *Somewhat prefer,* would be OK to use and develop this skill

3 = *Really enjoy,* want to use and develop this skill

4 = *Special favorite,* very important to use and develop this skill

SKILLS ASSESSMENT GRID

I. Functional Skills

A. Manual/Technical	1	2	3	4	5	CATCH-ALL 6	PREFERENCES 7
Assembling/installing							
Constructing/building							
Fixing/repairing							
Manual dexterity							
Mechanical reasoning							
Working with animals							
Using hand tools							
Operating machinery or equipment							
Driving vehicles—cars, trucks, buses, tractors, etc.							
Moving materials by hand							
Horticulture skills—working with plants							
Landscaping and groundskeeping							
Physical stamina							
Outdoor labor							
Other _____							

B. Analytical/Problem Solving	1	2	3	4	5	6	7
Analyzing/diagnosing							
Researching/investigating							
Interpreting data							
Classifying/organizing/systematizing							
Evaluating/assessing							
Scientific/technical writing							
Logical decision making/analytical problem solving							
Financial analysis							
Mathematical/numerical reasoning							
Using facts/evaluating							
Separating important from unimportant facts							
Putting facts, figures, or information into logical order							
Scientific curiosity/thinking							
Using logic or rational reasoning							
Other _____							

C. Innovative/Original	1	2	3	4	5	6	7
Using your imagination to create							
Graphic designing							
Using intuition							
Designing programs, events, activities							

I. Functional Skills (cont'd.)

C. Innovative/Original (cont'd.)	1	2	3	4	5	CATCH-ALL 6	PREFERENCES 7
Originating ideas							
Creative showmanship/acting/performing							
Creative writing, self-expression							
Possibility thinking							
Artistic sense/aesthetics							
Drawing/artistic designing							
Creative movement/dancing/miming							
Synthesizing—putting facts and ideas together in new, creative ways							
Being innovative or inventing something new or different							
Composing music, songs, lyrics							
Other _____							

D. Social/Interpersonal	1	2	3	4	5	6	7
Listening skillfully/hearing							
Developing rapport/understanding							
Counseling/helping/guiding/mentoring							
Drawing people out/interviewing							
Instructing/training/educating							
Social grace/putting others at ease							
Group facilitating							
Communicating tactfully							
Being of service/responding							
Providing information/advising							
Cooperating with others							
Showing warmth and caring							
Being supportive or cooperative							
Healing/nursing/nurturing/curing							
Other _____							

E. Detail/Data	1	2	3	4	5	6	7
Working with numerical data							
Proofreading/editing/technical writing							
Inspecting/examining/inventorying							

SKILLS ASSESSMENT GRID (cont'd.)

I. Functional Skills (cont'd.)

E. Detail/Data (cont'd.)	ACHIEVEMENTS 1	2	3	4	5	CATCH-ALL 6	PREFERENCES 7
Word processing/typing							
Following directions/ procedures accurately							
Being exact and accurate/careful							
Doing math quickly and accurately							
Scheduling/organizing events or activities							
Completing details on schedule							
Accounting/keeping track of data or numbers							
Categorizing/sorting/ placing items in the right places							
Remembering numbers or specific facts							
Attending to details							
Filing, classifying, recording, retrieving							
Other _____							

F. Managing/Influencing	1	2	3	4	5	6	7
Administering a program or resources							
Directing/supervising others							
Making business-related decisions							
Negotiating/contracting with others or groups							
Selling/persuading/ influencing							
Convincing others through force of personality							
Overseeing programs/ projects/activities							
Organizational/group goal setting/planning							
Undertaking entrepreneurial activities							
Organizing and managing an activity, task or project							
Exercising leadership in a group							
Taking risks in a public setting							
Negotiating deals or transactions							
Coordinating people and activities to work together							
Other _____							

II. Self-Management Skills

	ACHIEVEMENTS 1	2	3	4	5	CATCH-ALL 6	PREFERENCES 7
Assertive							
Authentic							
Cautious							
Cheerful							
Conforming							
Concentration							
Cooperative							
Determination/drive							
Deliberate/careful							
Dynamic (high energy level)							
Diligent							
Easy-going/calm							
Enthusiastic							
Ethical							
Fast and expedient							
Flexible							
Friendly							
Helpful							
Honest							
Initiative							
Integrity							
Kind							
Loyal							
Optimistic							
Orderly							
Patient							
Persistent							
Poised							
Polite							
Punctual							
Reliable, dependable							
Self-controlled							
Self-confident/self-assured							
Sense of humor							
Sincerely							
Strong willed							
Spontaneous							
Tactful							
Thrifty							
Tolerant							
Trustworthy							
Resilient							
Versatile							
Other _____							

Your Priority Skills

After completing the Skill Assessment Grid, prioritize your top ten functional skills and your top ten self-management skills. Your top ten should come from those skills that you have both used consistently (given scores of 3 or more in columns one through five) and have assigned a rating of 4 or 5 in column 6. List your results below. (Note: if you have identified any different functional or self-management skills from other methods, you might want to include them on your list as you develop your final prioritized lists below).

My top ten (most preferred) skills are:

Functional Skills	Self-Management Skills
1.	1.
2.	2.
3.	3.
4.	4.
5.	5.
6.	6.
7.	7.
8.	8.
9.	9.
10.	10.

My least preferred skills, those I don't want to use (these should come from the skills you have used but gave low ratings to in column six):

Functional Skills	Self-Management Skills
1.	1.
2.	2.
3.	3.
4.	4.
5.	5.

Your Preferred Family of Skills

The exercises above required you to identify your most preferred individual skills. It is also helpful to identify the groupings of functional skills that you most enjoy using. To do that, count the total number of points that you have assigned in column 6 of the Skill Assessment Grid for each of the six groupings of functional skills identified. There are 14 skills listed for each of the six groups, plus any that you may have added. Your total score for Manual/Technical skills (A) will be obtained by adding up all the numbers that you have assigned in column six for skills that you have actually used, those to which you have assigned a 3 or above in columns 1–5. Your preference ranking will be determined by your total scores, i.e., the group receiving the highest total becomes your # 1 preference under *My Preference Ranking*. These results will be included in an exercise that you will do later in Chapter 4.

My Preferred Family of Skills		
Skill Family	*My Total Score*	*My Preference Ranking*
A. Manual/Technical		
B. Analytical/Problem Solving		
C. Innovative/Original		
D. Customer/Public Service		
E. Detail/Data		
F. Managing/Influencing		

USING YOUR SKILLS GROUPS TO CHOOSE A CAREER

How does ranking your top skills get you any closer to making a career decision? Knowing your preferred skills gives you a starting point from which to begin identifying career options suited to your unique blend of skills. The task is to learn what kinds of careers and what particular jobs require your combination of preferred skills. It is also useful to be aware of your least preferred skills, or poorest skills, so that you stay away from career options where these types of skills would be called for. Chapter 8 covers occupational research in detail.

Researching also means asking people (i.e., neighbors, relatives, friends, classmates) for their ideas and advice about careers requiring your particular skills. Often a casual conversation can uncover an exciting option that you would not have considered or known about.

Web Connect

You may have previously used library references, such as The Guide to Occupational Exploration (GOE) and The Dictionary of Occupational Titles (DOT) to explore careers. Now, however, these references have been replaced by a dynamic and useful online program called O*NET. The O*NET Online can be found at <http://online.onetcenter.org>. This site will be helpful in exploring career options with regard to the skills, knowledge and abilities needed in the job, educational requirements, relevant occupations, and tips and links to help you find the right career activities for your interests and skills.

THE RELATIONSHIP OF WORK TO DATA, PEOPLE, AND THINGS

Figure 3.1, the Functional Skills Hierarchy,[2] illustrates the relationship of skills to data, people, and things as well as the different levels of these skills. These various ways of working with data, people, and things can occur in many work settings. For example, analyzing reports (data) is done in health clinics, environmental agencies, schools, and company offices. Operating copying machines (things) is done in department stores, computer assembly companies, and museums. Instructing (people) is done in homes, churches, schools, government offices, and health spas. The service or product at the work site may change, but the basic function—what you do with data, people, and things—does not.

The performance requirements for skills related to data, people, and things range in degree of ability from lesser, at the bottom of the diagram, to greater, at the top of the diagram. Successfully moving up from a lower-level skill to a higher-level skill requires increasing ability as the complexity of the skills increases.

For instance, in the data column on the diagram, the lowest skill, "comparing," is a fairly simple task involving examining two or more items for similarities or dissimilarities. The highest skill, "synthesizing," on the other hand, is very complex and involves combining diverse concepts into a coherent

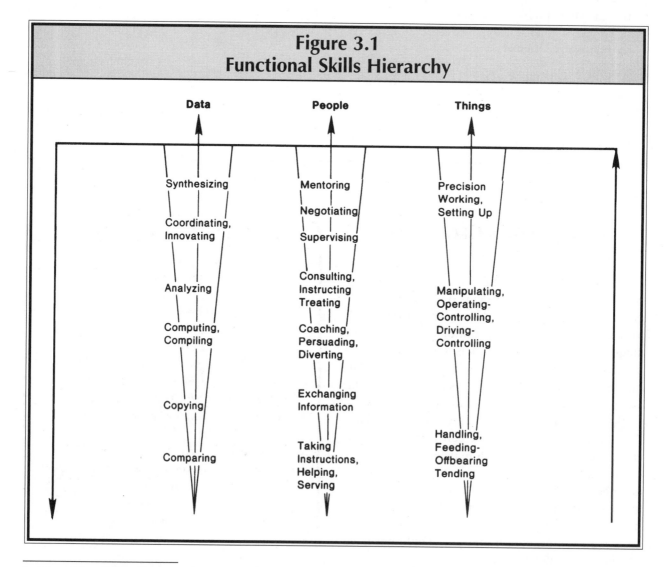

Figure 3.1
Functional Skills Hierarchy

Data	People	Things
Synthesizing	Mentoring	Precision Working, Setting Up
Coordinating, Innovating	Negotiating	
	Supervising	
Analyzing	Consulting, Instructing Treating	Manipulating, Operating-Controlling, Driving-Controlling
Computing, Compiling	Coaching, Persuading, Diverting	
Copying	Exchanging Information	
		Handling, Feeding-Offbearing Tending
Comparing	Taking Instructions, Helping, Serving	

[2.] Adapted from Richard N. Bolles, *The Three Boxes of Life and How to Get Out of Them* (Berkeley, CA: Ten Speed Press, 1978) 146.

whole. The skill of synthesizing is a complex and high-level skill because it incorporates all of the skills that precede it in the data column.

The diagram shows that the lower the skill level required in a job, the more the work duties are prescribed by someone else. What that means is that people performing jobs using only lower-level skills will have very little discretion in determining what they do and little chance to use their own judgment and creativity. People who feel more secure when the procedures and duties are well defined and predictable might be more comfortable working at the lower skill levels. Entry level jobs often begin at the lower skill levels but provide opportunity for advancing to the higher skill levels with experience.

The higher the skill level involved in a job, the fewer the duties and regulations that are prescribed by someone else. This affords employees more freedom to decide how they are going to spend their time. Far more is left to employees' judgment, creativity, and decision making. Of course, along with greater self-determination comes greater responsibility in ensuring that an organization's goals are met. Jobs requiring higher skill levels tend to pay higher salaries.

DEFINING DATA, PEOPLE, AND THINGS

Data skills always involve interaction with some types of symbols, details, or information. Data are related to numbers, words (anything you can read or write), facts, or ideas (any creative work that goes on in your head). People skills may include working with various kinds of people or with a specific group of people. It is important to note that information, facts, and statistics about people are data-related functional skills and should not be confused with people-related skills. The people-related skills involve actual interaction with people.

Skills related to things involve interaction with objects, tools, machines, and/or materials. Such things may include desktop items such as telephones, calculators, or computers. Skills associated with things may also involve spaces, buildings, and manual labor.

Skills involved in working with animals may be classified under the "things" column when the work-related function is strictly utilitarian, as in producing cattle for beef. Working with animals may also be in-

cluded as a people skill when the work involved is in a helping or caring role. The veterinarian, for example, interacts with animals in a helping role, and the skill orientation would therefore be classified under the "people" category for functional skill identification purposes. In contrast, medical lab technicians may need to relate to animals as objects of medical science research, which would be a "data" orientation.

FUNCTIONAL SKILLS VERSUS SELF-MANAGEMENT SKILLS

Self-management skills are your specific behavior responses or character traits. They describe the way in which you manage yourself and relate to others. Along with functional skills, self-management skills are important components of what people have to contribute in the world of work. Of the two, self-management skills are more widely recognized because they are often easier to observe and identify in work settings. Functional skills, however, are more basic to the actual performance of work tasks.

Knowing your specific functional skills can help you determine how qualified you are to perform the actual tasks of a particular job. Being clear about your self-management skills can suggest how adaptable you would be to the working conditions of a specific job.

THE IMPORTANCE OF SELF-MANAGEMENT SKILLS

According to John Crystal, functional skills are usually the personal attributes that get us hired, and self-management skills are those that get us fired.[3]

Web Connect

For ideas on additional self management skills, go back to **Creative Job Search's Online Guide** at: http://www.amby.com/worksite/cjs/cjsbook2/skill6d.htm and scroll down to the second section titled "Self Management Skills."

[3.] John C. Crystal, Career Planning Workshop, Prince George's Community College, Largo, Maryland, Spring, 1979.

EXERCISE 3-D. DATA-PEOPLE-THINGS PREFERENCE _____

The following exercise will show you how your functional skills preferences are distributed under the data-people-things categories.

1. Place your #1 functional skill, from Exercise 3-C, under the appropriate heading below. If you are unsure where to list a skill, ask yourself, "With whom or what would these skills be used—data, people, or things?" Continue filling in the table with all ten of your preferred functional skills.

Data	People	Things

2. After you have listed your "top ten" preferred skills on the table, add your least-preferred functional skills to the same table. When you do this, be sure to use a different color ink for these skills so that you won't confuse them with your preferred skills. The contrast between your most and least-preferred skills may begin to give you a picture of what types of careers fit and don't fit your particular profile.

3. Assessing your data-people-things preferences:

   a. Under which heading(s) are your preferred functional skills listed?

   b. Under which heading(s) do your least-preferred skills cluster?

   c. Based on this exercise, begin making a list of the kinds of careers that might be associated with your preferred skills and also list a few to stay away from—those associated with your least-preferred skills.

Careers Associated with Your Most Preferred Functional Skills	Careers Associated with Your Least-Preferred Skills

_____

This is true, of course, only when our self-management skills do not fit well with the conditions associated with a particular work setting. For example, the artist's or creative thinker's emotional self-expression and spontaneity might cause conflicts in a business office where working conditions involve highly structured activities, orderly task perfor-mance, and an emotional climate of relative calm. It is important, therefore, to really understand your self-management skills and assess how well they might fit with a particular job or work situation that you might be considering.

The importance of self-management skills for job survival can clearly be seen from glancing at any supervisory evaluation form. The majority of evaluation criteria measure self-management skills. Self-management skills that many employers or supervisors particularly value include initiative, resourcefulness, cooperation, dependability, flexibility, and loyalty. A deficiency in one or more of these skill areas will probably cause poor performance evaluations. Consistently low periodic evaluations can lead to a failure to be promoted, a demotion, or even an outright dismissal by an employer.

Self-management skills alone will not qualify you for any positions, except possibly the lower skill-level jobs. Usually people qualify for certain jobs or occupations primarily because they possess certain required functional skills, special knowledge, and have relevant work experience. However, in addition to reviewing your written qualifications, a prospective employer or employer's representative will interview you. This interview or series of interviews allows you to display self-management skills to your advantage. Your self-management skills or deficiencies are also important aspects of references from former employers or associates. If the self-management skills you display and your employment references emphasize are particularly valued in the new work setting, you might be hired over any number of equally or even more qualified candidates. Conversely, just one serious self-management deficiency can knock you out of the running. For example, an employer who is seeking a counselor generally requires the functional skills of listening and speaking effectively, sensitivity to others' emotional needs, and ability to analyze an individual's practical needs and offer appropriate advice. Job applicants who, in addition, display complementary self-management skills such as friendliness, sincerity, warm humor, and cheerfulness will have an edge on their competition, all other qualifications being equal. Notice that in people-oriented occupations, self-management skills are often part of the actual job requirements. In other words, they overlap with functional skills in some careers.

Here's another real-life example to stress just how important it is to match the unique blend of an individual's skills to what's required for a job. To function effectively as a public relations (P.R.) manager, you would need to possess a number of skills, including the functional skills of creative writing and public speaking and the self-management skills of gregariousness, tact, and flexibility. We know of an individual who was hired as a P.R. manager at a fairly large organization because of her excellent knowledge of P.R. work, her impressive functional skills, and the self-management skills she demonstrated impressively during the interview process. What the hiring process could not reveal, however, was an inability on her part to work compatibly and cooperatively with her staff and associates. On the job, she turned out to be a disaster. She was constantly squabbling with someone over minor issues that any effective P.R. manager should have easily been able to handle. After putting up with her poor self-management skills for about a year, the organization was eventually forced to fire this talented and hardworking woman. In retrospect, she should have either recognized this self-management deficiency and corrected it or obtained a job where she could have put her best skills to productive use in a setting where getting along with staff and peers was not a critical requirement of the job.

OBSERVING SELF-MANAGEMENT SKILLS

Self-management skills are the first skills that an employer can observe when initially meeting job applicants in face-to-face interviews. Imagine, for example, that you are a job seeker and have arranged an interview with a potential employer. Here are some of the opportunities that employer has to observe your self-management skills.

You have arranged your appointment at 9 A.M., but you arrive at 8:45 A.M. The potential employer already has learned something about your *punctuality, dependability,* and, perhaps, *eagerness.*

Upon greeting the interviewer you step forward *confidently* and greet the person *warmly,* at the same time expressing your *enthusiasm* at this opportunity to convince the interviewer of your potential worth to the organization. You have taken care that your *dress* and *grooming* are neat and appropriate for the occasion. In addition, you have taken the *initiative* to research carefully the potential employer's company or organization and have used your *resourcefulness* to identify a special problem within that organization that you feel capable of resolving. All these actions can be planned to convey to the prospective employer your interest in and suitability for the position.

Thus, in the course of perhaps an hour's interview, you have demonstrated to this prospective employer a number of self-management skills. (The *italicized* words in the above paragraph are self-management skill words.)

Not all self-management skills are so readily observable in an interview situation. Some, like *loyalty, reliability,* and *resilience,* can be assessed only after a substantial period of time on the job. Because they are so personal, most people have trouble accurately assessing their self-management skills. It is particularly difficult to evaluate self-management deficiencies without being defensive when they are associated with negative or painful experiences. Rely on other people's observations to learn more about your self-management skills, but always look for consistent observations. Get feedback from a variety of people or at least from the types of people likely to be your employers or coworkers.

 ## EXERCISE 3-E. IDENTIFYING YOUR SELF-MANAGEMENT SKILLS _____

1. From the following partial list of self-management skills, circle those that you think of and that others have consistently mentioned as being most characteristic of you. Keep in mind that while a given self-management skill may be characteristic of you, it does not mean necessarily that you are that way in every situation. Add to the end of the list any self-management skills you have that are not included.

Self-Management Skills

Adventuresome	Courteous	Friendly
Alert	Curious	Generous
Assertive	Decisive	Helpful
Astute	Dependable	Honest
Attentive	Diplomatic	Initiative
Authentic	Discerning	Insightful
Aware	Discreet	Integrity
Calm	Dynamic	Kind
Candid	Eager	Loyal
Cheerful	Easygoing	Methodical
Collected	Empathetic	Open-minded
Committed	Enthusiastic	Optimistic
Composed	Energetic	Orderly
Concentration	Ethical	Outgoing
Concerned	Expressive	Patient
Conscientious	Firm	Perceptive
Cooperative	Flexible	Persistent
Courageous	Focused	Playful

Poised	Responsible	Sympathetic
Polite	Risk-taking	Tactful
Precise	Self-confident	Thorough
Punctual	Self-controlled	Thrifty
Quiet	Self-reliant	Tolerant
Reliable	Sensitive	Trustworthy
Resilient	Sincere	Unique
Resourceful	Spontaneous	Versatile
Respectful	Steadfast	Vigorous

2. Prioritize your top ten self-management skills from those that you have identified as most characteristic of you. Place them in order of preference below.

My top ten (most characteristic) self-management skills are:

1.

2.

3.

4.

5.

6.

7.

8.

9.

10.

RELATING SELF-MANAGEMENT SKILLS TO WORK SETTINGS

Some self-management skills are advantageous in almost any work setting. For instance, cheerfulness, cooperation, enthusiasm, friendliness, good judgment, honesty, kindness, and sincerity are universally appreciated attributes. It is possible, however, for some positive self-management skills to be inappropriate or misunderstood in some kinds of job situations. For example, although cheerful, joking behavior by an employee could be taken as a lack of sensitivity in the office of a funeral director, a very serious and sober demeanor in a counselor might be considered cold and unresponsive in a therapy center. Different work settings require different combinations of self-management skills. For instance, assertiveness, adventurousness, ambition, enthusiasm, and dynamism are important skills for salespeople to possess. Concentration, astuteness, curiosity, deliberateness, and precision are traits more likely to be found in the work setting of engineers or researchers. Knowledge of your unique combination of self-management skills can help you reach an appropriate career decision.

 EXERCISE 3-F. SELF-MANAGEMENT SKILLS AND WORK SITES _____

Review your list of self-management skills and make some assessments on how to capitalize on those most characteristic of you and also those least characteristic of you.

1. How might you capitalize on your most preferred self-management skills in the workplace? How could you use them to help yourself and others?

2. Review the list of self-management skills on pages 54–55 and identify the five least characteristic of you. List them below.

3. Indicate some things that you might wish to keep in mind about your least-preferred self-management skills both in terms of career choice and on-the-job behavior.

_____

Distinguishing the Three Types of Skills

	Functional Skills	*Self-Management*	*Special Knowledge*
How they are acquired	As natural talents or aptitudes we possess from birth	As basic abilities we learn by relating to significant people early in our development; acquired later in life only through great effort	Learning
How they develop	Through practice and further refinement at any time in our lives	Through responses we make to the conditions imposed on us by significant people (parents, peers, etc.) and social institutions (schools, church, etc.)	Repetition and memory
What they are related to	People, data, and things	Life environments (family, school, work) and their conditions that force us to adapt	Specific work situations

ASSESSING YOUR SPECIAL KNOWLEDGE SKILLS

We all have acquired mastery of certain kinds of knowledge over the years. Perhaps you are acquainted with someone who knows a lot about certain kinds of sports such as football or tennis (special knowledge) even though that person may or may not be able to play them well (functional skills). As you begin identifying your list of possible career options, it's a good idea to take stock of your favorite special knowledge to see how important it might be to pursue a career that would enable you to apply a favorite body of knowledge.

One career changer, for example, had developed a great deal of knowledge about art and also about marketing (special knowledge), was good at selling (functional skill), and had a strong love of art (strong personal interest). He realized, however, that he was not an artist himself. After carefully considering his interests and assets, he decided to pursue a career as an art merchandiser. He is now making a very nice living as an art consultant for organizations looking to enhance the aesthetic appeal of their business offices. His role is to help his clients identify what kind of art would enhance a particular work setting and then negotiate with artists to purchase or obtain on consignment the needed artwork. As you can see, this individual was clever at seeing how to capitalize on his assets and interests. You too may be able to discover clever ways of combining your unique assets in a career in which you can earn a good living.

Web Connect

Still stumped? If you're struggling to come up with a list of special knowledge skills, try going to one of the major online job banks, such as Monster.com **www.monster.com** and search for job descriptions that may represent work, leisure, intern, volunteer, or other activities in which you have engaged during your life. Next, review the jobs and see if you can cull skills from the job descriptions. As for identifying knowledge gained through learning, try going onto your school's web site and searching for descriptions of previous courses you have taken.

Do the following exercise to help identify the special knowledge you have acquired over the years and to determine if there are any particular ones that you might wish to pursue in your career. This exercise is generally more helpful for mature adults who have acquired substantial bodies of special knowledge over the years than for younger individuals seeking their first career.

However, we recommend that you give the exercise a try even if you are a younger student, for you could discover an important piece of self-knowledge that might suggest a career path for you when considered with the other assessment data you will be acquiring. As you do this exercise, it can be useful to survey the entire spectrum of your life's history in search of special knowledge skills. Perhaps you will find a clue from childhood that will help put you on the road to a new career. We know of one person, for instance, who loved sports as a child. He played football, watched every football game he could find, and was an expert in professional football. Even though he wasn't talented enough to play at college, he still followed the game and continued to learn everything he could. He is now working for a professional football team in their public relations department. He is able to use his special knowledge and is very happy and successful in his job.

EXERCISE 3-G. DISCOVERING YOUR SPECIAL KNOWLEDGE ⎯⎯⎯⎯⎯⎯⎯

1. Divide a piece of paper into three columns headed *Work, Learning,* and *Leisure.* Then begin listing all of the special knowledge you have acquired over the years in each of these three categories. Be as thorough as you can, keeping in mind that some of your special knowledge may not be readily apparent. You may have to do some mental digging to uncover these. You might even need to do a careful memory search to recall that you learned a lot about gas combustion engines while working on your car as a teenager or that you found out how to conduct formal meetings while serving as a class officer in school.

   Other special knowledges are less subtle. You might, for example, have learned a lot about computer operations through taking formal courses, or you may have picked up a great deal of knowledge on your own through trial and error in working with your own computer. Special knowledges are often acquired by attending classes or workshops, reading books or manuals, or watching how someone else does something. Remember, you were not born with these kinds of skills: you acquired them through learning.

2. After identifying your own list of special knowledge, go back over your lists and circle your favorite knowledge. Work with this list until you have narrowed it down to the ten special knowledge skills that seem most important to you, the ten that you might want to use in the next phase of your career.

3. Prioritize your list of ten, using the prioritizing process described in Appendix B of the book. As you go through the prioritization process, ask yourself, How much do I value this special knowledge and how important might it be for me to use it in my career?

4. List your top five special knowledge skills below, then list some career options in which you might put your knowledge to use.

Your Top Special Knowledge Skills	Possible Career Options
1.	
2.	
3.	
4.	
5.	

SUMMARY

Everyone has unique talents and skills. Our skills can be categorized into three groups—functional, self-management, and special knowledge. Functional skills are aptitude-related and are transferable from one job, career, or profession to another. Your abilities to work with data, people, and things are defined by your functional skills. By identifying your top functional skills and by knowing your preference for working with data, people, and things, you can both discover and then effectively communicate what you have to contribute to a job or a career. Self-management skills relate to how we cope with or relate to people, conditions, and situations in our world, including our work. Our special knowledge skills are what we have learned and what we know.

Knowing what level of skills you possess and prefer is helpful in understanding yourself and identifying suitable career options. The more you know about your skills, the better decisions you can make in your career, educational, and job choices. In this regard, the more you know about yourself, the better you can capitalize on your unique assets as a person and prevent your shortcomings from becoming major obstacles.

CASE STUDY
CYNTHIA

Cynthia is an example of someone who used her transferable functional, self-management, and special knowledge skills to change from one career to another. Tired of her secretarial job, Cynthia decided to look for a new position where she would have more responsibility and opportunity to make decisions. She undertook a systematic inventory of the skills she used in her job. In addition to her typing and shorthand transcription skills, she found that her boss frequently asked her to compose correspondence and memos, as well as schedule and arrange meetings with other management staff.

Cynthia was popular among the other secretaries because of her functional and self-management skills. She was such a good listener, negotiator, communicator, and advisor that sometimes she was called on, informally, to arbitrate an office disagreement. She was very effective at summarizing each side's views, helping them to resolve their differences, and helping them to reach a compromise satisfactory to all. They considered Cynthia honest and fair.

More and more, Cynthia was dissatisfied with her primary duties of typing and answering the phone. She was spending too much time working with machines rather than with people. After she had assessed her skills, Cynthia realized that she had high-level human relations skills that could be transferred to other fields without extensive retraining. She narrowed down her alternatives to several good possibilities: an office manager, an Equal Employment Opportunities (EEO) personnel specialist, a labor relations assistant, a program coordinator for a convention center, a hotel public relations director, and a travel industry representative.

After doing extensive research on these careers and on actual opportunities in her own city, Cynthia decided that a position in hotel public relations was her most interesting and potentially satisfying option. She investigated five large hotels and discovered that two of them were lacking in strong, dynamic public relations programs. Using what she knew about her skills and the knowledge she had acquired in her research, she prepared a proposal outlining what she thought she could do to meet a hotel's needs.

Cynthia obtained interviews at those two particular hotels and was very excited to be offered positions at both. Today Cynthia is challenged by her job and much more satisfied with her new position as the hotel's assistant coordinator of public relations. She is using most of the functional and self-management skills that she identified in her secretarial job. She is also applying some of the special knowledge she acquired in her previous position (such as word processing, telephone answering techniques, and correspondence and office procedures) while learning new ones associated with the hotel business and public relations.

ASSIGNMENTS

1. Brainstorm with your family and/or friends to find names of people they know who use preferred skills similar to yours in their work. If they don't know anyone personally, perhaps they might refer you to someone else who does.

2. Begin talking with people who use the kinds of skills in their work that you prefer using.

3. Think back to some of the jobs you've had in the past (volunteer or paying jobs) and answer the following questions:

   a. What were some conditions of the work environments to which you were required to adapt?

   b. Were your self-management skills compatible with the conditions of the work environments?

   c. If they were not compatible, did that incompatibility contribute to your quitting or leaving?

   d. If they were not compatible but you stayed on the job, what adjustments did you make in order to be more compatible?

 Similar to small businesses that open and close, Web sites come and go. This means that some of the Web sites listed in this book will probably change during the time you are reading this material. Therefore, we have created a page on the Web where you can go to ensure you have the most up-to-date links for each of the chapters. To find these links, go to **www.CareerKiosk.org** and click on "Updated links for *Your Career*." These links will ensure that you have accurate links and access to great sites on the Web!

ADDITIONAL RESOURCES FOR SKILL IDENTIFICATION

Eureka Skill Inventory
The California Career Information System
Room 408
130 33rd Street
Richmond, California 94804
Telephone (415) 235-3883

The Job Hunting Map by Dick Bolles
Ten Speed Press
900 MODOC
Berkeley, California 94707

Motivated Skill Card Sort
Career Research and Testing
2005 Hamilton Avenue
San Jose, California 95125
Telephone (408) 559-4945

Skill Sort Cards
(See Appendix E)

Your Thinking Style in Work and Learning

How we think influences how we communicate, solve problems,
deal with relationships and make decisions.
—Ned Herrmann

Do you know people who—

☑ Are great at analyzing facts and coming to logical conclusions?
☑ Think best when thinking aloud while interacting with others?
☑ Are brilliant at coming up with unique ideas and new ways of doing things?
☑ Approach problems in a structured way and "follow the book" in making predictable decisions?

If so, you know people who process information and experiences in uniquely different ways because of their different thinking styles.

Rodney had scored exceptionally high in risk taking on his thinking style assessment

TRADITIONAL MEASURES OF INTELLIGENCE

What is your IQ? Do you think of yourself as a genius, highly intelligent, about average, or not too smart? Most people decide how smart they are when they are young and spend the rest of their lives, consciously or unconsciously, making their achievements conform to this imagined potential—their self-concept. Your concept of your abilities probably came from early interactions with significant people like parents, family, teachers and friends. Rarely do children base their self-concept on their own observations.

Thereafter, your intellectual concept probably was changed or reinforced by various IQ tests of general abilities and other tests of general knowledge. Do you remember tests like the Iowa tests or California Test of Achievement? Or the SAT, ACT, or GRE exams? These tests are objective measuring tools of intelligence, but are they the true indicators

Web Connect

Emotional intelligence is increasingly a topic of interest in business and industries around the world. More and more research is contributing to this interest, including research that demonstrates how emotional intelligence is related to IQ and career success. To read an interesting article on this, visit the ERIC site at **http://ericacve.org/docgen.asp?tbl=tia&ID=1327.**

of personal ability and human potential? The problem with IQ tests and general knowledge tests is that they turn out to be fair predictors of only one thing—academic success—for only one standard population. "At best, IQ contributes about 20 percent to the factors that determine life success, which leaves 80 percent to other forces."[1]

IQ scores are not a measure of true human potential. High IQ scores are not a guarantee of material or life success. But this is not surprising since many people with high IQ scores may be motivated by values other than wealth. It's more surprising that people with the highest IQ scores often fail to meet their intellectual potential as well. The issue is further clouded by stories of "mentally handicapped" children or adults with very low IQ scores who turned out to be unusually gifted in one specialized area. Clearly, other elements are involved in human potential.

In fact, no one really knows what an IQ is. Mind power is more than a matter of the natural abilities you have at birth. Your concept of your intelligence and the ways you learn how to use your mind are equally important influences—positive or negative. Recent research on brain injuries has shown that people use only a small portion of their brain. Research also shows that latent brain cells can take over the functions of damaged brain cells. Unless your brain is either physically impaired or psychologically damaged beyond correction, you have the capacity for intellectual accomplishment beyond anything you have demonstrated so far in your life. Consider the possibility that you just might be more intelligent and creative than you have ever dared to imagine.

Gerald felt that by allowing his son Ralphie to get his education on the Internet he had really encouraged him to express his individuality.

---

[1] Goleman, Daniel, *Emotional Intelligence: Why it can matter more than IQ* (New York: Bantam Books, 1994) p. 34.

Words of Wisdom

Effective thinking and intellectual success are held prisoner by negative expectations. Open your mind and let out your full human potential.

But what does this have to do with career planning and success? A great deal! First, doesn't it make sense to understand the way you think—your thinking style—to become a more successful learner? After all, this is the Information Age, where learning and creative problem-solving have become a way of life and a lifelong activity. Also, if you want to choose an occupation that puts your best abilities to use, it's important to determine how your mind works best. The content and exercises in this chapter are designed to help you do just that.

INFLUENCES ON YOUR THINKING

Becoming your intelligent best involves at least three types of awareness. First, you should become aware of how pressing needs and values can have a major but hidden influence on your thinking and decision making. Understand this influence to ensure that you use this self-awareness to positive advantage in your career decision making. Needs and values are especially relevant as you decide what particular work or academic environment is the best place for you to implement your career. Accordingly, needs and values are covered before you explore your career alternatives in Chapter 6, *Discovering What Motivates You.*

It's also useful to understand how negative attitudes hinder clear thinking as people try to carry out perfectly appropriate career decisions and plans. Some people turn totally passive, waiting for the world to come to them. Others get sidetracked easily and frequently, never committing to the decision, goals, and plans they have chosen. Still others resort to unnecessarily extreme or premature changes trying to reach their goals. This topic will be addressed fully in Chapter 10, *Empowering Yourself to Succeed.*

The third influence on your thinking is your unique style of learning. This influence can be assessed, and the result is considerably more useful to career planning than traditional IQ tests. Simply defined, your thinking style is the general approach you prefer in seeking to understand information or experience. This chapter is designed to help you determine and understand your own primary thinking and learning style. By choosing a career involving primary activities that require your dominant thinking style, you will refine and expand your mental powers. You will also be able to perform the tasks involved more easily than someone of equal or higher IQ who is intellectually mismatched to the job.

RECENT RESEARCH ON THE BRAIN

Researchers like Nobel Prize winner Roger Sperry and his associates studying "the split brain" and Carl Pribram's studies on the holographic brain have produced startling new insights into how the human brain works. Harvard psychologist Howard Gardner's research suggests that human intelligence is far broader than the simple verbal, linear, and sequential activities measured by IQ tests.[2] Another Harvard psychologist, Robert Rosenthal, an expert on empathy, has shown that when people administering IQ tests treat their subjects warmly, the test scores are higher.[3] Educational researchers are applying their research discoveries to enhance learning. Bulgarian psychotherapist Gregory Lozonov, for example, has demonstrated new learning approaches involving "whole brain" activities that accelerate learning performance and tap into little used creative abilities.

These discoveries about the human brain indicate that we all have learned to access our brains in characteristic ways. In other words, we have acquired "favorite" ways of thinking. Since our unique modes of thinking share common characteristics, various researchers have classified the approaches into thinking or learning styles. Ned Herrmann's model of thinking styles based on recent brain research has been particularly accurate in predicting which occupational tasks will be easier to perform for any individual. The *Herrmann Brain Dominance Survey* tests your preferred thinking styles and divides them into four categories. The exercises in this chapter are adapted from Herrmann's work.[4]

[2.] Gardner, H., *Frames of Mind: The Theory of Multiple Intelligences* (New York: Bask Books, 1983)

[3.] Cooper, R. K., and Sawaf, A., *Executive EQ: Emotional Intelligence in Leadership & Organizations* (New York: Grossett/Putnam, 1996), p. xxxiv.

[4.] Herrmann, Ned, *The Creative Brain* (Lake Lure, NC: Brain Books, 1988).

OUR TWO MINDS

In a way we seem to have two minds—one that specializes in thinking and the other in feeling. As a result of the past several decades of brain research we now know that the two hemispheres of the human brain tend to specialize in different styles of thinking. In general, the left brain specializes in a logical, linear, analytical mode of thinking that is best suited to activities such as fact finding, analyzing data, mathematical computation, and performing technical and procedural tasks. The left brain is often considered to be the seat of objective, dispassionate, computer-like thought process.

The right brain is the realm of nonlinear, holistic, spontaneous, and intuitive thinking. This is the kind of mental process best suited to creative expression and in relating to others with empathic warmth and intuitive understanding. The right brain is considered to be the center of feelings, subjective thought, mysticism, and "heartfelt" spirituality.

Our two minds operate together in close harmony, for the most part. The interactions of these two minds, or brain hemispheres, functioning together provide our perceptual understanding of the world and our unique orientation to reality. There are times, of course, when one mind takes management control over our behavior. We commonly think that our logical brain is in management control of our learning and our emotional brain of our affections and loving. Management control can quickly change from one function to the other, as most of us are well aware in recalling those times when our logical mind has suddenly been overwhelmed by emotion when something has "grabbed" our feelings.

For reasons we don't yet understand, most individuals acquire a preference for either left- or right-brain thinking. While there are some individuals who feel equally comfortable with both left- and right-brain thinking, they appear to be the exception. Knowing our thinking preference can be of great value in making life choices. There is rather strong evidence that we do our best work, and experience our greatest energy when the activities we are engaged in correspond with our preferred style of thinking. Ned Herrmann refers to this as knowing our "smart" zones and our "dumb" zones.

No one is equally smart across the entire brain spectrum, concludes Herrmann, based on his career-long observations of the styles of people as General Electric's director of corporate management and training.[5] He noticed that those inclined towards a

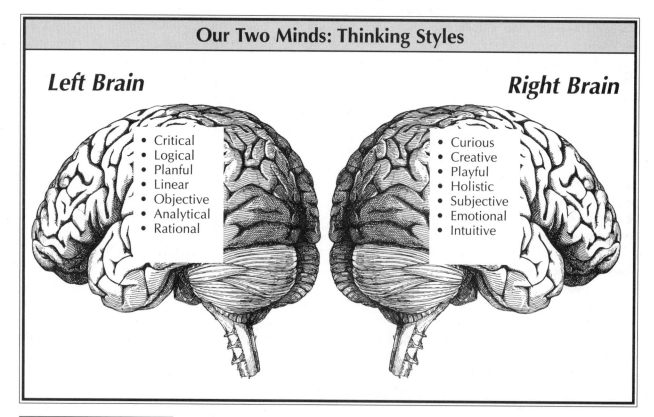

Our Two Minds: Thinking Styles

Left Brain

- Critical
- Logical
- Planful
- Linear
- Objective
- Analytical
- Rational

Right Brain

- Curious
- Creative
- Playful
- Holistic
- Subjective
- Emotional
- Intuitive

---

5. *The Creative Brain*, pp. 117–129.

EXERCISE 4-A. ASSESSING YOUR THINKING STYLE _____

We suggest that you now complete the *Thinking Style Assessment Inventory,* located at the end of this chapter. In completing the inventory, keep these points in mind:

☑ The more accurately your responses reflect your actual way of thinking, the more quickly and decisively you can identify your best assets.

☑ There are no "bad" outcomes or "bad" thinking styles that can result from this exercise. You are simply discovering your preferred mode of thinking.

---

left-brain style approached problem solving very differently than those favoring a right-brain orientation. Left-brainers went about problem solving in a fact-based, analytic, and step-by-step manner that favored words, numbers, and facts presented in logical sequence. In contrast, the right-brainers' way was to seek out insight, images, concepts, patterns, sounds, and movements, which they then synthesized into an intuitive solution.

THE FOUR STYLES OF THINKING

Have you already noticed how differently various people think? You are probably aware of certain predictable behavior or responses in your friends and associates. Perhaps you know someone who is highly creative or someone who always seems to be very organized. After years of research and observation, Ned Herrmann concluded that just four different styles are associated with brain functioning or how people access their brains.

Herrmann uses the names of physical regions of the brain to name his thinking styles. These regions are the left and right sides of the outer "cerebral" brain and the inner, "limbic" brain. His model is based on research showing that specific areas of the brain are associated with specific kinds of thinking activities. The limbic system appears to specialize in fundamental thinking activities associated with bonding and taking care of ourselves. The cerebral system is associated with higher level, abstract thinking. The codes being used in this chapter are adapted from Herrmann's work

Table 4.1	
The Brain—Four Styles of Thinking	
Analytical	*Intuitive*
• Left Cerebral	• Right Cerebral
Controlling	*Feeling*
• Left Limbic	• Right Limbic

Analytical Thinker

Analytical/Left Cerebral. This style of thinking is characterized by a careful, logical analysis of all available facts and information to produce answers or insights. This is the kind of thinking that IQ tests like SATs, ACTs and Graduate Record Examinations

> ### Web Connect
>
> If you're interested in additional information about how the brain works and how it impacts your health, emotions, career, IQ, success, and other areas of your life, you may be interested in looking at the information available through the International Brain Research Organization at **http://www.ibro.org** as well as the numerous interesting articles available on Brain.com at **http://www.brain.com/**

What happens when you put an intuitive right cerebral person in an analytical left cerebral job.

(GREs) measure. Those who favor this kind of thinking conclude that logical observation is the only way to determine reality, so truth cannot be determined until the "facts prove it so." This thinking style relies on a rigorous and critical thought process.

Analytical thinkers are inclined to question everything until they are convinced through careful examination of the available evidence. They are not swayed by emotional arguments or unexamined "good" ideas. They want the "cold, hard facts," and they want to know cause and effect. This approach is effective with problems and decision-making situations that can be resolved by finding the "one best answer" and where all the required facts are available for analysis. As an example of this thinking style in action, visualize a detective putting all the pieces together to determine "who done it," or an M.D. weighing the data to diagnose a medical condition and diagnose the likely outcome. Much of our scientific and technological advances have evolved out of this kind of thinking.

The Left-Brain Analytic—The BRIGHT and DARK Sides

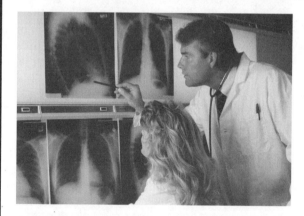

At their best they are logical evaluators of the facts who make their judgment and decisions on the basis of dispassionate reason.

At their worst they may become overly exacting or cynical, and become bogged down in meaningless analysis.

The Left Brain Controller—The BRIGHT and DARK Sides

At their best they are practical thinkers concerned about observable outcomes and effective task managers.

At their worst, they may micromanage details or become heavy handed about procedures and "going by the book" with little concern for others.

The Right-Brain Feelers—The BRIGHT and DARK Sides

At their worst, they may become overly emotional and irrationally impulsive or indecisively conflicted.

At their best, they are warm and caring individuals able to empathize, connect, and communicate with all kinds of people in all kinds of situations.

At their best they are wonderfully creative and imaginative.

At their worst, they're out of touch with reality and live in a fantasy world.

The Controlled Thinker

Controlling/Left Limbic. This kind of thinking is characterized by a one-step-at-a-time or sequential process. Those who favor this kind of thinking prevent problems through careful organization and planning. The controlled thinker avoids risks wherever and whenever possible. This style of thinking concentrates on details, dominance, and managing events through planning.

Controlled thinkers tend to be conservative in outlook and efficient and reliable in their daily activities. They like to have specific tasks to perform and a time frame for completing the job. Any kind of ambiguity or formlessness is annoying. Since this kind of thinker proceeds with tasks in an organized and planned way, time is well managed and things get done step-by-step on schedule. To get a better picture of this kind of thinking in action, imagine a person "debugging" a computer program, a highway patrolman determining who was "at fault" in a traffic accident based on the relevant traffic laws, or a manager working out a plan to control employee pay, vacation, and benefit policies. Left limbic oriented thinkers are great at getting things done in an efficient, timely manner.

Like predominantly analytical thinkers, the predominantly controlled thinkers do not see themselves as creative and don't trust emotions or intuition in making decisions. Controlled thinkers can be overly conventional and rigid or "tight" in their thinking. Occupations that require this kind of thinking style include many supervisory or middle management positions, police, secretarial, and many computer specialist positions.

The Feeling Thinker

Feeling/Right Limbic. This thinking approach involves paying attention to emotions, feelings, and the spiritual self. Feeling individuals tend to be empathetic, charitable, personable, and conversational. In problem-solving and decision-making situations, they work best in interacting with others, "talking out" a problem. These thinkers want to get in touch with any emotions involved and to understand the situation through verbal interaction. Right limbic thinkers also tend to be in touch with their spirituality and to be highly responsive to music. They may look for "inner guidance" as well as to "outer discussion" in their thought process.

For examples of this kind of thinking in action, visualize a counselor assisting a client in a problem-solving situation through the process of "talking about it" and being attuned to the nonverbal communications. Or imagine a teacher who is able to influence and motivate a student through patient understanding and caring interaction. Right limbic dominant individuals tend to excel in thinking that involves awareness of feelings and emotions. They are responsive to people and to the "inner world" and excellent at establishing rapport through communications. Feeling thinkers are inclined to trust their feelings over facts. For that reason, they can tend to be overly "soft" or uncritical, unsystematic thinkers or even "bleeding hearts." Occupations that require feeling-oriented approaches include:

- ☑ counseling,
- ☑ social work,
- ☑ teaching,
- ☑ nursing,
- ☑ human resource development,
- ☑ music.

The Intuitive Thinker

Intuiting/Right Cerebral. Right cerebral thinking is characterized by possibility thinking and creativity. Intuitive insights are often portrayed as a sudden flash of light. The thought process leading to that apparently sudden insight is not fully understood. Intuitive thinking tends to be "big-picture" or holistic thinking, where different elements from various sources are synthesized or simultaneously brought together.

Intuitive thinkers often have grand ideas about innovative new ways of doing things or creative redesigns of old methods, products, or services. Intuitives are visionaries who see creative possibilities in situations and get excited about their ideas for the future. To visualize right cerebral thinking in action, imagine an artist conceiving of an idea and bringing it to completion on canvas, or Beethoven evolving his "Fifth Symphony," or a manager coming up with a new employee development program or simultaneously seeing a creative, flexible solution to a long-standing problem. Intuitive thinkers are great at coming up with ideas, insights, and possible solutions to problems. They often get their best ideas in unstructured situations and places like reading, dreaming, walking, driving, or listening to music.

However, purely intuitive thinkers tend to work on their own inner time frame and don't work well on regular schedules. They tend to approach problem solving in an unstructured way and let their brain incubate on a problem until they have a flash of ideas. Intuitives are inclined to come up with many ideas, of varying quality. Intuitive thinkers are not inclined to prove their ideas through a careful consideration of the facts. Instead, they are usually anxious to try them out or get on to the next challenge. People with primarily right-cerebral thinking styles do well as:

- ☑ artists,
- ☑ creative writers,
- ☑ entrepreneurs,
- ☑ program developers.

YOUR THINKING-STYLE PROFILE

Your own thinking-style profile consists of some degree of preference (or avoidance) for all four thinking styles described above. There are a total of 71 different four-digit code possibilities. Perhaps you are uncomfortable labeling your mind with a single "four-digit" code. If so, we don't blame you. But this simplified code is a useful tool for helping you develop a list of occupational alternatives.

By helping you understand what thinking styles are dominant in your own mind, your code also helps you capitalize on your best assets and understand what thinking styles could be developed further. Having the versatility to use different thinking styles for different situations is a great asset to most people.

Figure 4.1 Sample Thinking Style Profiles

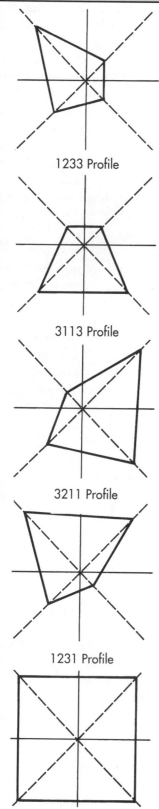

1233 Profile

3113 Profile

3211 Profile

1231 Profile

1111 Profile

1133 Profile. "The Technician"

The initial "1" indicates strong left-cerebral, analytical thinking with a preference for logical problem solving. The "1" score in controlled thinking indicates the capacity for organization, planning, and efficiency, when needed. The "3" in the feeling sector and intuitive sector shows this person avoids feelings, interpersonal interactions, and creative, big-picture ideas. Individuals with this profile work well with problems requiring a step-by-step analysis of the facts.

3113 Profile. "The Organized Friend"

This profile with "1" in both the controlled thinking and feeling sector shows a strong preference for order, planning, and control as well as a strong preference for interpersonal relationships and a trust for feelings. Individuals with this profile prefer planned activities with others. A reliable worker and a caring friend. This person avoids analytical and intuitive activities.

3211 Profile. "The Creative Helper"

This profile with a "1" in both right-brain sectors (feeling thinker and intuitive thinker) shows a possibility thinker and creative problem solver. Who loves to help people and enjoys interactive communication. The "2" in the controlled thinking sector shows the capacity for organization and planning when needed. Individuals with this profile avoid analytical thinking.

1231 Profile. "The Abstract Thinker"

This profile featuring a "1" in both cerebral sectors shows a thinker who loves to hypothesize based on facts, devise ideas, designs, and strategies and then analyze them for logical consistency. The "2" score in controlled thinking shows the capacity for planning and efficiency, if required. Individuals with this profile avoid personal feelings and close personal interactions.

1111 Profile. "The Executive"

A multi-dominant profile, showing an individual who enjoys all kinds of activities and thinking. This person can experience conflict between analyzing and feeling and risk taking and safe keeping. Individuals with this profile relate well with different thinking styles, and with the right skills, can become an effective leader if able to match up or balance different thinking styles appropriately to the situation at hand. This person must also be able to delegate thinking tasks to others to take maximum advantage of the profile.

Figure 4.1 Sample Thinking Style Profiles (continued)

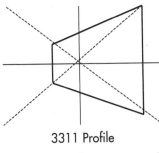

3311 Profile

3311 Profile. "The Self-Expressive Creator"

This profile features a strong right-brain preference for creative abstract thought combined with expressive feeling. The great strength of this style of thinking preference is in heartfelt and innovative expression. Individuals with this profile tend to avoid rigorous organized thought in favor of intuitive expression and connecting with feelings.

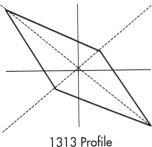

1313 Profile

1313 Profile. "The Humane-Analyst"

This individual is attuned to both thinking and feeling. Because these two orientations are opposite mental processes, individuals with this thinking style may often be conflicted between issues involving the head and the heart, or pulled between objective analysis and subjective emotion. When these two preferences work together, the resultant output can be human-centered rationality.

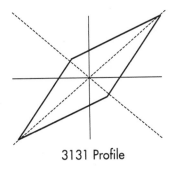

3131 Profile

3131 Profile. "The Innovative Implementer"

This profile features a dual preference for structured-procedural and intuitive-abstract thinking. An individual with this preference may often feel conflicted between the desire to take a creative risk and the need to "play it safe." When these two opposite styles of thinking are integrated, the result can be a creative output that is implemented through a careful plan. The challenge for this individual is generating the creative ideas first, before getting too concerned about practicality.

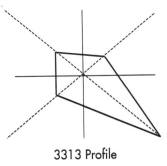

3313 Profile

3313 Profile. "Person of the Heart"

This is the profile of a warm, caring feeler. Individuals with this preference may feel strongly moved by music, spirituality and relationship. Because they feel so strongly, they may have little patience with left-brained, abstract thought, which is likely to seem cold and impersonal to them. At their best, persons of the heart care deeply and connect with their own emotions and those of others.

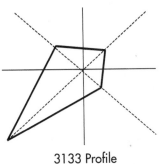

3133 Profile

3133 Profile. "The Traditionalist"

This profile features a very strong preference for structure, order, and convention. A great strength of individuals with this profile is their ability to take things one step at a time, being careful to follow procedures and established policies. They prefer to "go by the book" and are loyal to the "tried" and the "true." A weakness of this style can be a stubborn avoidance of new ideas, feelings and impatience with abstractions. They like to have things boiled down to the "black and white" of issues without a lot of fancy talk in getting there.

It's true that some conflicts may be encountered by the rare people who have 1111 thinking style codes, with strong preferences for all approaches. But such versatility will be a strength in any high-level occupation, as long as the individual can use the different thinking styles appropriate to the particular problem or situation at hand. What conclusions can you draw from your own profile? Figure 4.1 illustrates five different thinking-style profiles and summarizes how these varying preferences are likely to work together.

PUTTING YOUR PROFILE TO WORK

At this point, the relationship between thinking style and career should be clearer. Herrmann concludes that competence in your career depends upon performing activities that fully involve your most preferred thinking style(s). When you do that, you are likely to enjoy your work and be productive at it, a good combination for success at work. Without this compatibility, both employer and employee are likely to suffer. Herrmann's research suggests that one of the main causes of drug and alcohol problems on the job is the failure to match personal thinking-style preferences with job activities.

To help you find occupations requiring thinking styles compatible with your own profile, Table 4.5 contains a listing of sample occupations reflective of the four modes of thinking. Any occupation, however, is likely to involve all four of the thinking styles in varying proportions. What is important to note are your dominant thinking styles. The occupations in Table 4.4 (page 91) are placed in categories on the basis of the most dominant thinking styles.

As you do the following exercise, it is important to remember that there is no single perfect way to find the best career for you. Thinking style is just one of several tools used in the book to help you identify a fairly lengthy list of career possibilities that are "right for you." In a later chapter we will show you how to narrow down your list and to select your best choice. For now, however, begin the process of identifying career possibilities by going on to Exercise 4-B.

BEING YOUR SUCCESSFUL BEST

If you truly want to develop your total mind power, you will not only capitalize on your best assets, but you will also effectively "manage your deficits." In this regard, consider what you avoid and what might be your deficits. Your thinking deficits are not nec-

 ## EXERCISE 4-B. SELF-INSIGHTS AND CAREER PROSPECTS _____

1. Review your thinking-style profile and your four-digit code, and then list personal insights acquired. Be as specific as you can about what you prefer and what you should avoid in your work, education, relationships, and life. List a few words from Appendix A1 that will remind you of the most important aspects of your thinking style.

2. Using Table 4.5, identify those occupations that fall within your preferred mode(s) of thinking. Circle any that are of interest and involve skills you have identified in Chapter 3.

   First, go through the list corresponding to your strongest preference. If your code is a 1132, for example, you would look for occupations in the *Analyzing* column. Circle any occupations of interest to you. Then go back to the individual columns corresponding to the next strongest preferences and circle occupations of interest there.

   After you have circled a number of occupations, narrow that number down to the 10 or 12 that you like best and that probably require some of your best skills. Transfer these to the *occupations of interest* section of Appendix A2.

   (*Note:* Leave the *Holland code* column blank; you'll find out how to obtain that in Chapter 6.)

Table 4.2
Developing and Capitalizing on The Thinking Styles

Analyzing
- Be totally objective—get the facts right
- Decide and solve problems logically
- Question your assumptions and conclusions
- Play devil's advocate
- Be exact and precise in communications
- Treat others with detached fairness and justice

Controlling
- Keep a schedule calendar
- Reach conclusions in an orderly and step-by-step way
- Prioritize tasks and do the most important first
- Keep a "to do" list and follow it
- Be organized, punctual, and reliable
- Appreciate procedures, rules, and policies

Intuiting
- Read widely and randomly to stimulate ideas
- Look for unique and novel associations
- Trust your instincts and hunches
- Work in bursts of energy—then relax
- Use mental imagery, fantasy, dreams
- Stimulate creativity with play, dance, and art

Feeling
- Nurture and support yourself and others
- Appreciate your feelings and trust them
- Understand others from your feelings
- Listen to music for mood and harmony
- Decide with your heart and soul
- Express your feelings and relate with warmth

essarily "ability" deficits. If you have a fully functioning brain, you can develop your ability in all four styles of thinking. It is difficult, however, to develop a competence in an area in which you lack interest. It's a bit like learning how to swim when you dislike or fear the water. It is difficult, but possible, for people who fear the water to overcome their bias and learn how to swim—even well.

You are going to be the most successful when you are engaged in activities that fully utilize and develop your preferred skills, thinking preferences, and personal interests in pursuit of what you truly value. Generally people are far more successful in activities that fully use their preferred thinking style and require little or nothing of their least preferred style. It makes sense, therefore, to effectively put your preferences to productive work. Table 4.2 lists some suggestions for activities that capitalize on the strengths within each of the four areas.

How do you overcome mental biases? Do you hate mathematics, for instance? Stop saying you can't do it, and consider that you are dealing with a mental preference, which probably has little to do with the functioning capabilities of your brain. Do you believe you are not creative or can't get along with people? Remember, these attitudes are learned, often from isolated experiences that left a deep impression.

A good reason to develop your "least preferred" thinking skills is that multidimensional or whole-brain thinking is simply more powerful than one-track thinking. Whole-brain thinkers can do more things well than those who use only a small portion of their brain power potential. Think, for example, of the analytical thinker trying to solve a problem when only limited facts are available and many solutions are possible, each controversial to some people in the organization. Many problems in business and in life are like that. It's really only in rare situations that all the facts are available and there is only one right answer.

What if you are a great intuitive thinker who is always coming up with terrific ideas but can't get any of them off the drawing board into action? Wouldn't it be nice to be able to tap into the left limbic controlling portion of your brain for some productive planning, organizing, and structuring? Consult Table 4.2 for ideas on how to develop your preferences in the four areas. Sometimes you can change an avoidance area to one of relatively more comfort by experimenting with the activities associated with your nondominant quadrants. You can upgrade your limited thinking-style preferences in the same way.

THE VALUE OF KNOWING YOUR THINKING STYLE

Why bother taking the *Thinking Style Assessment Inventory* or finding out your brain dominance profile? There are good reasons for doing so. These have to do with motivation, self-understanding, self-concept enhancement, career decision making, and understanding how you might be a more successful performer in your career, your education, and your life. Let me, Dr. Borchard, offer a personal example of why I make such a claim. Several years ago I enthusiastically accepted a college position where I assumed I was going to be engaged in my dream job. In many ways that turned out to be so—but there was a big problem. No matter how hard I tried, I seemed unable to connect with my administrative colleagues in a way that was very satisfying. This was extremely frustrating to me because the need for stimulating intellectual collegiality was a primary reason I had chosen this kind of work. It wasn't that I was any more or less intelligent than my colleagues or that we disliked each other. It was that we were different, but how? An administrative retreat with my colleagues revealed the answer. The retreat featured the *Herrmann Brain Dominance Survey*, a thinking-style preference instrument similar to the one you take in this chapter. From this experience I discovered that I was a "right-brainer." Not only that, but I was the one and only right-brainer in that whole division of 16 administrators. My colleagues and I were essentially operating on different wavelengths. Their interests were focused primarily upon the ob-jective and practical management of the everyday business—a left-brain focus. What grabbed my attention, on the other hand, was the creative possibilities in developing new programs. My colleagues were pragmatists and I, an idealist. We were operating in different perceptual worlds. We all came away from this retreat with useful and interesting new insights. One was that we now understood why and how we were so different. That experience greatly enhanced our respect for our differences and we learned how to more effectively relate and work together. After that I no longer went to them expecting to engage in interesting, to me, discussions on the theoretical, the idealistic, or the possible. I did go to them, however, for advice and suggestions on how to make an idea more effective, and more importantly, how to make it more palatable to the left-brain-oriented executives to whom I needed to sell the 'thing.' They, on the other hand, would often look to me for creative input to problems being confronted. As a result of the insights acquired from this retreat my colleagues and I were able, in essence, to link the right brain harmoniously to the left, producing a more holistic and effective operation along with a more pleasant working environment.

While I could share numerous other stories of individuals who benefited from the results of their thinking-style assessment, I shall refrain. I do want to offer just two short stories, however, as examples of the value in knowing your style. To begin let us introduce Michelle, an ex-lawyer and now bookstore owner. We will close with a short story about Joe, our cartoonist, an ex-soldier turned artist-educator.

CASE STUDY
MICHELLE

Michelle became a lawyer, not because she was particularly interested in law, but because she was strongly encouraged to do so by her parents and teachers. As an excellent student who had high SAT scores, she opted to take the LSATs. She did well on those, so that settled it—she got a degree in law. Michelle then began her career as an attorney with the federal government. She had been advised to go this route because a government position was secure, at least it was thought to be back then, and it came with a good salary and excellent benefits. She discovered, however, that there was more to a career than job security. She found her work to be routine and boring. For a while she thought all work must be that way. Nonetheless, she found herself dreaming about other possibilities. One of her prime interests had always been books. Often she would find herself browsing through bookstores in her leisure, losing herself there for hours on end in reading and exploring. Eventually she began dreaming about owning a bookstore. The more she thought about it, the more she was captivated by the idea, so much so that she thought she might actually do it. And, while it didn't happen overnight, she eventually decided to make the leap. Leaving a secure government position for such an uncertain venture shocked her colleagues, who strongly advised her against such a seemingly irrational act. In spite of their dissuasions, however, she went on to develop her passion as a bookstore owner. Exhibiting some marketing savvy, she chose to set up shop in a small, upscale town with a college community and a government training center. Her assumption was that this would be a location where there would be enough book-reading people to make a "go" of it. She was right, although she had to work hard to make her business a success. Today she is thoroughly enjoying life and her work even though she clears a bit less money than she would have had she stayed with the government.

As you might have guessed, Michelle is a risk-taker, with strong entrepreneurial leanings. She is a right-brainer in her activity preferences, with strongly developed left-brain skills. Had she understood these things about herself earlier in life, she probably would have decided against law and a career based primarily upon security. She might have been better able to visualize a career path more suited to her unique interests and personality. Michelle's story highlights this important point: it is usually better to make your career decision on the basis of deep-seated interests and personality style than strictly upon general intelligence and/or academic achievement.

CASE STUDY
JOE

As you might have guessed from his cartoons in this book, Joe is a little unusual. Joe became an advocate of the *Thinking Style Assessment* several years ago and has been using the insights he acquired from it professionally with his art students and informally with friends ever since. Here is why understanding brain dominance and thinking-style differences are important to Joe. While today he is a very successful artist, art teacher, and cartoonist, Joe has come a long way since his earlier days from a broken home in a Pennsylvania steel town. To escape the difficulties of his early life, Joe joined the Army and ended up as a cryptographic technician. Upon his eventual departure from military life, Joe began looking for what to do next. He had been offered a technicians job with the National Security Administration (NSA) in Tokyo and decided to take it, even though that kind of work never felt right to him when he'd being doing it in the Army. He took his first art courses just to pass the time until the date he was to report for work in Tokyo. At that time he had no idea that he had a special talent for art, although he had become aware of an art interest. He had been in art school about two months when the call came to report to NSA headquarters for indoctrination. He had 24 hours to make his choice between the NSA job and continuing in art school. In mulling over these two options he realized that something had come alive within himself when he began making art. There was a joy that he had never experienced before. On that basis, he jumped into the life of an artist knowing only that it seemed "right' for him.

Now, years later, with a master's degree in art from a top art institute and a successful career as a college art professor under his belt, Joe is at the peak of an extremely rewarding career. He says this about the insights he acquired from the *Thinking Style Assessment*:

When I first saw my assessment results, it was like a new light dawned. Because I had not been so great at math in my early life, I concluded that I must not be very bright—even though I had been successful in college and graduate school. Old self-doubts about my mental ability hung over me like a black cloud. I had to be clever to earn my masters and bachelors degrees without running into insurmountable problems in 'left brain' courses. It got dicey a couple of times. Working out the glaze formulas in an advanced ceramics course required finding a left brainer to help me through. When I saw my assessment results, however, I realized—hey I'm a strong right-brainer, without much going on in the left side! (Joe's thinking style is a 3311.) While I may not be so great at some left brain activities like math, finances and schedule books, I'm brilliant at right brain activities. Seeing those results and understanding what they meant affected my whole self-concept. Ever since understanding this, I have felt great about who I am, rather than depressed about who I'm not. That assessment boosted my self-confidence. Since discovering that, I've been using this whole-brain stuff with my art students. I help them understand that being a right-brainer is OK and show them techniques for accessing both hemispheres of the brain to become better artists. In fact, when you accept who you are and develop skills in line with your interests; you can even be brilliant—like me!

Needless to say I haven't become rich as an artist but I find every day of my life exciting, challenging and satisfying. My message to the world is . . . if you are a dominant right brainer get the heck out of the left brain career track before it's too late!

Words of Wisdom

A brain strained by a new idea never returns to its original shape.
Oliver Wendell Holmes

ing-style spectrum. There is no one way to be that is better than any other. The important issue is who you are, what your gifts are, how you capitalize on these, and how you can share them happily in the world. When you can do that, you too can become brilliant—just like Joe (actually, you can become brilliant—just like you!).

Joe's comments contain several valuable insights. First, Joe was indeed lucky to stumble into a profession in which he had great, but unrealized talent and passion. How many people have been so fortunate? Undoubtedly there are thousands who have never discovered their career-motivating interests and thinking-style talents. There are also far too many who have stumbled into the wrong kind of job, educational program, or career path where their interests and talents have not had the opportunity to develop and bloom. A second point from Joe's story worthy of highlighting is this: when you know and accept yourself, you are on the road to self-confidence and self-esteem. These are not only essential ingredients to feeling good about yourself, they are key in being successful in your career, in your relationships, in your learning, and in your life. It makes no difference if you are more of a right-brainer than a left, a controller rather than a creator, or that your preferences are distributed equally across the think-

SUMMARY

Old ideas about intelligence and creativity are being altered by modern brain research. It is now clear that most individuals have considerably more potential than formerly realized. One way to develop that potential is to discover and develop your preferred thinking style. A thinking style is a favorite way of thinking or processing information and experience.

Ned Herrmann has devised a thinking-style model that identifies four types of thinking—analytical, controlling, feeling, and intuiting. This can serve as valuable input for career planning because various occupations emphasize various thinking styles. If you want to be both motivated and successful in your career, it's important to select an occupation involving activities that use your dominant thinking-style preference or preferences. Knowledge of thinking styles can also help you develop your total "whole-brain" potential.

ASSIGNMENTS

1. Read the description of ten occupations that most interest you from your work in this chapter in the *Occupational Outlook Handbook (OOH)* (you can access an Internet version of the OOH at **http://www.bls.gov/ocohome.htm**). Attempt to identify the four-digit thinking-style profile code of these occupations, using the model explained in this chapter. Compare your thinking style profile code with these other codes. How would they appear to fit your thinking-style preferences?

2. Conduct information interviews with two or three people in careers of possible interest to you. Ask them questions about the nature of their problem-solving and information-processing activities to learn about the thinking styles their professions require. Compare your own thinking-style profile with these, and make assessments about any possible match.

REFERENCES

The Herrmann Brain Dominance Survey and *The Creative Brain*. Brain Books, c/o Applied Creative Services, 2075 Buffalo Creek Road, Lake Lure, N.C. 28746.

Goldman, Daniel. *Emotional Intelligence: Why It Can Matter More Than IQ*. New York: Bantam Books, 1997.

Cooper, R. K., and S. Ayman, Executive EQ: *Emotional Intelligence in Leadership & Organization*. New York: Grosset/Putnam, 1996.

Gelb, Michael J. *How to Think Like Leonardo da Vinci: Seven Steps to Genius Every Day*. Dell, 2000.

THE THINKING STYLE ASSESSMENT INVENTORY

This assessment will help you identify your brain-dominance preference and link your preferred style of thinking with career options that bring out your best. This assessment is based upon the work of Ned Herrmann, who as manager of management education within General Electric Corporation pioneered the study of the brain in the field of business—specifically, how individuals' thinking preferences, or "brain dominance," affect the way they work, learn, and communicate.

The assessment consists of four sections:

- ☑ **Part 1**: *Trait Comparisons* (defining traits that fit you best and those that fit you poorly)
- ☑ **Part 2**: *Ranking Your Preferences* (rank ordering traits that best describe you)
- ☑ **Part 3**: *Preferred Work Activities* (identifying work activities of greatest and least interest)
- ☑ **Part 4**: *Developing Your Thinking Style* (summarizing the results of the above three assessments into a profile that graphically depicts your thinking-style preference)

PART 1. TRAIT COMPARISONS

Use this scale to rate how well the traits listed below describe you.

Rating Scale	
4	Most like me
3	Next most like me
2	Somewhat like me
1	Least like me

DIRECTIONS

1. Read the table across from left to right for each of the ten rows. In row 1, decide which of the four words appearing across in Columns A, B, C, or D best describes you. Assign 4 points to that word by writing "4" in the box preceding it. Then decide which word is the next best description, and give that word 3 points by writing "3" in the preceding box. Repeat this ranking, assigning "2" points to the next closest description, and finally 1 point to the word that is the least descriptive word in that row.

   Example: For row 1, Ben decides that *Dreamer* best describes him, *Sociable* next most, and *Logical* the next most, and *Orderly* the least. He assigns scores for Row 1 as follows:

	A	B	C	D
1.	2 Logical	1 Doer	3 Sociable	4 Dreamer

Rank and score the words in the following summary table in the same manner to indicate how closely they describe you. Consider each row separately. Then add up the totals for each column, and record these in the *Totals* boxes at the bottom of each column.

If you are not sure what some of the terms in the table mean, check the *Definition of Terms* section after the table.

Part 1. Summary Table

	A	B	C	D
1.	☐ logical	☐ doer	☐ sociable	☐ dreamer
2.	☐ analytical	☐ detail-oriented	☐ cooperative	☐ intuitive
3.	☐ factually precise	☐ orderly	☐ tender hearted	☐ original
4.	☐ critical	☐ conventional	☐ spiritual	☐ imaginative
5.	☐ reserved	☐ practical	☐ warm hearted	☐ creative
6.	☐ verbally accurate	☐ straightforward	☐ genuine	☐ individualistic
7.	☐ exact	☐ cautious	☐ tactful	☐ big picture thinker
8.	☐ studious	☐ efficient	☐ outgoing	☐ innovative
9.	☐ rational	☐ systematic	☐ sympathetic	☐ futuristic
10.	☐ questioning	☐ planner	☐ accepting	☐ possibility thinking
	☐ A Total	☐ B Total	☐ C Total	☐ D Total

Your total scores for box A+B+C+D should equal 100.

DEFINITION OF TERMS

Analytical: Making logical sense of things by carefully examining the facts and data.

Authentic: Committed to being honest with yourself and genuine with others (what you see is what you get).

Big-picture thinker: Understanding things conceptually; seeing how many pieces might fit together in the whole.

Conceptual: Able to mentally conceive designs, ideas, plans, and programs.

Controlling: Managing events and situations through efficient plans and by following the rules and procedures.

Conventional: Abiding by the usual, the traditional, or standard way of doing things.

Critical: Judging the value of an idea or product, discriminating, finding fault.

Empathetic: Ability to appreciate how another sees, understands, and feels about things.

Entrepreneurial: Undertaking a business venture; assuming the risk for the sake of profit. Having an intuitive sense about a product or service that would be a good investment risk.

Evaluative: Making judgments through careful observation of the available facts.

Emotive: In touch with your feelings and freely expressing them.

Futuristic: Possessing facility in thinking about the future and imagining what it may bring.

Ingenious: Clever, resourceful, original, or inventive.

Impartial: Favoring no one side or party more than another. Being fair or just.

Innovative: Able to come up with new or novel ideas, methods, actions, or devices.

Intuitive: The immediate knowing of something without the conscious use of reasoning.

Instantaneous: Knowing. Flash of insight.

Investigative: Seeking after the facts, examining them in detail.

Orderly: Proceeding about things in a careful and effective manner.

Rational: The ability to think clearly and draw reasonable conclusions from the facts without being influenced by your emotions.

Resourceful: Cleverness in coming up with new and original ways of solving problems or ways of doing things.

Sequential: Dealing with things and ideas one after another or in numerical order.

Spiritual: Pertaining to divinity or soul as opposed to the body or material; feeling a deep sense of awe and reverence for the divine.

Systematic: Following an orderly plan. Doing things one step at a time.

Visionary: Having a knack for seeing forward in time and knowing how to take advantage of future possibilities.

FURTHER DIRECTIONS

2. Now that you have rated the descriptive words above, review each row to find the items you have assigned a score of "4" because they were most self-descriptive. Decide which one word best describes you, and change the score of "4" to "10" for that description. Then decide which of the remaining words next best describes you, and change that description's number from a "4" to an "8." Finally, decide which characteristic next best describes you, and change that number from a "4" to a "6."

3. After completing Step 1, retotal the columns. Your new grand total for columns A+B+C+D should equal 112.

PART 2. RANKING YOUR PREFERENCES

DIRECTIONS

1. In the following list of twenty traits, circle the ten (10) that you think best describe you.

Part 2. Traits Table

	Trait	Ranked Value		Trait	Ranked Value
1.	Investigative		11.	Deliberate	
2.	Conceptual		12.	Controlled	
3.	Risk taking		13.	Impartial	
4.	Evaluative		14.	Patient	
5.	Conservative		15.	Analytical	
6.	Objective		16.	Musical	
7.	Organized		17.	Entrepreneurial	
8.	Harmonizing		18.	Ingenious	
9.	Helping		19.	Resourceful	
10.	Personal		20.	Spiritual	

2. Now rank the ten traits you have circled from 1–10 in numerical order, assigning the highest number ("10") to that trait which is most like you, on down to "1" to the trait that is relatively the least like you.

3. After completing your rankings, place your *Ranked Value* numbers in the boxes of *Part 2. Your Ranked Value Summary Table*. Place your ranked value for each number item in the unshaded box. Place a "0" in the boxes for those items that were not among your top ten ranked value traits.

   Example: Ben assigned his highest ranking ("10") to *Risk taking* and his next highest ranking value ("9") to *harmonizing*. His Summary Table would look like this:

Part 2. Sample Summary Table

Item #	Trait	Ranked Value			
		A	B	C	D
1.	Investigative	0	/ / / / / / / / /	/ / / / / / / / /	/ / / / / / / / /
2.	Conceptual	/ / / / / / / / /	/ / / / / / / / /	/ / / / / / / / /	0
3.	Risk Taking	/ / / / / / / / /	/ / / / / / / / /	/ / / / / / / / /	10
4.	Evaluative	0	/ / / / / / / / /	/ / / / / / / / /	/ / / / / / / / /
5.	Conservative	/ / / / / / / / /	0	/ / / / / / / / /	/ / / / / / / / /
6.	Objective	0	/ / / / / / / / /	/ / / / / / / / /	/ / / / / / / / /
7.	Organized	/ / / / / / / / /	0	/ / / / / / / / /	/ / / / / / / / /
8.	Harmonizing	/ / / / / / / / /	/ / / / / / / / /	9	/ / / / / / / / /

4. After completing your Summary Table below, add up the totals for each of the four columns.

Part 2. Your Ranked Value Summary Table

Item #	Trait	A	B	C	D
1.	Investigative		/ / / / / /	/ / / / / /	/ / / / / /
2.	Conceptual	/ / / / / /	/ / / / / /	/ / / / / /	
3.	Risk Taking	/ / / / / /	/ / / / / /	/ / / / / /	
4.	Evaluative		/ / / / / /	/ / / / / /	/ / / / / /
5.	Conservative	/ / / / / /		/ / / / / /	/ / / / / /
6.	Objective		/ / / / / /	/ / / / / /	/ / / / / /
7.	Organized	/ / / / / /		/ / / / / /	/ / / / / /
8.	Harmonizing	/ / / / / /	/ / / / / /		/ / / / / /
9.	Helping	/ / / / / /	/ / / / / /		/ / / / / /
10.	Personal	/ / / / / /	/ / / / / /		/ / / / / /
11.	Deliberate	/ / / / / /		/ / / / / /	/ / / / / /
12.	Controlled	/ / / / / /		/ / / / / /	/ / / / / /
13.	Impartial		/ / / / / /	/ / / / / /	/ / / / / /
14.	Patient	/ / / / / /		/ / / / / /	/ / / / / /
15.	Analytical		/ / / / / /	/ / / / / /	/ / / / / /
16.	Musical	/ / / / / /	/ / / / / /		/ / / / / /
17.	Entrepreneurial	/ / / / / /	/ / / / / /	/ / / / / /	
18.	Ingenious	/ / / / / /	/ / / / / /	/ / / / / /	
19.	Resourceful	/ / / / / /	/ / / / / /	/ / / / / /	
20.	Spiritual	/ / / / / /	/ / / / / /		/ / / / / /
	Totals				

Note: Your totals for columns A+B+C+D should add up to 55 points.

PART 3. WORK ACTIVITIES

DIRECTIONS

Using the same scale as in Part 1 above, decide for each of the following situations which type of work activity is of greatest interest to you (your preferred activity). Then assign the highest score to that situation by filling in its box with "4." Then decide what your next preferred work activity is, and assign that a score of "3." Decide which is your least preferred activity, and award that a "1." The remaining item then gets a "2."

1. Working with people as a:

   A. ☐ financial planner

   B. ☐ supervisor

   C. ☐ teacher or counselor

   D. ☐ creativity consultant

2. Working primarily with:

- A. ☐ facts and information
- B. ☐ plans and procedures
- C. ☐ emotions and feelings
- D. ☐ ideas and possibilities

3. If I were to work at a large plant nursery, I would prefer to be:

- A. ☐ business manager/accountant
- B. ☐ plant and garden supervisor
- C. ☐ customer assistant
- D. ☐ plant and flower arranger

4. If I were the manager of a company, I would be most concerned about:

- A. ☐ making decisions logically based on hard data
- B. ☐ establishing clear and efficient procedures
- C. ☐ employees getting along well and feeling good about their work
- D. ☐ the future possibilities of the company

5. In my ideal work setting, I would like to:

- A. ☐ work alone doing research with sophisticated equipment
- B. ☐ plan, organize, and manage the daily business activities
- C. ☐ be involved in team projects working with friendly people
- D. ☐ work alone in a quiet setting generating ideas for innovative applications

6. I prefer to use the computer for:

- A. ☐ performing complex analytical functions
- B. ☐ increasing office efficiency and productivity
- C. ☐ communicating with others via electronic mail
- D. ☐ creating graphic design possibilities or writing up ideas for new programs

7. I would prefer to be:

- A. ☐ a scientist or technical specialist
- B. ☐ a midlevel manager or supervisor
- C. ☐ an educator or talk-show host
- D. ☐ a "think tank" specialist or fiction writer

8. I would rather:

- A. ☐ analyze technical data
- B. ☐ get the bugs out of computer programs
- C. ☐ give talks and presentations
- D. ☐ develop innovative concept papers (idea papers)

9. If in the military, I would rather be:
   A. ☐ an intelligence expert or military historian
   B. ☐ a helicopter pilot or tank driver
   C. ☐ a chaplain or medical support professional
   D. ☐ a strategic campaign planner or designer of new weapons systems

10. If you were to be assigned to a large, inhabited, orbiting space station, would you prefer to be a:
   A. ☐ nutrition research scientist evaluating the health benefits of colony-grown foods
   B. ☐ space-colony events manager who plans, schedules, and oversees events and activities
   C. ☐ space station psychologist helping people adjust to space-colony life
   D. ☐ business entrepreneur designing products and/or services to meet the needs of the colony residents

Note: After completing items #1–10 above, tally up all of your scores on the *Part 3. Summary Table*.

Part 3. Summary Table

Question	Points awarded for item			
	A	*B*	*C*	*D*
1.				
2.				
3.				
4.				
5.				
6.				
7.				
8.				
9.				
10.				
Totals				

Note: Your totals for Column A+B+C+D should equal 100.

PART 4. DEVELOPING YOUR THINKING-STYLE PROFILE

DIRECTIONS

1. After completing Parts 1, 2, and 3 above, summarize your scores for Exercise 3-A below using the combined summary scores table. Fill in the rows for Parts 1, 2, and 3 by entering the subtotal scores for each choice. Then add up grand totals for each column.

   Example: Ben's total "A" score from the Part 1 summary table was "20." Accordingly, Ben looks for the Part 1 row on the combined summary table, and enters "20" in the *Choice A* column.

Combined Summary Scores for Exercise 3-A, Parts 1, 2, and 3

My summary score from	*Choice A*	*Choice B*	*Choice C*	*Choice D*
Part 1 Trait Comparisons				
Part 2 Traits				
Part 3 Work Activities				
Grand Total				

2. Use the grand totals for your Choice A, B, C and D scores to plot your thinking-style profile. To do that, first mark your combined "A" score on the A diagonal of the profile. Then mark your combined "B," "C" and "D" scores on the corresponding diagonals.

3. Draw your profile by connecting your plotted marks on the "A," "B," "C" and "D" diagonals. The resulting profile represents a graphic visualization of your thinking-style profile.

YOUR THINKING-STYLE PROFILE

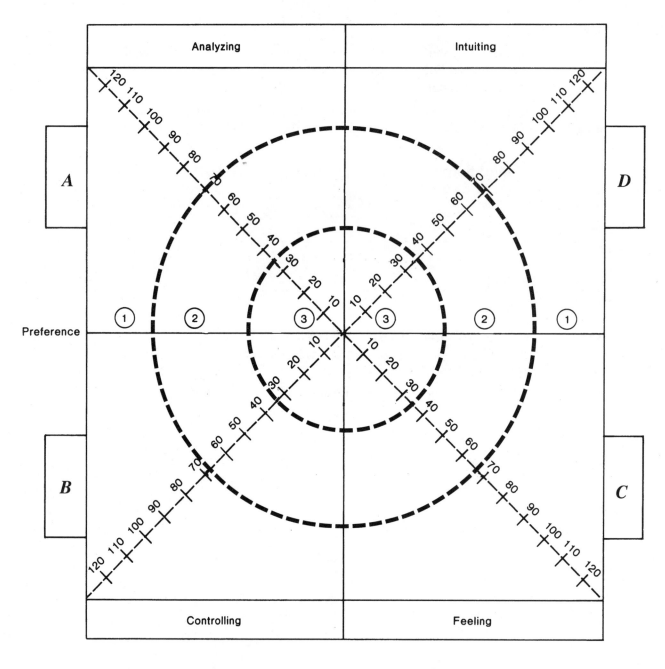

Note: This graphic is adapted from Ned Herrmann's Brain Dominance Model. For information about the Herrmann Brain Dominance Instrument visit: http:www.hbdi.com/who.html

Understanding Your Mental Powers

The Three Thinking Predilections		
Number	Biases	Range of Scores
1	Prefer	70 and over
2	Use	35–69
3	Avoid	0–34

IDENTIFYING YOUR PROFILE

Your thinking-style profile provides clues about the way you think and perceive. This information can be helpful in identifying occupations that will allow you to capitalize on your preferred style of thinking. You will also see what kinds of learning activity might help you further develop other styles of thinking.

Your profile provides you with a visual representation of your unique style of thinking and perceiving. The numerical code identifies your degree of preference for each of the four different kinds of thinking. Table 4.3 defines the degrees of preference represented in your thinking-style code. Table 4.4 describes the uniquely different kinds of thinking represented by the four thinking styles.

Table 4.3 Thinking-Style Degrees of Preference Codes		
Code	Degree of Preference	Description
1	Prefer	Strong preference; a favorite style of thinking
2	Use	Comfort zone; you use this kind of thinking whenever needed, but have no particular bias for or against using it
3	Avoid	Resistance zone; you avoid this kind of thinking. You probably use this kind of thinking only when absolutely required and may avoid developing skills in this kind of thought process.

Note: This scoring model is developed from Ned Herrmann's Brain Dominance Assessment model.

EXAMPLE

A 1232 profile indicates a person who strongly favors logical thinking, pays some attention to intuition and plays it safe.

DIAGRAM OF A 1232 PROFILE

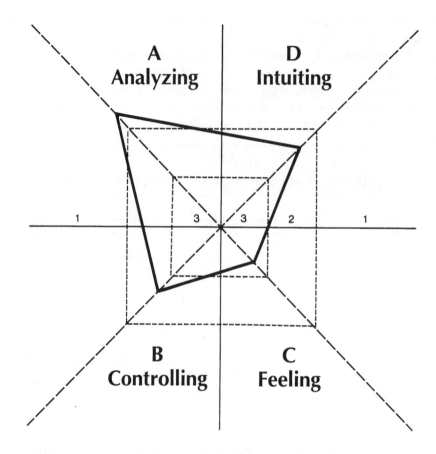

Question: What kind of occupations might be appropriate for a person with this kind of profile? What kind of learning activities and/or subject matter would he/she favor? Avoid?

 ## EXERCISE 4-C. WHAT'S YOUR NUMBER?

Using the numbering system from Table 4.3 and the combined scores that you plotted on *Your Thinking-Style Profile,* complete the table below. Note the correct score ranges for degree of preference (prefer, use, avoid) at the bottom of the *Thinking-Style Profile.*

My Four-Digit Thinking-Style Code

Herrmann's Model Quadrants	A	B	C	D
Thinking Style	Analyzing	Controlling	Feeling	Intuiting
My numerical preference (1, 2, or 3)				
General tendency of my preference Prefer, Use or Avoid				

Table 4.4 Characteristics of the Four Styles of Thinking

Quadrant	A *Analyzing*	B *Controlling*	C *Feeling*	D *Intuiting*
Thinking process	Logical analysis of facts to form rational conclusions	Step-by-step sequential proceeding from A to B to C	Inner awareness Attuned to the inner state of emotions and feelings	Inituitive understanding of the "big picture"
Traits most valued	intelligence logic rationality factual analytical reason	conventional security efficiency control loyalty	harmony empathy communicating touching relationship	ideas and concepts vision risk-taking creativity possibility
Traits least valued	feelings emotions subjectivity	intuition abstract ambivalence	detached rationality "cold facts" impersonal	conventional procedural sequential
Some favorite leisure activities	chess science history computer games or logic	cards fishing bowling spectator sports yard work	clubs music cooking dancing social events	self-expressive arts creative writing reading fiction art museums
Some favorite subjects	history mathematics economics physics science	business management computer programming accounting	humanities drama music religion psychology	art literature design philosophy metaphysics
Skills	examine data scrutinize observe research read for information evaluate test analyze quantify solve problems logically estimate evaluate assess critique see flaws in ideas	budget make arrangements plan organize schedule maintain records monitor proofread implement plan follow through expedite classify supervise coordinate details trouble shooting	act as liaison counsel communicate entertain perform interview for information serve as host/hostess discuss feelings mediate motivate promote teach, train negotiate treat, nurse sell	design conceptualize generate ideas compose music, poetry imagine possibilities integrate portray images prognosticate initiate change synthesize visualize write develop scenarios solve problems creatively

Table 4.5 Occupations Grouped by Thinking Style

Left-Brain Dominant Occupations

A Analyzing	B Controlling
Accountant	Accounts manager
Artificial intelligence engineer	Air traffic controller
Biologist	Auto mechanic
Chemist	Automobile dealer
Computer scientist or engineer	Administrative assistant
Computer systems analyst	Bookkeeper
Criminal investigator/detective	Bank manager
Dentist	Bookstore manager
Economist	Bureaucrat
Engineer (e.g., agricultural, automobile, aeronautical, electronics)	Computer technician
Etymologist	Computer programmer
Financial analyst, administrator, or planner	Credit advisor
Geologist	Database manager
Horticulturist	Driver (bus, taxi, train)
Lawyer	Electronics technician
Market researcher	Emergency medical technician
Mathematician, math instructor	Factory supervisor
Mechanical diagnostician	Firefighter
Medical researcher	Hotel/motel manager
Meteorologist	Health care manager
Military strategist	Human resources compensation and benefits manager
Neurologist, neurosurgeon	Insurance agent
Nutritionist	Law enforcement officer
Optometrist	Librarian
Orthodontist	Marketing manager
Orthopedic surgeon	Manufacturing manager
Osteopath	Military line and technical officer, enlisted, petty officer
Pathologist	Medical records technician
Physician (medical doctor)	Merchant mariner
Pharmacist	Office manager
Physicist	Paralegal
Printer technician	Pilot
Psychologist (research)	Proofreader
Radiologist	Purchasing agent
Researcher (technical)	Real estate agent
Scientist, science teacher	Research assistant
Statistician	Restaurant manager
Stockbroker	Retail manager
Strategic planner	Robotics technician
Veterinarian	School administrator
Web master, web analyst	Technical writer
	Telemarketer
	Travel agency route planner, manager
	Tugboat skipper
	Warden

Table 4.5 Occupations Grouped by Thinking Style *(continued)*

Right-Brain Dominant Occupations

C Feeling	D Intuiting
Actor, performer	Advertising designer
Humanities teacher, instructor	Architect
Child-care provider	Art administrator
Chiropractor	Art museum curator
Coach (athletic, speech, drama)	Artist
Communications specialist	Cartoonist
Comedian	Choreographer
Cosmetologist, hairdresser	Creativity consultant
Counselor (drug, eldercare, education, family, geriatrics, marriage)	Culinary experimenter
Customer service representative	Designer (creative, nontechnical)
Dancer	Director of stage, motion picture, TV or radio productions
Day-care center associate	Editor (book, journalist)
Diversity trainer	Entrepreneur
Funeral counselor, director	Exhibit designer
Human resource development (HRD) specialist	Fashion designer
Humanities professor	Filmmaker, producer
Hospice counselor, manager	Floral arranger
Massage therapist	Futurist (nontechnical, theoretical)
Mediator, arbitrator, conflict resolution specialist	Graphics designer
Minister, priest, rabbi	Humorist
Musician, music teacher	Interior designer
Newscaster	Landscape architect
Nurse	Literary agent
Occupational therapist	Manager of creative and/or intuitive enterprises
Ombudsman	Musical composer
Organizational development consultant	Playwright
Parole officer	Philosopher (theoretical: abstract as opposed to logical-analytical)
Performer	Novelist
Pediatrician	Movie set designer
Physical therapist	Mythologist
Psychologist (counseling, school)	Poet
Psychotherapist	Psychiatrist
Public relations specialist	Physicist (theoretical)
Recreational therapist	Set designer
Religious education director	Strategic designer, theorist
Roman Catholic nun	Software developer, concepts innovator
Salesperson (not technical)	Theorist (creative, nontechnical)
Social worker	Toy designer
Sociologist	Web site designer
Special education teacher, consultant	Writer (nontechnical, science-fiction, creative)
Teacher (elementary, special education)	
Therapist (art, music, dance)	
Translator/interpreter	
Training and development specialist	
Vocational rehabilitation specialist	

Note: Individual occupations are placed into categories based on the predominant style of thinking most often required in the workplace. The groupings should be thought of as approximations rather than absolutes because in actual practice: (1) most occupations use all of the thinking styles to varying degrees, and (2) the nature of the work activity can vary a great deal from one work setting to another.

Understanding Your Personality and Interests

*The degree of satisfaction that you get from your work directly affects
the degree of health and vitality in the rest of your life.*
—Tom Jackson
Guerrilla Tactics in the Job Market

Do you know people who—

☑ Are physically active and enjoy engaging in activities requiring manual agility and body conditioning?

☑ Are inquisitive and are energized by solving abstract problems requiring mental concentration and persistence?

☑ Are creative and feel compelled to express themselves with originality and distinctiveness?

☑ Are social and enjoy interacting with, supporting, and encouraging others?

☑ Are gregarious and outgoing and take pleasure in exercising influence and persuasion?

☑ Are organized and like systematic work involving details, data, and numbers?

If so, you know people whose motivational interests reveal six classically different styles of personality.

THINKING STYLE VERSUS PERSONALITY STYLE

While Chapter 4 focused on your brain, or the way you think and perceive, this chapter deals with your personality and what energizes your interests. We're not talking about good and bad personalities here, but about personality styles. You are born with certain neurological characteristics that cause you to prefer one type of thinking over others. You can actually change the neurological structuring of your brain through cerebral exercise; we're talking about learning and mental skills development here. Your personality, on the other hand, probably develops through a combination of genetic programming and early life experiences. Research on personality styles informs us that by the age of about twenty-one your personality has crystallized; we're talking maturation here. Since personality shapes what engages your interests and what doesn't, it is very probably that after the age of twenty-one your personality-style-based interests will remain fairly constant. For this reason, understanding your personality is a key factor in career and life planning. In this chapter you will have an opportunity to clarify your personality style and discover the kinds of interests associated with your style, along with those of six general styles of personality.

DO OPPOSITES ATTRACT?

Have you noticed that people tend to associate with those who share similar interests? Do you accept the commonly held belief that opposites attract? If that's what you believe, there is a little test we would like you to take. Consider how enjoyable it is for you to interact for any prolonged period of time with people with whom you can find no common interests. That's a lot of fun right? Of course, there are some who can seem to communicate effectively with just about anybody, and even enjoy that. But we're talking about genuine sustained interpersonal, interactive, invigorating interest. How long do you really believe that you can actively remain engaged, attentive to, and attracted to others with whom you share no strong mutual interests?

When we have a choice, we either consciously or unconsciously seek out others who share at least some of our interests. In contrast, you may notice that sooner or later you pull away from people who don't respond to your interests. While opposites may attract, at least initially, they are not likely to "click," at least for the long run.

The belief that opposites attract is true for magnets, but the dynamics are more complex for humans. Our values or needs may motivate initial attraction to our opposites. However, when our interests are truly opposite, we can expect compatibility challenges. This is true in relationship and it is true also in work. For sustained interest in career, choose work that is compatible with your interests.

PERSONALITY AND CAREER CHOICE

During our formative years, we develop interests linked to the uniqueness of our environmental experience, our cellular biology, and the times in which we live (people in the Middle Ages didn't get excited about space travel, and today we don't think much about exploring the seven seas in manually rowed galley ships). Your interests crystallize, or become ingrained patterns, with maturity. These distinctive patterns of interests thereafter determine what energizes you and what depletes you. For example, some people love scientific investigation, while others hate it. Some prefer unstructured creativity such as visioning a fantasy story in their minds, while others are far more attracted to structured activities like keeping close watch over their finances. Some enjoy social activities, while others prefer solitary endeavors. Some prefer working with their hands, others with their minds, and other with their personalities.

Because your mature personality reflects your crystallized interests, you're likely to feel motivated

Web Connect

A popular assessment with college students is the **Career Key** at **www.ncsu.edu/careerkey**. This assessment looks at interests, abilities, and values. It provides a Holland code in the results with job titles that reflect the interests of others who share that code. The job titles are linked to information in the *Occupational Outlook Handbook*.

when engaged in favorite activities and unmotivated in things alien to your personality. In fact, just discussing your favorite interests with others who share them can arouse your attention and spring those brain cells into stimulating activity. Unfortunately, too many people overlook their personal interests in career planning, focusing exclusively upon their "practical" skills and/or what's popular in today's media. The problem with this is that skills don't necessarily connect directly to your interests or to the careers popularized by the media. We have seen many clients who have been engaged in work nicely matched to their skills, but hate what they are doing. Speaking of motivation, have you ever noticed how hard it is just to get out of bed on those mornings when you have nothing you are looking forward to? You don't want to spend your entire working life, about 11,880 days of life for a twenty-year old, dreading Mondays. Most of us need things to look forward to if our days are to be pleasurable experiences.

Knowing your interests and what kinds of activities engage them allows you to develop career plans that are realistic and likely to produce both success and enjoyment. An additional plus of developing a career based on interests is a health benefit. People who enjoy their work tend to be healthier, both physically and emotionally, than those who view work as a "rat race" or just another boring day at the office. We need to add a disclaimer here; what we are advocating is developing your career goals around your deep-seated interests. We are definitely not suggesting that you develop only skills associated with your strongest interests. The world does not, of course, allow us to do only what interests us. We need to develop a broad range of skills, but focus our career direction around our sustainable interests.

IDENTIFYING YOUR PERSONALITY STYLE

What's unique about you? What are the strengths and shortcoming of your personality? In thinking about your career future, it is important to be able to answer questions such as these. In fact, in most interview situations for professional and managerial positions you will be asked these kinds of questions. So, how do you describe your personality in career-relevant terms? While there are several methods for assessing and clarifying personality styles, we recommend four well-known inventories—the *Myers-Briggs Type Indicator* (MBTI), the

Web Connect

If you don't have access to the MBTI, Personality Type.com at http://www.personalitytype.com/quiz.html provides a mini-version of this assessment to help you quickly self-identify your "type." There is no cost involved, but note that this is not a reliable nor valid personality instrument either. Once you identify your type, the site then provides useful information related to your personality and interests. This quiz is part of the site designed by Barbara Barron-Tieger and Paul Tieger who have written many books about personality type and its relevance to careers. Also, once you do know your MBTI four-letter personality type, you might find Type Logic's site of interest at **www.typelogic.com**

A popular personality assessment with college students is the **Kiersey Temperament Sorter II** at **www.advisorteam.com/user/ktsintro.asp**. This tool aims to assess temperament by asking 70 questions and providing personality information very similar to that of the Myers-Briggs Personality Type Indicator.

Strong Interest Inventory (SII), the *Holland Self-Directed Search* (SDS) and the *Campbell Interests and Skills Survey* (CISS). These inventories are available in most college career-development centers and through most career-counseling practices. If you plan to take these inventories be sure to review them with a professional counselor who has training and experience with the instruments.

Whether or not you choose to take the SII, SDS or CISS, the following exercises should be helpful in evaluating your personality-related interests. Do Exercises 5-A, B, C, and D before skipping ahead to further reading. Reading ahead may alter the way you respond to the questions and give inaccurate results. In doing these exercises, be as frank and honest with yourself as you possibly can. Respond to each item the way it really is for you rather than the way you would like it to be or the way you think it should be.

EXERCISE 5-A. SOUTH SEA ISLAND FANTASY[1]

For this exercise, imagine that you are flying an airplane alone, having taken off for a day's pleasure excursion.

After flying for some time, you find yourself approaching six remote islands. Suddenly, your plane develops engine trouble, and you realize that you are going to have to make a forced landing on one of the islands.

Imagine that Figure 5.1 is an aerial view of these islands. From the information available, you know that highly civilized and advanced people populate each island. They have moved to these locations to associate with other compatible people and to enjoy the balmy climate.

The people on each island have the characteristics described in the diagram. You realize that you will be on the island for a long time since ships make only infrequent visits. You also know that transportation between these six islands is nonexistent. Where you land, therefore, determines what kind of people you will be staying with for a long while. Therefore, you will want to choose your landing spot with care.

Which group of people would you prefer as companions for a significant amount of time? Write the letter for that island in the box below marked *first choice*.

Then assume that for some reason you cannot land on your preferred island. Which group of people would be your *second choice* as companions? *Third choice? Fourth choice?* Write the letter of the island for each choice in the boxes below:

☐ First choice ☐ Third choice

☐ Second choice ☐ Fourth choice

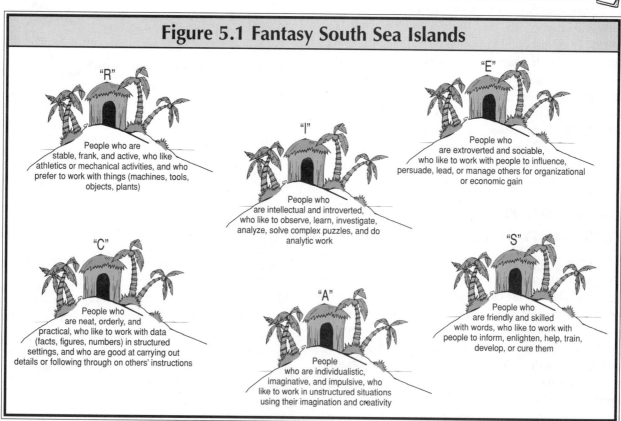

Figure 5.1 Fantasy South Sea Islands

"R" People who are stable, frank, and active, who like athletics or mechanical activities, and who prefer to work with things (machines, tools, objects, plants)

"I" People who are intellectual and introverted, who like to observe, learn, investigate, analyze, solve complex puzzles, and do analytic work

"E" People who are extroverted and sociable, who like to work with people to influence, persuade, lead, or manage others for organizational or economic gain

"C" People who are neat, orderly, and practical, who like to work with data (facts, figures, numbers) in structured settings, and who are good at carrying out details or following through on others' instructions

"A" People who are individualistic, imaginative, and impulsive, who like to work in unstructured situations using their imagination and creativity

"S" People who are friendly and skilled with words, who like to work with people to inform, enlighten, help, train, develop, or cure them

---

[1] Adapted from Richard N. Bolles, *The Party Exercise* (Berkeley, CA: National Career Development Project, n.d.).

EXERCISE 5-B. MY FAVORITE KINDS OF PROBLEMS

Problem solving can be stimulating, but different people have different preferences in the types of problems they like to grapple with. The following exercise describes six kinds of problems. Assume that you have a job involving 100 hours of your time. You have the option of spending those 100 hours working with any of the six kinds of problems.

You might, for example, decide that you would prefer to spend 50 hours of time working with the "A" types of problems, 30 hours with the "S" types, and 20 hours with the "I" types. In that case, you would mark 50 in the "A" box, 30 in the "S" box, 20 in the "I" box, and 0 in the "E," "C," and "R" boxes. You are free to choose to spend all of your time working with just one instead of several kinds of problems.

Do not place the same amount of time in more than one box. Take a moment to decide which one you really want to spend at least a little more time doing. Make sure that your combined score for the six boxes adds up to 100.

I prefer to spend my 100 hours of time working with and solving the following kinds of problems:

☐	R	Problems that involve using your hands to resolve challenges like operating a piece of equipment, putting an addition onto a house, or building a computer from scratch.
☐	I	Problems of a scientific or mathematical nature that require mental concentration, fact finding, analysis, and logical thinking.
☐	A	Problems that can be solved by combining various concepts or artistic elements to create new approaches, methods, programs, art forms or literature.
☐	S	Problems that involve situations where you are interacting with others for assistance in solving their personal problems, providing difficult feedback to improve their behavior, or helping them improve academically.
☐	E	Problems associated with persuading and/or motivating others to accomplish the objectives of an organization or a community-based project.
☐	C	Problems that can be solved through organization and orderly use of data (information, words, records, numbers) or through carefully applying appropriate policies or regulations.

Total Score (This total must equal 100.)

EXERCISE 5-C. INTEREST AND ACTIVITY ASSESSMENT _____

This process is designed to help you assess your personality-style-related preferences. Decide whether you like or dislike each of the listed activities. Using the following scale, assign a numerical value to your like or dislike for each activity. The greater your like or dislike is, the higher the number. Be sure to focus on your known or suspected interest rather than whether or not you believe you would be good at it.

Like	Dislike
1–2 like a little	1–2 dislike a little
3–6 like considerably	3–6 dislike considerably
7–10 love it	7–10 hate it

Example

If your reaction to *home repairs like carpentry, plumbing, etc.* is that you definitely already enjoy or would likely enjoy the activity, then place a number between 7 and 10 in the *LIKE* box for *Home repairs,* depending upon the intensity of your preference for this particular or similar type activity.

If you know or are fairly certain that you would dislike designing your own web page, you would place a number between 1 and 6 in the *DISLIKE* box, depending upon the strength of your dislike or your probable dislike based on experience with similar activities.

LIKE   DISLIKE

☐ ☐ R_1 Home repairs like carpentry, plumbing, etc.

☐ ☐ I_1 Designing my own web page

☐ ☐ A_1 Playing a musical instrument

☐ ☐ S_1 Going to social functions and actively interacting with other people

☐ ☐ E_1 Organizing and leading a club, conference, or business meeting

☐ ☐ C_1 Keeping detailed accounts of personal expenses

☐ ☐ R_2 Reading magazines like *Popular Mechanics* and *Hot Rod* or *Aviation Week* and *Space Technology*

☐ ☐ I_2 Studying the stars through a telescope

☐ ☐ A_2 Writing a novel or a piece of music

☐ ☐ S_2 Working as a hot-line counselor at an addiction center

☐ ☐ E_2 Persuading others to buy a product, service or idea you are selling

☐ ☐ C₂   Completing business tasks and projects by studying and carefully following procedures and policies

☐ ☐ R₃   Performing maintenance work on your car

☐ ☐ I₃   Reading science magazines like *American Scientist, OMNI,* or *Discover*

☐ ☐ A₃   Acting or singing in a play or musical

☐ ☐ S₃   Reading children's stories at a day-care center

☐ ☐ E₃   Meeting and getting acquainted with influential people

☐ ☐ C₃   Preparing reports and documents using spread sheet applications such as EXCEL

☐ ☐ A₄   Reading poetry, philosophy, or fiction

☐ ☐ S₄   Serving on a social events committee

☐ ☐ E₄   Debating an issue or delivering a presentation

☐ ☐ R₄   Doing hands-on work in a plant nursery or fish hatchery

☐ ☐ I₄   Solving math or logic puzzles

☐ ☐ C₄   Taking accounting or business ethics courses.

☐ ☐ A₅   Expressing an idea with a sketch pad or computer design program

☐ ☐ S₅   Teaching games to children

☐ ☐ E₅   Following politics and working on a political campaign

☐ ☐ R₅   Operating a piece of equipment such as a backhoe, bulldozer, or army tank

☐ ☐ I₅   Taking a science course like geology, astronomy, or biology

☐ ☐ C₅   Programming your computer

☐ ☐ A₆   Decorating the interior of a house

☐ ☐ S₆   Helping others deal with personal problems

☐ ☐ E₆   Developing a business plan for a commercial venture you would start and manage

☐ ☐ C₆   Analyzing fiscal expenditures and compiling budget reports

☐ ☐ I₆   Collecting and examining rocks and minerals

☐ ☐ R₆   Working as a deckhand on a large oceangoing sailboat

☐ ☐ A₇   Generating innovative ideas for an advertising campaign

☐	☐	S_7	Taking a course in psychology, religion, or sociology
☐	☐	E_7	Leading a work team or managing a group of people
☐	☐	C_7	Sorting and categorizing data, records, or files
☐	☐	I_7	Surfing the Internet for scientific news
☐	☐	R_7	Playing fast-paced computer games that require quick reactions and physical dexterity
☐	☐	A_8	Creating eye-pleasing arrangements with flowers, pictures, furniture, etc.
☐	☐	S_8	Reading self-help or personal-development books
☐	☐	I_8	Doing work with a microscope
☐	☐	E_8	Reading the *Wall Street Journal* or magazines like *Fortune, Money,* or *Success*
☐	☐	C_8	Keeping an accurate appointment calendar for a busy office
☐	☐	R_8	Taking a home maintenance course to learn how to make home repairs and do home improvements
☐	☐	A_9	Painting with watercolors as a highly enjoyable pastime
☐	☐	S_9	Participating as a team member on projects providing a useful social service
☐	☐	I_9	Playing chess and/or doing highly complex crossword puzzles
☐	☐	E_9	Giving a business presentation to a group of important people
☐	☐	C_9	Proofreading documents and putting them in final form
☐	☐	R_9	Working as a technician in a mechanical engineering laboratory

After you have assigned numbers to each of the above items, use Table 5.1 to record and add up your total LIKE and DISLIKE scores. The code numbers on the left of this table correspond to the numbers found beside each of the six letters in the exercise. For example, if you put a 7 in the *LIKE* box for home repairs (R_1), you would put a 7 in the *L* column directly under *R* in row labeled *1*.

L = LIKE; D = DISLIKE

	R		I		A		S		E		C	
	L	D	L	D	L	D	L	D	L	D	L	D
1												
2												
3												
4												
5												
6												
7												
8												
9												
Total												

Web Connect

Take a look at the interests and profiles of others who match your personality type by playing the **Career Interests Game** at **http://career.missouri.edu/holland** This game was designed by the University of Missouri-Columbia and is an adaptation of Holland's RIASEC model.

✎ Exercise 5-D. Identifying Interests from Skills

This exercise is based on the *Skill Assessment Survey* you completed in Chapter 3. Based on the insights acquired from that process, decide what percentage of time you would like to spend using each of your preferred families of skills in your work. Make sure that your percentages add up to 100.

My Top Five Skills-Family Percentages

R The percentage of time I prefer to use my manual/technical skills in work. ☐ %

I The percentage of time I prefer to use my analytical/problem solving skills in work. ☐ %

A The percentage of time I prefer to use my innovative/creativity skills in work. ☐ %

S The percentage of time I prefer to use my social/interpersonal skills in work. ☐ %

E The percentage of time I prefer to use my managing/influencing skills in work. ☐ %

C The percentage of time I prefer to use my organizing/data skills in work. ☐ %

✎ Exercise 5-E. Compiling My Personality-Style Profile

Having completed four exercises to explore your personal preferences, you can now develop your own personality-style profile. This profile will help highlight your unique interest patterns and provide valuable career- and life-planning insights. To develop your profile, complete the following steps.

1. From Exercise 5-A, list the letters for your first four choices below.

	Island Letter	*Points*
The island of my first choice	_____	20
The island of my second choice	_____	15
The island of my third choice	_____	10
The island of my fourth choice	_____	5

Notice that each letter you have listed above has a corresponding point value. After you rank the island letters, put the point value for each of the Island Letters in the designated space on the *Combined Scores Table* below.

Example

1. If the island corresponding to your first choice was "R" and your second, third, and fourth choices were "I," "C," and "E," write the number "20" in the *R* Column of the *Combined Scores Table* on the Exercise 5-A line or row. Also write "15" under *I*, "10" under *C* and "5" under *E*. Leave blank spaces on this line for the other two letters you did not select.

2. Transfer the scores you listed in each of the six problem boxes to the *Exercise 5-B* line of the *Combined Scores Table*. Be sure to place all six scores on the *Exercise 5-B* line, each in the appropriate column.

3. In Exercise 5-C you added up the totals for all the scores you listed under the *LIKE* and *DISLIKE* boxes in the table provided. Transfer your LIKE scores for each of the six letters to the *Combined Scores Table*. Do nothing with your DISLIKE scores for now; we will discuss those later.

4. Record your scores for Exercise 5-D on the *Combined Scores Table*.

5. After recording all your scores in the *Combined Scores Table,* total each column and record the sums of all in the *Total Score* row.

Combined Scores Table

	R	I	A	S	E	C
Exercise 5-A Island Fantasy Scores						
Exercise 5-B Favorite Problem Scores						
Exercise 5-C Activity Preference Scores						
Exercise 5-D Preferred Skills Scores						
Total Score						

6. After you have determined your total scores, use them to form a bar graph on the *My Personality-Style Profile* grid. To do that, first find the number corresponding to your total *R* score along the side of the grid. Then form a bar in the *R* column by filling in with pen or colored marker from the bottom of the grid up to your total "R" score. Do the same for each of the remaining scores.

MY PERSONALITY-STYLE PROFILE

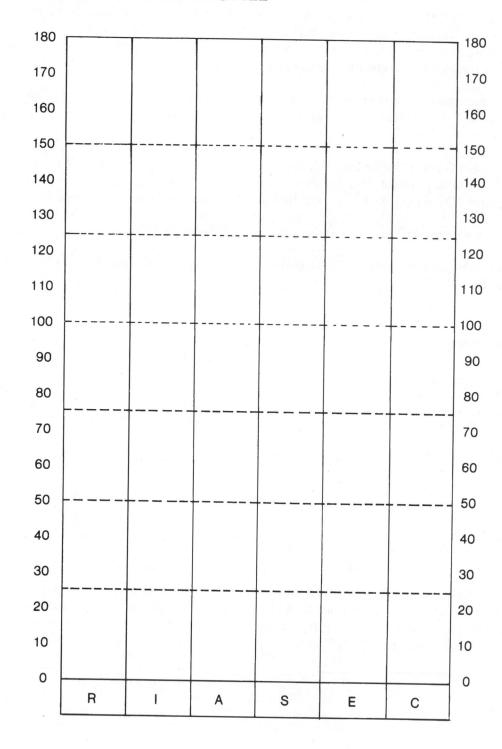

WHAT YOUR PROFILE SHOWS

Developing your personality-style profile provides a graphic picture of your personality-style-related interest patterns. This profile and the proceeding exercises are based upon the work of Dr. John Holland (*Making Vocational Choices: A Theory of Vocational Personalities and Work Environments*). Dr. Holland's work informs us that in our formative years we develop preferences for certain groups of related activities. These preferences develop as a result of environmental influences (family, community, ethnic background, socioeconomic status, religion, race), the nature of our early life, and our genetic make-up. By the age of twenty-one, these preferences have shaped your personality, and your personality determines your general preferences (likes and dislikes). A mature personality remains fairly stable throughout the remainder of life, which means that once crystallized, your general interests are very likely to remain fairly constant thereafter. What tends to engage your primary interests in your twenties is likely to be similar in general terms, to what engages your interests when you are forty, and even when you are sixty. Your preferences guide your behavior, including what you are inclined to do and how you do it. For these reasons, you can probably see the importance of knowing yourself in terms of personality-style-related preferences for career-planning purposes.

No matter how hard Louise tried to be a successful programmer, she knew inside that she would always be a wild flower.

Holland identifies six personality styles, giving them the following labels:[2]

R Realistic

I Investigative

A Artistic

S Social

E Enterprising

C Conventional

Look at the short description of each of the six personality styles below. In the box to the left of the appropriate description, place the number "1" next to the letter with the highest score on your personality-style profile.

Then read that description and evaluate how well it fits you. Place the number "2" in the box corresponding to your second-highest personality-style score. Then read and assess this description. Do this with each of the remaining styles.

R You enjoy physical activity and prefer outdoor work. You like working with your hands using tools, operating mechanical equipment, and seeing the concrete results of your work.

I Intellectual things turn you on. You prefer to analyze situations and solve challenging mental problems. You prefer to work alone and are attracted to scientific pursuits.

A Creative modes of self-expression suit you. You enjoy unstructured and free-flowing environments where you can express your originality and innovative ideas.

S You like to work with people— helping, teaching, or training them. You prefer to resolve problems through discussion.

E You enjoy exercising influence with people and feel comfortable in situations where you are in authority and control. Economic objectives are important to you.

---

2. John L. Holland, *Making Vocational Choices: A Theory of Vocational Personalities and Work Environments*, 2nd ed. (Odessa, FL: Psychological Assessment Resources, Inc., 1992).

☐ **C** You like to know exactly what is expected of you and prefer to do well-defined tasks. You are organized, efficient, practical, good with number and data, and are precise in doing things accurately and thoroughly.

Did you notice that the description for the letter corresponding to your highest score, your #1 letter, sounds the most like you, and your #2 letter the next most like you? And conversely, did you notice that the description corresponding to your lowest score, your #6 letter, was the least like you?

Study Table 5.1 *Comparison of the Personality Types,*, to learn more about the six interest-based personality types.

Table 5.1
Comparison of the Personality Types

	Realistic	Investigative	Artistic	Social	Enterprising	Conventional
Characteristics	Stable Physical Practical Frank Self-reliant	Analytical Independent Curious Intellectual Precise	Imaginative Idealistic Original Expressive Impulsive	Cooperative Understanding Helpful Tactful Sociable	Persuasive Domineering Energetic Ambitious Flirtatious	Conscientious Orderly Persistent Conforming Efficient
Likes	Outdoor work Mechanics Athletics Working with plants, tools, and animals	Abstract problems Science Investigation Unstructured situations Working alone	Ideas Self-expression Creativity Unstructured situations Working alone	People Attention Discussion Helping Socializing	Power People Status Influencing Managing	Order Carrying out details Organizing Structure Working with data
Dislikes	Educational activities Self-expression Working with people	Repetitive activities Rules Working with people	Structure Rules Physical work Details Repetitive activities	Physical work Working with tools Working outdoors	Systematic activities Precise work Concentrated intellectual work	Unsystematized activities Lack of structure Ambiguity
Orientation	Hands-on activities	Problem solving	Idea creating	People assisting	People influencing	Detail and data
Preferred Skills	Building Repairing Making and growing things	Problem solving Analytical reasoning Developing models and systems	Creating Visualizing Unstructured tasks Imagining	Interpersonal activities Establishing rapport Communicating Helping	Leading Managing Persuading Motivating others	Detailed tasks Following directions precisely Repetitive tasks
People Who Characterize the Styles	Thomas Edison The Wright Brothers Antonio Stradivari Chris Evert Lloyd Johannes Gutenberg Neil Armstrong Amelia Earhart Arthur Ashe Michael Jordan Jackie Joyner- Kersee Tiger Woods Willy Mays	Albert Einstein Sherlock Holmes George Washington Carver Marie Curie Sigmund Freud Charles Darwin Admiral Grace Hopper Charles Drew W.E.B. Dubois Carl Sagan Dr. Jonas Salk	Alex Haley Beverly Sills Ludwig von Beethoven Michelangelo Luciano Pavarotti William Shakespeare Mikhail Baryshnikov Emily Dickinson Frank Lloyd Wright Maya Angelou Stevie Wonder Duke Ellington Toni Morrison	Helen Keller Carl Menninger Kenneth Clark Florence Nightingale Mother Theresa Mahatma Gandhi Albert Schweitzer Jaime Escalante Coretta Scott King Desmond Tutu Marian Wright Edelman Jimmy Carter Leo Buscaglio	Henry Ford Winston Churchill Martin Luther King, Jr. Margaret Thatcher Lee Iacocca Golda Meir Cesar Chavez Barbara Jordan Nelson Mandela Oprah Winfrey Madeleine Albright Colin Powell Laura Ashley	E. F. Hutton Dr. Watson (Sherlock Holmes' assistant) Noah Webster (dictionary) Melvil Dewey (Dewey decimal system) Herman Hollerith (keypunch card) Carolus Linnaeus (botanist) Clarence Thomas Miss Manners

Exercise 5-F. Likes and Dislikes as Guides

In Exercise 5-C you identified a profile of your likes and dislikes, useful information in career- and life-planning. You can use your top interests to choose compatible careers, jobs, and goals, just as you can use your dislikes to determine what activities you will want to avoid in your work, leisure, and learning. Review Exercise 5-C, and record below your insights from that exercise.

My favorite LIKES were:

1)

2)

3)

4)

5)

My major DISLIKES were:

1)

2)

3)

4)

5)

I can use that information in planning to:	I can use that information to avoid doing:

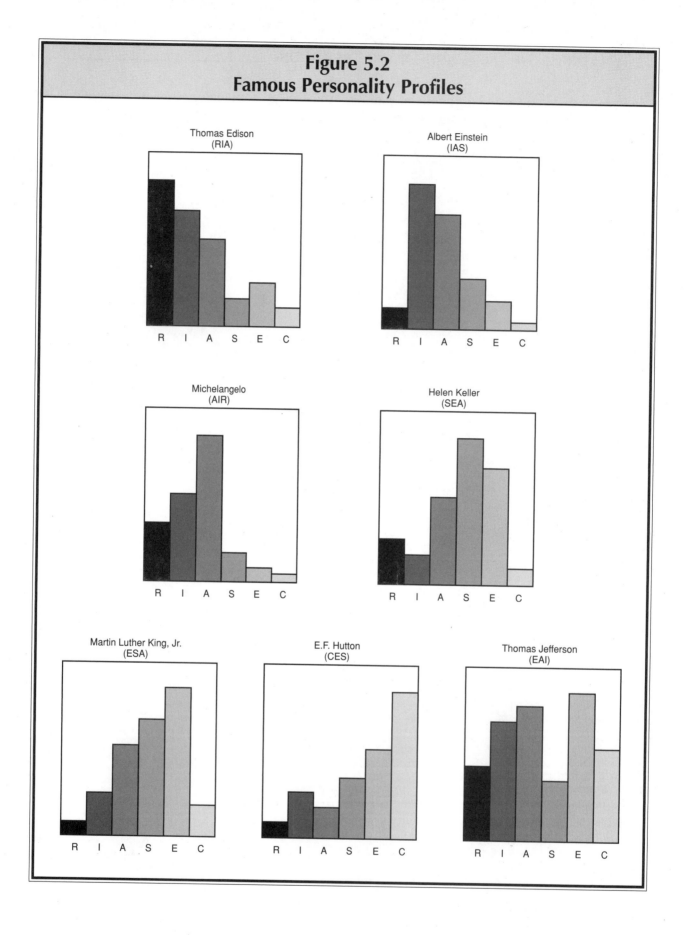

Figure 5.2
Famous Personality Profiles

ASSESSING FAMOUS PERSONALITY PROFILES

Figure 5.2 shows our best guess as to the personality styles of a few famous individuals. The Thomas Alva Edison ("RIA") profile, for example, portrays Edison as a hands-on inventor, relentlessly trying out applications ideas until he eventually finds the one that works. The "RIA" code attributed to Edison represents a career pattern dominate in working with one's hands to invent things (an "R" activity). We know that Edison almost lived in his laboratory where he created hundreds of inventions such as the phonograph and light bulb. But Edison was also an idea person, creating a stream of ideas for new technology ("A" activity). But these ideas had to be analyzed and tested. Edison would not have persisted in developing his ideas beyond the thought stage without a passion for investigative research and rational problem solving ("I" activity).

The Michelangelo ("AIR") profile represents this magnificent artist-scientist as first and foremost a creative genius ("A"). Secondly, he was an analytical problem solver in many respects, creating abstract ideas in marble and paint, and complex architectural designs (both "A" and "I" activities). Michelangelo is assigned an "R" to reflect the hands-on type of activity that was involved in actually sculpting a David or painting the Sistine Chapel.

Some famous people are represented by nearly all the styles because they were such multifaceted personalities. Take Thomas Jefferson, for example. We have listed Jefferson as "EAI" on the assumption of a dominant "E," which he probably would have had to want to be the President of the United States. He was also an architect, talented writer, and music lover ("A" activities), as well as a scientific thinker ("I"), a cataloger of data ("C"), a gardener ("R"), and a humanitarian ("S").

Career/life planning is much easier for those who have only one or two peaks in their interest profile from which to make career decisions. While a profile like Jefferson's represents great natural gifts, the problem multiinterested people find is in narrowing down their choices. If all these interests do not find an outlet, conflict and frustration result. However, intelligent career/life planning can balance the range of favorite interests in a combination of work, leisure, and learning activities.

THE PERSONALITY-STYLE HEXAGON

Holland's six personality styles are geometrically arranged in the shape of a hexagon (see Figure 5.3). The shape of this figure is significant because it shows important relationships among the six different styles, such as:

☑ Personality types that are adjacent to each other on the hexagon share some similar characteristics. For example, strong "R," "A," "I" types generally prefer working alone while strong "S," "E," and "C" types tend to enjoy close personal interactions with others. The "A" and "I" types prefer unstructured activities that involve working with the mind and ideas. The "S" and "E" types are verbally oriented, gregarious, and personable. The "C" and "R" types prefer structured work settings where expectations are clear and procedures are well established.

☑ Personality types that are opposite each other on the hexagon share few characteristics. For example, the "S" and "R" types are opposite: "S" types dislike work that gets their hands dirty, while "R" types don't seem to mind that a bit; "S" types like social situations with groups of people, while "R" types prefer a more solitary, out-of-doors lifestyle.

☑ The distance separating types on the hexagon represents the degree of similarity or difference between types. The closer the types are, the more alike they are. The farther apart the types are, the more different they are. For example, since "R" and "I" are next to each other, they are somewhat alike. They share some common characteristics such as a preference for solitary activity and a nononsense preference for the hard facts. While there are differences between the two types, they are not as great as the differences between "I" and "E," represented by their opposite positions on the hexagon.

Figure 5.3
The Six Personality Types

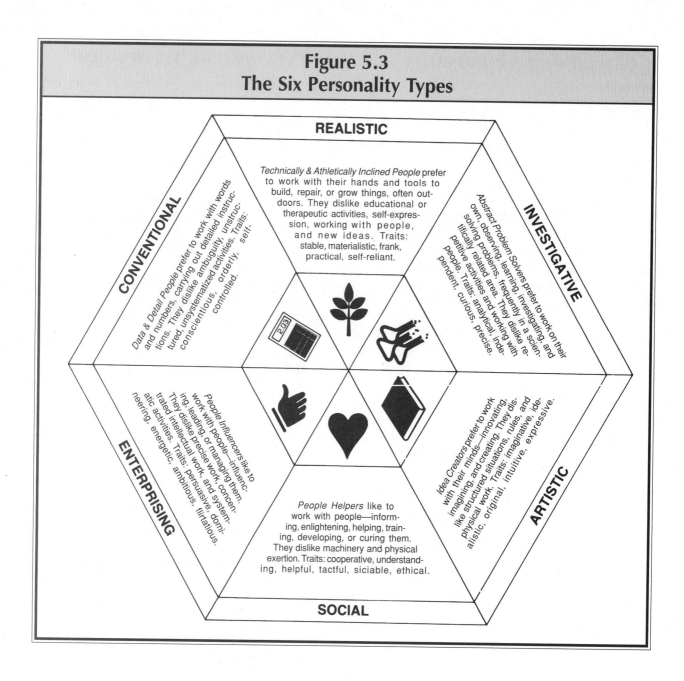

REALISTIC

Technically & Athletically Inclined People prefer to work with their hands and tools to build, repair, or grow things, often outdoors. They dislike educational or therapeutic activities, self-expression, working with people, and new ideas. Traits: stable, materialistic, frank, practical, self-reliant.

CONVENTIONAL

Data & Detail People prefer to work with words and numbers, carrying out detailed instructions. They dislike ambiguity, unstructured, unsystematized activities. Traits: conscientious, orderly, self-controlled.

INVESTIGATIVE

Abstract Problem Solvers prefer to work on their own, observing, learning, investigating, and solving problems, frequently in a scientifically related area. They dislike repetitive activities and working with people. Traits: analytical, independent, curious, precise.

ENTERPRISING

People Influencers like to work with people—influencing, leading, or managing them. They dislike precise work, concentrated intellectual work, and systematic activities. Traits: persuasive, domineering, energetic, ambitious, flirtatious.

ARTISTIC

Idea Creators prefer to work with their minds—innovating, imagining, and creating. They dislike structured situations, rules, and physical work. Traits: imaginative, idealistic, original, intuitive, expressive.

SOCIAL

People Helpers like to work with people—informing, enlightening, helping, training, developing, or curing them. They dislike machinery and physical exertion. Traits: cooperative, understanding, helpful, tactful, siciable, ethical.

EXERCISE 5-G. LEARNING FROM YOUR PROFILE _____

After considering these illustrative examples, see what new insights you have gained from studying your own profile. Answer the following questions regarding your profile.

1. Do I have a narrow range of interest areas, or do they spread across several areas?

2. Who are some people who have profiles similar to mine? What kinds of activities and/or interests did/do they seem to have? Does this provide clues for new activities and interests to investigate?

3. How do I feel about my profile? In what ways does it seem to be an accurate reflection of me? What does it confirm about me and what surprises me?

CASE STUDY
FROM NAVAL OFFICER TO CAREER COUNSELOR

The following case study is presented to demonstrate the usefulness of the Holland model as a career/life-planning tool.

One of this book's authors spent several years serving as a U. S. Naval officer. At one point, he was assigned to a two-year stretch as the hangar deck officer aboard an aircraft carrier. His responsibilities included managing a division of seventy men in moving aircraft in and out of the hangar to support flight operations. He was also responsible for the security of a vast array of vehicles, machines, supplies, equipment, and people on the hangar deck.

This two-year job proved to be an extremely unhappy time in the life of the author. While he enjoyed the great liberty in ports visited by the ship, he found his required work activities highly disagreeable. He vividly remembers a particular incident that highlighted his general discontent with this job. One morning, on one of his countless inspection tours of the hangar deck, he met another officer coming from the opposite direction who was whistling happily.

The other officer instantly greeted the author by saying, "Isn't this a great life!" and "Aren't we lucky to have such great jobs!" The author was shocked by this encounter because he had been feeling depressed, wishing that he were somewhere else, and counting the days until this tour was over. He wondered how there could be so much difference in the feelings of two people about this same lifestyle. Could there be something wrong with him? Or maybe the other guy was just plain crazy!

A few years after that incident of revelation about differences, the author needed to make the transition from military to civilian life. He used a career assessment and counseling service to help him decide where to go with his career. From these assessments, he became familiar with the Holland model and learned that his code was "AIS." Then, for the first time he understood why he had been so terribly unhappy in his shipboard assignment as hangar deck officer. Now he understood the enthusiasm of his fellow officer. No doubt the officer and the job description shared matching Holland codes.

The work activities he had been performing in that military assignment would be classified as "ECR" by the Holland system. Clearly the hangar deck job was simply a terrible mismatch for his particular personality style. It was reassuring to realize that there had been nothing wrong with him in being so discontent and depressed. That particular job was just totally unsuited to his unique interests. Someone else with interests more clearly matched to the job would have thrived in the same position.

Through these career assessments, the author realized that he must get into a career that would enable him to express his creativity, investigative, and social interests. This story has a happy ending. The author loves his work as career counselor and life-planning specialist where he gets to create programs, assist people with their career and life goals, and do some human development research and writing. A pretty good career match for an AIS, don't you think?

SUMMARY

Personalities and interest patterns can be grouped according to six personality types. While most of us have characteristics from all six types in our personalities, we tend to favor one style over others. We have a primary, a secondary, and a tertiary preference. The strength of the difference from our primary to secondary preference may be great, as it probably was for a Michelangelo, or slight, as it seems to have been for a Thomas Jefferson.

Identifying your own personality style will help you know what kinds of people you are likely to be more energized by, what kinds of activities you most enjoy, and where your strongest career and educational interests lie. With this understanding, you are in a better position to appreciate your style of personality and make intelligent career and educational decisions.

ASSIGNMENTS

1. List your top hobbies and identify their Holland codes.

2. From the list of personality characteristics below, check those that you would prefer in your co-workers.

intellectual	creative	cheerful
idea oriented	emotional	popular
analytical	impulsive	controlled
self-reliant	imaginative	orderly
independent	impraticable	data oriented
curious	nonconforming	practical
reserved	sociable	conforming
adventurous	understanding	serious
energetic	helpful	a loner
aggressive	idealistic	frank
argumentative		involved with things
other _____	_____	_____
_____	_____	_____

3. Summarize in Appendix A1 the most important insights you obtained from this chapter. What did you learn about yourself? What ideas did you get for career possibilities?

RESOURCES

Cohen, Joyce and Caela Farren. *It's in the Cards*. Links 52 occupations to eight industries and color codes occupations to things, data, ideas, and people.

Hammer, Allen L. *Introduction to Type and Careers*. Palo Alto, CA: Consulting Psychologists Press, 1993. Helps you use your Myers-Briggs Type Indicator profile to choose or change your job/career. Order from Consulting Psychologists Press, Inc., 3803 E. Bayshore Road, Palo Alto, CA 94303 or call 1-800-624-1765.

Knowdell, Richard L. *Occupational Interests Card Sort Kit*. Helps you identify and rank occupational interests from 110 occupational interest cards. Both this card sort and the one above can be ordered from Career Research & Testing by calling 1-800-888-4945 or in California 1-408-559-4945.

The Passion Revealer. An on-line, 3-part assessment developed to assist adults in understanding their deep-seated interests and comparing them with their developed skills and current work activities. (http://passion.career-nsite.com)

Connecting Your Personality to Work

. . . your career–is going to determine how you live.
—David P. Campbell
If You Don't Know Where You're Going,
You'll Probably End Up Somewhere Else

Do you know people who—

☑ See their work as little more than a necessary evil to support weekend escapes into leisure?

☑ Enjoy their work so much that they look forward with enthusiasm to getting to their jobs on Monday mornings?

☑ Frequently call in sick to avoid going to work because they find their jobs so draining?

☑ Find their educational coursework so fascinating that they are inspired to work hard out of pure interest rather than just to obtain good grades?

☑ Keep changing their academic major, hoping to find one that connects with their interests?

If so, you have become aware of the difference that making a career choice that is compatible versus one that is incompatible with your personality style can make in your overall motivation and success in life and work.

So Miss Anderson, do you feel your personality is suited for a career as a corporate attorney?

CASE STUDY
HELEN

Helen, a forty-year old mother, decided her children were old enough that she could begin a new career. She wanted to get into something that was secure, had good employment prospects, and was useful. She was advised that a special education specialty in speech pathology would accomplish her stated objectives, so, on that basis, that's what she decided to do. Helen had some indication that this kind of work might not be a great fit for her when she realized that the course work was not engaging her interests. But, overlooking this telltale clue of a personality style miss-match, she persevered to become certified and then to get a job as a speech pathologist. Now, one year into her new work, she has come to the sad realization that this profession just is not for her. She simply does not have the right temperament for it. At the time of this writing she is paying for the services of a career counselor for help in getting redirected into something that fits her better. Why, she asks herself, did I not seek this kind of assistance before investing so much time, money, and effort into something that fit me so poorly?

CASE STUDY
MERRILL

For several years Merrill had worked as an economist with the World Bank engaged in an extremely demanding field of poverty alleviation in the developing world. She loved being in a position of devising economic development projects for helping people move out of poverty. But after a few years of this work a major problem developed; she was working herself into a state of total exhaustion, emotionally and physically. Her health deteriorated to the point that she was forced to take a prolonged disability leave. During her recovery period she came to the realization that she could not continue with her economic development work—she needed to make a career change. For help in finding a career better suited to her unique personality and lifestyle needs she sought the services of a career counselor. Through various types of assessment activity she concluded, among other things, that she was a Holland code SAI and that she wanted to work with people in a much more direct way than she had been doing. She also knew that she needed to do much less traveling, to have more control over her time, and if at all possible, to work with animals. The desire to be involved with animals resulted from a long-term love of animals and the fact that pets had played a very important role in her own recovery and healing process. In putting all of these pieces together, she eventually decided to obtain a degree in social work. She is currently developing a unique practice as a social worker in creative association with a veterinarian. In her new profession, she has chosen to work with people dealing with serious emotional issues such as anoxia, autism, depression, and drug addiction. Often, in appropriate situations, she will prescribe treatments that bring her clients into association with the healing presence of animals. Through her explorations in seeking a new career direction she discovered that there was a developing body of research indicating that people dealing with emotional issues such as these seem to recover more quickly and more fully when they are caring for animal pets. Her work now seems to be an excellent way for connecting her personality, values and talents with work about which she is passionate and which provides her with a strong sense of purpose and meaning.

There are a number of career-relevant lessons to be gained from the above case studies. First, and most important, is the need to do what the title of this chapter suggests—connecting your personality to your work. By personality we mean those interest styles we discussed in the previous chapter along with your deep-seated values, needs, and your unique neurological wiring. Choosing a career strictly on the basis of good employment prospects, job security and pay may sound totally practical. As a strategy for choosing or changing your career, however, it is lacking because it fails to take your deeper personal needs and motivations into consideration. Helen, in the first example, is a vivid illustration. Because she failed to do enough self-assessment and occupational exploration before jumping into a new career, she ended up frustrated in her work and angry with herself. While speech pathology is a great fit for the right personality, it happened to be an exceedingly poor fit for Helen's.

Merrill, on the other hand, found a better fit for herself as an economist in poverty development work. What she hadn't realized, however, was that her passion for helping others, especially those living in poverty, would be so all-consuming that it would drive her to the brink of emotional and physical exhaustion. She came to realize, with the aid of counseling, that she was the type of person who needed to manage her obsessive inclination to be of service with awareness and care. Merrill also came to understand a deep-seated desire to combine working with people to therapeutic involvement with animals. The latter awareness came from her very positive experience with animals while she was recovering her health. During this period she obtained a horse and a cat for companionship and to draw her attention away from her health problems through caring for her pets. Through this experience she came to realize that there is great therapeutic benefit in tending animals. Her love for these animals, and we presume their affection for her, brought her out of her state of emotional exhaustion and helped to restore her in body and mind. Aware of the healing power that she had realized through her relationships with these delightful creatures, she longed to help others similarly afflicted. Her counselor suggested some ideas for how she might do this and encouraged her to look for innovative ways she might combine these interests by talking with people in the fields of human health and animal care. Finding the right connection between personality and work for Merrill took a combination of pain-induced awareness, self-assessment, exploration, and creativity. Her investment has paid dividends, however, in that she has found a productive way to make a good living by doing good work.

CONNECTING PEOPLE AND OCCUPATIONS

Having acquired a better understanding of your personality style in Holland code terms from the previous chapter, you will want to select a career direction that fits your unique personality-style-related interests. To do that, you need to have some way of matching personality style with occupations. Holland's system is particularly useful in this regard in that it facilitates relating your unique personality traits with the typical kinds of work activities involved in various occupations.

The Holland model profiles occupations in the same manner as personality styles were profiled in the previous chapter. So, for example, occupations primarily *realistic* in nature usually involve hands-on work activities like building, repairing, operating, maintaining, growing, checking, or producing things. Some typical realistic work tasks are operating a large crane, building a wooden cabinet, piloting an airplane, repairing an antique clock, and doing home repairs. Examples of primarily realistic occupations include: diesel mechanic, computer technician, civil engineer, carpenter, dental technician, National Park Service ranger, air-traffic controller, and industrial arts teacher.

Occupations primarily *investigative* in nature involve using mental effort to solve problems, understand cause-and-effect relationships, or make intelligent meaning out of facts and data through research, analysis and objective reasoning. (Referring back to the brain-dominance chapter, we're talking left-brain cerebral here.) Some typical investigative tasks are studying science journals, developing new computer programs, analyzing tissue cultures for laboratory research, engineering new computer systems, and analyzing demographic data from National Census Reports to understand the changing nature of the U.S. population. Examples of primarily investigative occupations include economist, computer scientist, biochemist, mathematician, medical researcher, NSA intelligence analyst, and astrophysicist.

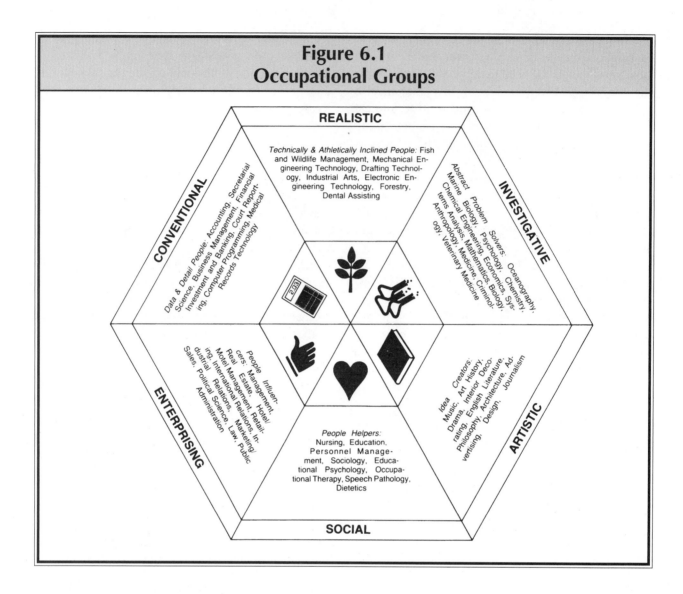

Figure 6.1
Occupational Groups

REALISTIC

Technically & Athletically Inclined People: Fish and Wildlife Management, Mechanical Engineering Technology, Drafting Technology, Industrial Arts, Electronic Engineering Technology, Forestry, Dental Assisting

CONVENTIONAL

Data & Detail People: Accounting, Secretarial Science, Business Management, Court Reporting, Computer Programming, Medical Records Technology Investment and Banking, Financial

INVESTIGATIVE

Abstract Problem Solvers: Oceanography, Marine Biology, Psychology, Chemistry, Chemical Engineering, Economics, Systems Analysis, Mathematics, Biology, Anthropology, Medicine, Criminology, Veterinary Medicine

ENTERPRISING

People Influencers: Management, Hotel/Real Estate, Hotel/Motel Management, Retailing, International Relations, Industrial Relations, Marketing/Sales, Political Science, Law, Public Administration

ARTISTIC

Idea Creators: Music, Art History, Drama, Interior Decorating, English Literature, Advertising, Philosophy, Architecture, Design, Journalism

People Helpers: Nursing, Education, Personnel Management, Sociology, Educational Psychology, Occupational Therapy, Speech Pathology, Dietetics

SOCIAL

Occupations primarily *artistic* in nature typically involve mental intuition in creating artistic renderings and innovations in the form of ideas, metaphors, images, musical and verbal expressions. (Again referring back to the brain-dominance chapter, we're talking right-brain cerebral here.) Some typical artistic tasks are generating cartoons for the *New Yorker* magazine, singing in the choir of a London stage production, drawing caricature portraits, developing designs for a toy manufacturer, creating advertisements for Apple computer, and producing scripts for TV sit-coms. Examples of some primarily artistic occupations include: literature teacher, children's book writer, landscape architect, organizational creativity consultant, film director, public relations director, art therapist, country music singer, and web site designer.

Occupations primarily social in nature usually involve exercising interpersonal intelligence in relating with people for the purpose of educating, healing, training, and providing general support and nurturance. Some typical social tasks include working as a Red Cross care provider, providing therapy in a health center, teaching first graders to read, mediating grievance disputes as an organizational ombudsmen, showing someone how to express feelings in a more socially acceptable way as an employee assistance specialist, and providing solace to people in the final stages of life as a hospice worker. Examples of some primarily *social* occupations include: vocational rehabilitation counselor, registered nurse, special education teacher, speech and drama teacher, and school psychologist.

Ya know what I like about computers . . . ya can't tell your words are slurred on e-mail.

Occupations primarily *enterprising* in nature commonly require a head for business and a facility in exercising influence with others, organizational decision making, risk-taking, and finding cost-effective and practical solutions to business-related operations. Some distinctive enterprising tasks include chairing an important civic committee, providing consultation services to managers, starting your own business, running for political office, leading a work team, acting as spokesperson for a group, and selling a product or an idea. Examples of some primarily enterprising occupations include National Park superintendent, real estate agent, bank manager, organizational development consultant, travel agency manager, captain of a cruise liner, and sales manager.

Occupations primarily *conventional* in nature commonly involve a facility for working with numbers and data, carrying out or developing detailed plans, managing client accounts, bookkeeping, relating policies to practice, and overseeing detailed operations. Some typical conventional tasks are keeping accurate fiscal records, preparing reports and

graphs, analyzing fiscal expenditures, and developing quality-control instructions. Examples of some primarily conventional occupations include proofreader, computer programmer, accountant, finance officer, procurement specialist, NASA space data technician, and credit analyst.

PERSONALITY PROFILES AND OCCUPATIONAL PROFILES

As we hope you will see from the above discussion, personality styles and occupational functions are relatives. For example, those of us who are strong "I's," primarily *investigative* in nature, are drawn to cerebral activities such as observing, scientific investigation, contemplating complex problems, analyzing and evaluating possible meanings from available data. Isn't it fortunate that investigative occupations involve functions such as observing, learning, abstract analytical problem solving, and seeking to understand the nature of things like the cosmos, the

Web Connect

The Computer Information Systems Interests Game **www.harper.cc.il.us/careers/assess.htm** is a unique interests assessment in that it is geared toward individuals who are interested in technology careers. If you're not sure where you fit in the world of technology, this assessment may give you some ideas of careers that may be of interest to you. This assessment was designed by William Rainey Harper College in Illinois. The assessment is based on Dr. John L. Holland's system that is discussed in "The Personality Style Hexagon" section.

brain, and bed bugs. Similarly, we *enterprising* types like to work with people, doing things like selling, leading, making business-related decisions, engaging in risk-taking adventures in launching new products or services, and motivating others to achieve goal-oriented results. *Enterprising* occupations fit "E" types nicely because in them we get to do things like make business decisions, persuade, lead, sell and influence others for gain, fame, fun, and—oh yes—profit.

John Holland assigned three-letter codes (referred to as Holland codes) to both people styles and occupational types.[1] The nature of work involved in a specific occupation can readily be appreciated and understood by its 3-letter code. Figure 6.2 shows characteristic profiles for a few selected occupations. Here is a little example to help show you how that works. In reference to Figure 6.2, the functions or activities performed by laboratory testers include using hands-on skills to set up and run testing equipment and instruments ("R" activities), analyzing materials to determine their chemical or physical properties ("I" activities), and performing tests according to prescribed standards ("C" activities). Laboratory testers, therefore, have "RIC" Holland code classifications because the primary functions of this work involve "R" activities, the secondary functions involve "I" activities, and the third-level functions characteristically are "C" activities. Does this not want to make you become a laboratory tester?

---

1. Holland, John L. *Making Vocational Choices: A Theory of Vocational Personalities and Work Environments,* 2nd ed. (Odessa, FL: Psychological Assessment Resources, Inc., 1992).

Figure 6.2
Typical Profiles of Sample Occupations

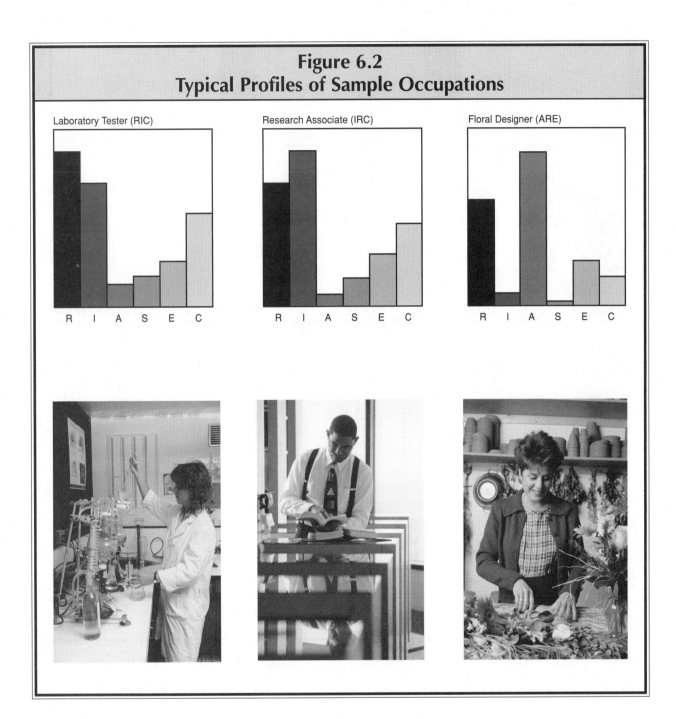

Laboratory Tester (RIC)

Research Associate (IRC)

Floral Designer (ARE)

R I A S E C

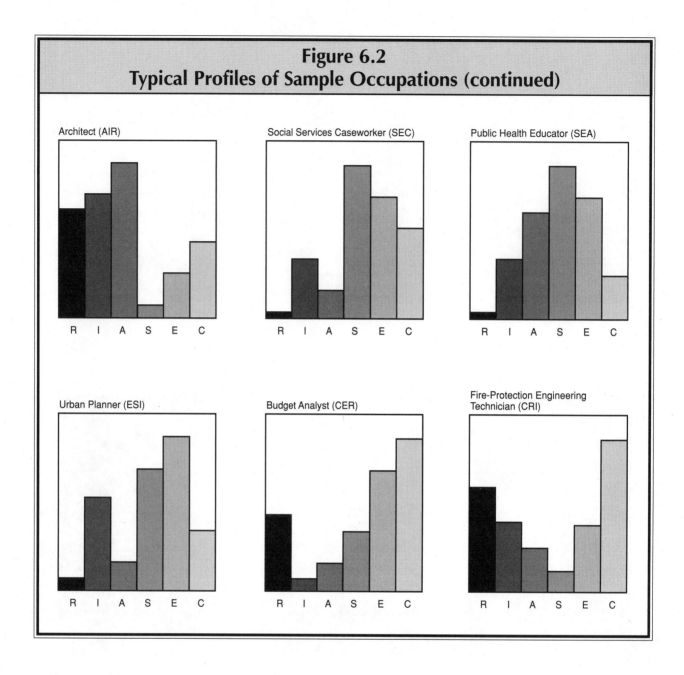

Figure 6.2
Typical Profiles of Sample Occupations (continued)

Three-letter Holland codes can be assigned to most occupations. An "SEC" code, for example, is assigned to social service caseworkers, since the chief set of functions of their work is counseling and assisting individuals and families ("S" activities). The secondary function is to influence their clients to utilize appropriate community resources ("E" activities). A third-level function is to complete forms, compile records, and do client follow-up ("C" activities).

A "CRI" code is assigned to the occupation of fire-protection engineering technician because this work first involves ensuring that fire-protection sys-tems conform to specifications and building codes, and drafting detailed drawings for fire protection systems ("C" activities). Secondary functions in-clude using and operating a variety of fire-fighting equipment ("R" activities). A third level function is analyzing blueprints prepared by architects ("I" activities).

FINDING A COMPATIBLE OCCUPATION

Don't let anyone talk you into pursuing a par-ticular career just because an occupational field of-fers good job opportunities and/or good pay. We're not suggesting that you forget about employment prospects or career development opportunities, nor even good salary prospects. Instead we encourage you, in addition to these things, to choose an occupation compatible with your personality! You have a far better chance of succeeding (getting promoted, getting salary increases, being self-motivated, having fun, and getting into more interesting challenges) in work compatible with your Holland code. To help you find work that matches your style, Mr. Holland spent years creating an elegant methodology for career choice. Aren't you glad you weren't trying to do this work 50 years ago before the fruits of Mr. Holland's work were available?

To find occupations that match your personality style, explore those with the same or similar Holland codes on Table 6.1 *Personality Types and Occupational Characteristics*. Since this is a rather short list of occupations see the reference section at the end of this chapter for additional sources of information. Also, we encourage you to consult with a career counselor for additional assistance.

When developing your list of occupational possibilities keep in mind that there is a great deal of variety among the different occupations associated with a particular field. Figures 6.3 and 6.4 illustrate by Holland code profiles the variety within two fields: library science and psychology. If you have a "CRS" personality profile and want to be a librarian, you might be inclined to reject such a career if you did nothing more than note that the code for librarians is listed as "SAI" (see Figure 6.3). But that might be too hasty a rejection. Notice that library classifiers have a "CRS" profile.

Web Connect

If you didn't take the chance to look at this site in the last chapter, you may want to take a look at it now. The **Career Interests Game** at **http://career.missouri.edu/holland** allows you to explore careers that match the personality style of those similar to you. This game was designed by the University of Missouri-Columbia and is an adaptation of Holland's RIASEC model.

Be sure also, to consider the long-term promotional opportunities within the fields you are exploring. We know of many career professionals who have both enjoyed and been successful in their early work experiences only to become derailed later on by getting promoted into work that is very different from their nature. Promotions are not always good things, especially if they promote you away from the kinds of work that taps your interests. Let's say, for example, that you are particularly interested in the career field of mechanical engineering because, as an "IRA" you find the intellectual, hands-on, and creative work of this field to be particularly interesting. After being in this field for some time, however, you may be looking for a promotion but see that the only way for that to happen is to move into management, which is likely to involve ESC work. If you take that promotion, you just might find that your work is no longer very enjoyable for you. In fact, this kind of thing happens very frequently. So think about both the short and the long range in making your career decisions.

The range of possibilities within a particular occupational field is illustrated in Figure 6.4 by the options available within the broad field of psychology. If you are highly motivated to help people live more effective and satisfying lives, you would probably want to consider the occupations of counseling psychologist or marriage and family counselor. If, on the other hand, you are interested in assisting people afflicted with severe emotional or thinking disorders, you might choose to become a psychiatrist or a clinical psychologist. Should you have strong research and investigative interests, you might choose to become an experimental or development psychologist. Or, if you are interested in using the study of psychology to assist industry in managing its human resources more effectively, you might decide to become an industrial-organizational psychologist.

PREDICTING OUTCOMES OF OCCUPATIONAL AND ACADEMIC CHOICES

In digesting the contents of this chapter, you should be better able to predict what is likely to happen if a particular personality type enters a specific occupation or academic program. Artistic personalities, for example are far more likely to experience satisfac-

Figure 6.3
Occupational Profile Variations Within the Library Science Field

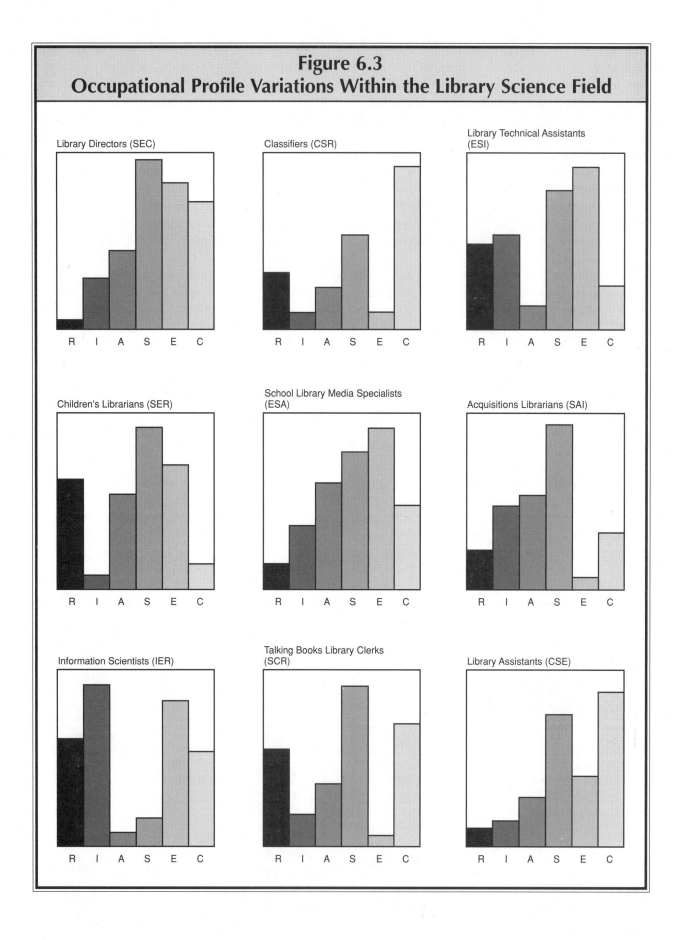

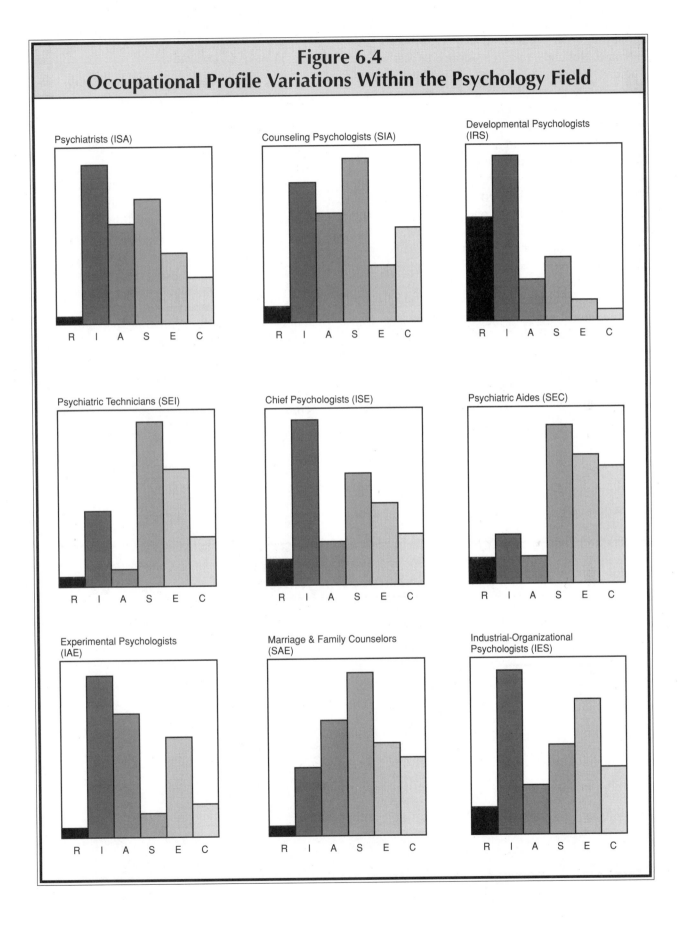

Figure 6.4
Occupational Profile Variations Within the Psychology Field

Psychiatrists (ISA)

Counseling Psychologists (SIA)

Developmental Psychologists (IRS)

R I A S E C

Psychiatric Technicians (SEI)

Chief Psychologists (ISE)

Psychiatric Aides (SEC)

R I A S E C

Experimental Psychologists (IAE)

Marriage & Family Counselors (SAE)

Industrial-Organizational Psychologists (IES)

R I A S E C

tion if they enter occupations that are primarily "A" in nature. Holland's research informs us that people who enter occupations compatible with their personality type are more satisfied in their work and happier in their lives—and don't you really want this for yourself?

What alternatives are available for people with Holland codes that are not adjacent on the hexagonal model? For example, what happens if the essentially artistic person with a primary "A" has a "C" or conventional code as the second or third letter in the personality profile? It is possible, with some creativity, to find occupations with unusual Holland code combinations, as the example of Merrill at the beginning of the chapter suggests. Another alternative is to select an appropriate creative occupation, but choose a more conventional, orderly working environment for the specific job. Still another alternative is to choose work compatible with your strongest Holland letter and reserve an enjoyable leisure activity for a lesser code letter. Read the following case study of Gene for an example of how this might be done.

Web Connect

You may already have the sense that you have chosen the right major, but still at a loss as to what type of work within that major would make you the happiest. **What Can I do with this Major?** found at **http://career.utk.edu/students/majors/majors.html** was developed by the University of Tennessee's Career Services. It is a great site to explore careers that are related to your major. It covers more than 40 majors and for each major, it provides information on common career areas, typical employers, and strategies designed to maximize career opportunities. In the section "Links" each major contains a listing websites that provide additional career-related information. If you don't find your major here, try the **University of Delaware's Major Resource Kits** (70+ majors covered) at <**www.udel.edu/CSC/mrk.html**>.

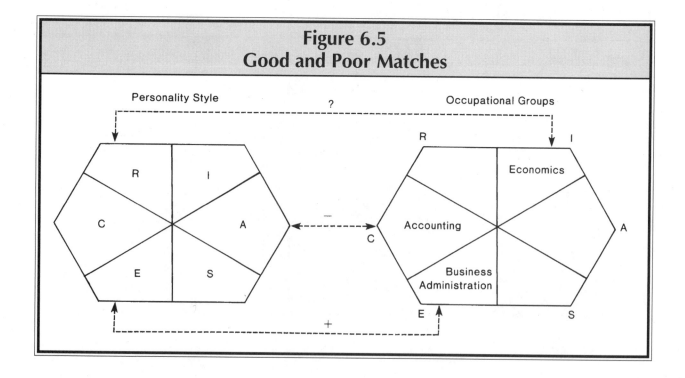

Figure 6.5
Good and Poor Matches

EXERCISE 6. PREDICTIONS OF SUCCESS _____

Make some predictions as to the most likely outcomes in each of the following examples. How satisfied and motivated do you think people are likely to be in each example? Why? Write down your thoughts, and then compare them with the authors' answers in Appendix B.

1. How successful and motivated is the "E"-oriented person likely to be who enrolls in a biology curriculum?

2. How successful and motivated is the "I"-oriented person likely to be who becomes a sales representative or a warehouse manager?

3. How motivated is an "A" personality type likely to be who enrolls in an interior design curriculum?

4. How engaged is a "C" type likely to be doing theater set design work? What personality style might be especially energized by this kind of work? Why?

5. How motivated are "S" types likely to be about their work if employed as electricians, surveyors, carpenters, or mechanical engineers? What if they were employed as organizational trainers, social workers, or college professors in the humanities?

Through his school years, Bill had always been interested in music. He played the piano, guitar, and electronic keyboard. He organized a musical group with some of his friends, and they often played until late into the night in his basement—usually until the neighbors complained or Bill's father yelled "Enough."

Bill aspired to a music career, visualizing himself as a concert pianist, playing before appreciative audiences all over the world. He allowed his dream to be squelched, however, by his well-meaning father. His father advised him to be more realistic about his career, warning that pursuing a career in music was impractical because of limited employment opportunities, which would make supporting himself or a family difficult, if not impossible.

Bill did what his father prescribed for him, which was to become an accountant. His father's reasoning for that was that Bill had always been good at math and that the employment outlook for accountants was excellent. After getting an accounting degree, Bill obtained a job with a large firm. He worked hard, and was rewarded with promotions and salary increases.

Eventually, Bill married his childhood sweetheart, and they had a child. He seemed to have all the ingredients for the good life—good job, steady income, great wife, family, home. But there was a problem—he felt terrible! He had become anemic, sickly, and had no energy. Eventually his deteriorating health forced him to see a doctor because he thought he must have diabetes or some other major problem. His doctor, unable to find anything physically wrong with him, advised Bill that the cause of his problem was probably mental rather than physical. Suspecting job-related stress and dissatisfaction, his doctor referred him to the nearby college career-counseling center.

Bill came into the center looking emaciated and tired. He was so thin that his suit hung on him like the drape on a scarecrow. In discussing his situation with a career counselor, Bill decided to enroll in a career planning class, where he discovered the source for his malady. He learned that he was an "ASR" on the Holland test and a primary reason for his unhappiness in his "CIE" accounting job was that the activities of his work in no way connected with any of his personality traits and top interests. Even though he had a good job and appropriate skills for it, this particular kind of work was draining his energy and vitality. He literally had to force himself to work each and every day. His career choice had pleased his father, but the cost to Bill had been severe.

On the basis of this awareness, Bill, with his wife's consent and support, decided he must make a major lifestyle and career change. Bill's wife went to work and he went back to college to pursue his first love—music. For awhile, they had to struggle by on less than their previous income, but they felt energized and optimistic about their career and life possibilities. Bill began putting on weight, and his health has improved. Today he has a job with a dot.com music company where he combines his love of music with his computer skills and musical knowledge. He also has organized a group of talented musicians in a blue-grass group and plays gigs on weekends for fun—occasionally they even generate a little extra spending money.

Gene, a fifty-something engineer ("IRC" code), came to a career-planning center to talk about a career change. There he learned, among many other things, that he was an "ASE." This was a major revelation to Gene, who had concluded, based upon comparing himself to his engineering colleagues, that he must be lazy and not nearly as bright as they.

Actually, Gene was an extremely bright man, but neither his interests nor his thinking style were compatible with the work of an engineer. With such a gap between his personality and the nature of his work, Gene simply had been experiencing a serious and prolonged lack of motivation. Gene's job used some of his skills, but they were not his best talents and the work certainly did not connect with his interests. There were some rather severe consequences that came with spending so much time in work ill-suited to his best talents and interest. It had taken a toll on his self-esteem, his dignity, and his sense of self-worth. That's often what happens when someone stays in work that's a misfit with their personality for too long.

In Gene's case the remedy he chose was not simply to change careers. He elected not to do this because he had only a few more years remaining to be eligible for a pension. Instead, he decided to stick with his current job but to make some constructive changes in other areas of his life. To find expression for his strongest interests he started acting in amateur theater productions, taking creative writing courses, and very actively participating in social/learning activities with his church.

Miguel got off to a shaky start with his career counselor.

Gene found a piano accompanist and began singing solos in his church, but singing mostly for the sheer fun of it. With a rich tenor voice and a strong Italian lineage, singing was something he had done a lot of in his earlier life but had stopped doing in the course of his career.

Through his new leisure activities, Gene was able to restore his energy and improve his self-confidence and sense of self-worth. By engaging in activities that matched his interest patterns, Gene literally transformed his life and created enough satisfaction through his leisure activities to carry over and energize him in his work. When you are able to energize one part of your life through uplifting activities, there is often a transferal that occurs in other areas of your life, even when those areas may not be very happy situations. That was the case with Gene, whom you can now often find singing his heart out in church and making his church's adult education program a very interesting learning opportunity.

Words of Wisdom

To experience satisfaction and fulfillment in your work and in your life, choose a career direction that allows you to pursue your top interests, engages your preferred style of thinking, and puts your preferred talents to productive work.

SUMMARY

The characteristics and activities that typify each of the six personality styles also apply to occupations and academic programs. Once you have identified your personality style, you are in a better position to select occupations and academic programs that are compatible with your personality-related interests. Pursuing an occupation or an academic program of study that is compatible with your personality type is an essential task for personal motivation, for self-concept development, and for career and academic success. It is crucial for life satisfaction as well, since your occupational choice plays a major role in your energy and emotional disposition.

ASSIGNMENTS

1. Following the suggestions provided in Appendix C, conduct information interviews with two or three people in occupations that match your personality style or with instructors in educational programs that seem to be good fits for your personality style.

2. In Chapter 5, you identified your 3-letter Holland code. Table 6.1 lists a number of occupations in each of Holland's six occupational groups. Scan down the list of occupations corresponding to the primary letter in your 3-letter Holland code and circle those occupations you find interesting. Then go on to the occupation groups corresponding to the second and third letters of your Holland code and circle any of these occupations that interest you. Write the names of occupations you have circled under *Career Possibilities* in Appendix A2.

 Similar to small businesses that open and close, Web sites come and go. This means that some of the Web sites listed in this book will probably change during the time you are reading this material. Therefore, we have created a page on the Web where you can go to ensure you have the most up-to-date links for each of the chapters. To find these links, go to **www.CareerKiosk.org** and click on "Updated links for *Your Career*." These links will ensure that you have accurate links and access to great sites on the Web!

REFERENCES

Holland, John. *The Occupations Finder: For Use With The Self-Directed Search, Career Options Finder; and The Leisure Activities Finder*. Odessa, FL: Psychological Assessment Resources, Inc.

Holland, John. "Short version of the Myers Briggs Temperaments." *The Self-Directed Search*. Online. Internet. http://content.monster.com/tools/quizzes/perfectcareer

Tieger, Paul & Barbara Barron. *Do What You Are: Discover the Perfect Career for You Through the Secrets of Personality Type*. Boston: Little Brown, 1995.

Table 6.1 Personality Types and Occupational Characteristics

Occupational Groups (Realistic)

Occupational Group	Occupation	Holland Code
REALISTIC "Hands-On" Technically Oriented	Access Coordinator, Cable TV	REI
	Airbrush Artist	RCA
	Animal Trainer	RES
	Architectural Drafter	RCI
	Auto Mechanic	RCI
	Biomedical Equipment Technician	RIE
	Cable TV Line Technician	REC
	Commercial Airline Pilot	ERI
	Computer Technician	RIC
	Dispensing Optician	RIS
	Emergency Medical Technician	RSI
	Electronic Technician	RIS
	Estimator	RCE
	Firefighter	RES
	Fish and Game Warden	RES
	Helicopter Pilot	RIC
	Historical Restoration Specialist	RIC
	Industrial Arts Teacher	REI
	Landscape Gardener	RIS
	Locksmith	REC
	Model Maker	REA
	MRI Technologist	RIC
	National Park Ranger	REI
	Nuclear Medicine Technologist	RIS
	Piano Tuner	RCS
	Prosthetist	RSE
	Quality Control Inspector	RSC
	Radiographer	RIS
	Robotic Machine Operator	RSE
	Ships Crew	RCI
	Solar-Energy-System Installer	RCI
	Sound Mixer	RCS
	State Highway Police Officer	RSE
	Tool Designer	RIS
	Ultrasound Technologist	RSI

Enduring Careers

Bionic limb technician

Robotic technician

Mechanics for new engines (solar, hydrogen, ion)

Space vehicle pilots

Holographic Imagery Technician

Communication satellite television

Occupational Groups (Investigative)

Occupational Group	Occupation	Holland Code
INVESTIGATIVE Abstract Problem Solving Science Oriented	Actuary	ISE
	Aeronautical Engineer	IRS
	Anthropologist	IRE
	Astronomer	IRA
	Astrophysicist	IAR
	Biologist	IAR
	Biomedical Engineer	IRE
	Chemist	IRE
	Computer Science Faculty Member	IRE
	Computer Scientist	IRC
	Criminalist	IRC
	Dentist	ISR
	Economist	IAS
	Exercise Physiologist	ISR
	Geologist	IRE
	Internal Auditor	ICR
	Laser Technician	IRE
	Market-Research Analyst	ISC
	Mathematician	IER
	Mechanical Engineer	IRS
	Medical Researcher	IAR
	Meteorologist	IRS
	Museum Curator	IRS
	Optometrist	ISE
	Pharmacist	IES
	Physician	ISR
	Physicist	IAR
	Psychiatrist	ISA
	Research Dietician	ISR
	Research Psychologist	IAE
	Science & Technology Writer	IAE
	Statistician	IRE
	Systems Analyst	IER
	Translator	ISC
	Veterinarian	IRS

Enduring Careers

Global economists

Genetic engineers

Artificial intelligence engineers

Ecology scientists

Information Architects

New products researchers

Table 6.1   Personality Types and Occupational Characteristics *(continued)*

Occupational Groups (Artistic)

Occupational Group	*Occupation*	*Holland Code*
	Actor/Actress	AES
	Advertising Manager	AES
	Architect	AIR
	Art Teacher	ASE
	Book Editor	AES
	Cartoonist	AES
	Columnist/ Commentator	AES
ARTISTIC	Commercial Designer	AER
	Copywriter	AIS
	Dancer	AER
	Drama Teacher	ASE
	English Teacher	ASE
Idea Creators	Entertainer	AES
	Exhibit Designer	ASE
Artistic and	Fashion Artist	AER
Self-Expressive	Graphic Designer	AER
	Illustrator (traditional and digital)	AER
	Landscape Architect	AIR
	Lawyer-Trial Counsel	AER
	Musician, Instrumental	ARC
	Music Teacher	AES
	Newswriter	AEI
	Paintings Restorer	ASR
	Pastry Chef	ASE
	Photojournalist	AEC
	Promotions Manager	AEI
	Prose Writer	AIE
	Public Relations Manager	ASE
	Reporter	ASI
	Sculptor	AER
	Set Designer	AES
	Stage Technician	ARS
	Technical Illustrator	ARI
	Web Site Designer	AIC

Evolving Careers

Creative directors
Actors, middle aged & multilingual
Web graphics production artist
Presentation graphics consultants
Cross-cultural writers

Occupational Groups (Social)

Occupational Group	*Occupation*	*Holland Code*
	Air-Traffic-Control Specialist, Tower	SER
	Athletic Trainer	SRE
	Athletic Coach	SEI
	Clinical Psychologist	SIA
	Corrections Officer	SER
	Counselor	SAE
	Elementary Teacher	SAE
SOCIAL	Employee Relations Specialist	SEA
	Equal Opportunity Officer	SRI
	Faculty Member, College/University	SEI
People/Plant/ Animal Helpers	Health Care Administrator	SER
	High School Teacher	SAE
Nurturing	Interpreter, Deaf	SCE
	Librarian	SAI
	Minister, Priest, Rabbi	SEA
	Music Therapist	SAE
	Nurse	SIA
	Occupational Development Consultant	SRE
	Occupational Therapist	SEI
	Organization Learning Specialist	SEI
	Passenger Service Representative	SEI
	Park Naturalist	SER
	Personal Coach	SEI
	Personnel Recruiter	SIA
	Physical Education Instructor	SCE
	Physical Therapist	SIE
	Probation-and-Parole Officer	SIE
	Professional Athlete	SRC
	Respiratory Therapist	SIR
	School Counselor	SEA
	Social Worker, Psychiatric	SEC
	Special Agent, Customs	SRI
	Speech Pathologist	SAI
	Teacher, Learning Disabled	SER
	Vocational Rehabilitation Counselor	SEC

Evolving Careers

Accelerated learning consultants
Actualization psychologists
Cultural diversity consultants
Conflict resolution mediators
Age 60+ career/relationship counselors/coaches
Corporate ethics consultants

Table 6.1 Personality Types and Occupational Characteristics (continued)

Occupational Groups (Enterprising)

Occupational Group	Occupation	Holland Code
ENTERPRISING People Influencers Power/Status/ Prestige Oriented	Airport Manager	ESR
	Budget Officer	ESI
	Business Manager	ESC
	Camp Director	ESA
	Chef	ESR
	College Administrator	ESC
	Criminal Lawyer	ESA
	Day Care Center Director	ESC
	Federal Government Executive	EIC
	Flight Attendant	ESA
	Food Services Director	EIS
	Fundraising Director	ESA
	Golf Club Manager	ECS
	Head Waiter/Waitress	ESA
	HMO Manager	ECI
	Hospital Administrator	ESC
	Hotel/Motel Manager	ESR
	Judge	EIA
	Lobbyist	ESA
	Media Marketing Director	ESR
	Merchandise Manager	ESR
	Military Officer	ECR
	Museum Director	ESR
	National Park Manager	ESR
	Newscaster	ESI
	Organizational Development Consultant	EIA
	Research and Development Director	ERI
	Real Estate Agent	ESR
	Sales Manager	ESA
	Salesperson, Clothing	EAS
	Sales Representative, Sporting Goods	ESA
	School Principal	ESI
	Securities Trader	ECS
	Tax Attorney	ESI
	Travel Agent	ECS
	Umpire/Referee	ESR
	Urban Planner	ESI

Evolving Careers

Hi-technology sales
Global trade attorneys
Medical Research Center managers
Multimedia Project managers
Coaches for Entrepreneurs

Occupational Groups (Conventional)

Occupational Group	Occupation	Holland Code
CONVENTIONAL Orderly and Efficient Data and Detail Oriented	Abstractor	CSI
	Account Manager	CSI
	Accountant	CSI
	Budget Analyst	CER
	Bursar	CEI
	Caseworker	CSE
	Central-Office Repairer	CRE
	Computer Security Specialist	CIS
	Computer Programmers	CIA
	Congressional-District Aide	CES
	Court Clerk	CSE
	Cost Accountant	CIE
	Customer Service Representative	CSE
	Customs Inspector	CEI
	Editorial Assistant	CIA
	Financial Analyst	CIA
	Fire Inspector	CES
	Insurance Underwriter	CSE
	Legal Secretary	CSE
	Library Assistant	CSE
	Loan Review Analyst	CSR
	Medical Records Technician	CIR
	Medical Secretary	CES
	Mortgage Loan Processor	CRS
	Paralegal Assistant	CIS
	Payroll Clerk	CRE
	Proofreader	CSI
	Quality Control Coordinator	CES
	Reservation Agent	CES
	Secretary	CSE
	Tax Preparer	CES
	Title Examiner	CSE
	Tourist Information Assistant	CSE
	Word Processing Supervisor	CES

Evolving Careers

Information system security experts
Robotic programmers
Office information system managers
Electronic information specialists
Space telemetering analysts

Discovering What Motivates You

*[A human] is a wanting animal and rarely reaches a
state of complete satisfaction except for a short time.*
—Abraham H. Maslow
Motivation and Personality

Do you know people who—

☑ Struggle through life barely maintaining a roof over their heads and enough to eat?
☑ Never feel part of a group because they have difficulty relating to others?
☑ Drive themselves to be equally successful at everything they attempt?
☑ Consider their work devoid of meaning and purpose?
☑ Are unsure about what is important in their lives?

If so, you know people who have not clarified their needs and values and turned them into
constructive influences.

I know I'm kind of old, Miss Recker, but I finally realized that the fashion industry is my calling!

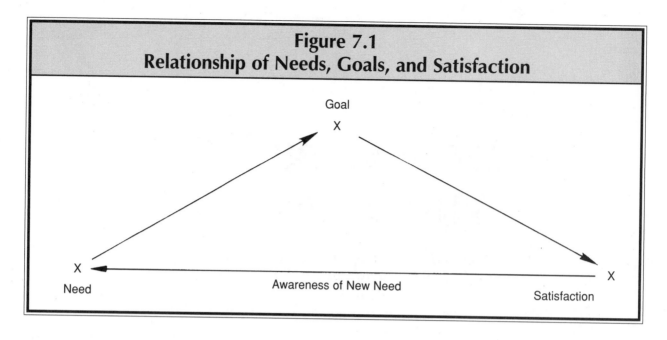

Figure 7.1
Relationship of Needs, Goals, and Satisfaction

Goal
X

X
Need

Awareness of New Need

X

Satisfaction

NEEDS AND VALUES

Of all the individual preferences explored so far, needs and values are the most deeply personal. When people are asked to talk about their own needs and values, they often give "socially acceptable" answers, rather than speaking frankly. Other people are confused about what needs and values actually are, since these forces have been totally unconscious influences in their lives. This is unfortunate because real needs and values are especially powerful motivators in most people's lives. Ignoring or distorting them in career/life planning can cause painfully wrong decisions and wasted effort. This chapter will help you clarify your own true needs and values and put them in proper perspective. Once this is accomplished, needs and values become invaluable "filters" for eliminating general career/life alternatives or specific environments that don't fit you.

NEEDS AND MOTIVATION

Have you ever seen anyone try to motivate somebody else by offering inducements or threats? The research of Abraham Maslow clearly demonstrates that this approach is useless in the long run. All people can be motivated, but motivation cannot be imposed from the outside. Instead, Maslow's work

shows us that all people are motivated by inner drives or impulses called needs.[1] A need is an urgent requirement for something that is essential. Because needs reflect some vital deficiency, a strong sense of inner discomfort motivates people to get their needs met.

Although some basic needs are shared by all, higher-level needs vary from person to person. You might, for example, be strongly motivated by a need to compete with others, while a friend might be highly motivated by the need to help others. Some people have needs for security and others for risk-taking. Some require independence, and others need dependency. Some needs may be readily fulfilled, but others remain unsatisfied for the greater part of our lives. Each of us, however, has a few dominant needs in our life at any one time.

NEEDS, BEHAVIOR, AND SATISFACTION

Your unsatisfied needs drive you; they provide the energy that directs your actions. Once you satisfy a dominant need, you reduce inner tension and experience fulfillment. You also cease to be motivated by any goals that were connected to this particular need. This dynamic is the reason it is a mistake to set up a career goal based solely on a temporary need. On the

---

[1]. Abraham Maslow, *Motivation and Personality,* 2nd ed. (New York: Harper & Row, 1970).

other hand, needs cannot be ignored because satisfaction itself is only a temporary experience. You undoubtedly know that it is human nature, once one pressing need has been satisfied, to quickly become aware of a new unsatisfied need. In this manner, the needs satisfaction process is cyclic, and everyone is destined to be motivated throughout life by needs. Perhaps that is fortunate. Wouldn't life be boring if all your needs were fully met, and you possessed no motivation at all?

UNACKNOWLEDGED NEEDS AND FALSE MOTIVATIONS

Your dominant needs motivate you regardless of whether you are consciously aware of them. And most people are not consciously aware of their real needs, even though they are revealed to others through actions. You may be ineffective at getting your needs met just because you need to clarify them.

Web Connect

Career Perfect's Work Preference Inventory at http:/www.careerpower.com/ CareerPerfect/cpWorkPrefInv.htm can help you identify your work preferences based on personal work values. This is a simple 24-question tool, which produces results that help understand better how you view different aspects of work, such as work style, management style, learning style and preferences for carrying out work tasks. If you are interested in additional insight with regard to work preferences, you may be interested in completing **The Princeton Review Career Quiz** at http://www. review.com/ career/career quizhoome.cfm? menu ID=0&careers=6

Early seminar in career planning.

Typically, when people lose touch with their real needs, they substitute a false need for a real one. For example, people who hunger for love and affection in their lives may substitute a false hunger for food. While these people appear to be motivated by the need for food, the underlying need is really for intimacy. Another example of "false" motivation is illustrated by people who mask a real need for security with a desire to dominate or to become subservient to others. None of the people represented by these examples are getting closer to meeting their real needs. Instead of fulfilling their deficiency, they are often creating other problems.

MASLOW'S NEEDS HIERARCHY

Research psychologist Abraham Maslow found that people have patterns of needs that make behavior predictable.[2] Abraham Maslow classified all needs into five basic categories. Maslow concluded that needs conform to a hierarchy; that is, they are structurally organized from a lower to a higher level of need. The five needs from lowest to highest are: physiological, safety, belongingness and love, esteem, and self-actualization.

Maslow's work shows that there is a natural progression and growth associated with the way that

---

Table 7.1
Steps of the Basic Needs System[3]

The Need System	1 (P) Physiological	2 (S) Safety	3 (B) Belongingness and Love	4 (E) Esteem 1) Self-respect 2) Esteem of Others	5 (A) Self-actualization
Type of Need	Personal Needs		Social Needs		Transcendent Needs
Specific Needs Involved	physical comfort food and water shelter warmth sexual gratification other bodily needs	avoiding risk feeling of being safe emotional security physical security harm avoidance predictability protection stability dependency freedom from fear need for structure and order, law, limits	friendship affiliation feeling part of a group belonging with someone else giving and receiving love affection relationships with people a place in a group or family intimacy	self-respect desire for acknowledgment demonstrate competency and mastery advancement recognition self-confidence independence and freedom reputation attention status sense of self-worth adequacy being useful and necessary	self-fulfillment achieving one's full potential desire to know and understand self realization personal growth meaning in life and work satisfaction through doing making a contribution serving a worthy cause

---

2. Maslow, p. 44.
3. Maslow, p. 45.

people experience their needs. This progression involves a step-like structure as illustrated in Table 7.1, page 140. The general tendency is for a person to move progressively from the lower to higher steps in the needs hierarchy. The lower steps represent deficiency needs for physiological survival and physical safety and then progress through emotional support to the need for self-esteem and self-fulfillment. People living at the highest need-level experience little difference between work and pleasure.

Maslow does not see these high-level self-actualization needs as deficiency needs. People become motivated by the self-actualization needs only when all of their deficiency needs have been satisfied as a general condition in life. Only then are people free to discover, explore, develop, and unfold their true potential. This upward moving tendency is what Maslow calls the growth process. Of course, not everyone grows at the same rate.

It is also possible to move downward on the needs hierarchy because of certain life events. For instance, the sudden, unexpected death of a spouse or loved one could result in belongingness and love reappearing as a strong motive when previously it had been satisfied. Or the devastation resulting from the loss of one's job and the inability to find another could plunge an individual all the way down the hierarchy to a personal need for safety and security.

THE BASIC NEEDS ON THE JOB

So far we have discussed the basic needs hierarchy in general terms. These needs also operate in the work setting to motivate characteristic types of behavior. The needs and behaviors are presented in Table 7.3, page 142. Study the table to see if you can identify on-the-job behaviors typical of you and of other people you know.

| Table 7.2 |
Key Points about Needs
• An unsatisfied need produces a state of inner tension or discomfort that motivates the individual to satisfy that need.
• Unsatisfied basic needs are the primary sources of motivation in life.
• Basic needs that have been essentially satisfied in life no longer create discomfort and cease to be prime motivators of behavior.
• There are five basic needs systems that operate to influence most of human behavior.
• The five basic needs are arranged in a hierarchy from lower to higher.
• There is a natural tendency to progress from the lower level need system to the higher level need system.
• A person becomes aware of a higher order need system only when a lower order need system has been essentially satisfied.
• Should the satisfaction of a basic lower order need be blocked, a person will not become aware of, or motivated by, a higher order need system.
• While no need is ever fully satisfied, there is some minimal level of satisfaction at which a particular basic need ceases to be a major discomfort in life. At that point, the lower level need ceases to motivate behavior and a new, higher level need begins to capture one's attention and motivate behavior.
• Living at the higher level of needs is healthier and more satisfying than living at the lower levels.

Table 7.3
The Basic Needs on the Job[4]

The Basic Need	Work Motivation/Behavior
Physiological	Concern for subsistence (making enough money to survive). Concern for adequate time for meals and rest breaks. Concern for the physical working conditions and avoiding bodily discomfort.
Safety	Concern for fringe benefits such as retirement/pension plan, hospitalization insurance, safe working conditions, seniority protection, clear and consistent working standards (knowing exactly what is expected of a person).
Belongingness and Love	Concern for good relationships, harmonious interactions with peers and superiors, being a member of a working team or group, giving and receiving nurturing.
Esteem	Concern for ways of demonstrating skills and proving self to others. Seeking out opportunities for advancement and promotion. Obtaining work assignments to demonstrate special knowledges and skills. Preoccupation with the best work in return for various types of rewards available (titles, salary, praise, promotions, recommendations, status).
Self-Actualization	A concern for testing one's self (challenge), proving something to one's self. Preoccupation with personal growth, along with a need to be involved in challenging and interesting work that allows learning, growth, creativity, productivity, and contribution to a worthwhile cause.

 ## CASE STUDY
BRAD

    After ten years with his company, Brad moved up to a position of considerable respect and responsibility. Then suddenly his life was thrown into chaos. Brad received notification that he was being laid off. Upon learning this, he was shocked, hurt, and frightened. How could he support his family? How could he obtain another job that would pay a comparable salary? How could he find work he liked and was interested in? How could he replace his friendships at work? Where could he have a comparable amount of responsibility and respect?

    At this point, Brad sought the help of a career counselor to assist him in deciding where to go with his life. Brad's primary concern was finding work that would interest him, best use his talents, and associate him with people he really liked. This latter concern, being with people he liked, was Brad's major preoccupation at this point. Primarily because of this need, Brad decided upon a new career as a career counselor. Once he had chosen his new career, Brad worked hard to implement it, first by getting the necessary education and then by obtaining a career-counseling position.

    When Brad acquired his new job, he was excited about it and very much involved. By belonging to an organization of his choice and by associating with clients and co-workers he liked, Brad's needs were being met. Gradually, however, Brad began losing his enthusiasm for counseling. In-

---

[4] Hall and Williams, *Work Motivation Inventory*.

stead, he noticed that he was skilled at designing counseling materials as well as planning and developing counseling programs. This new love eventually became a problem for Brad. People seeking his counseling services were filling up his time, which he thought could be better spent in program development.

Eventually, Brad applied for and obtained a position where he could spend most of his time and efforts designing, planning, and developing programs. At this point, Brad re-experienced the interest and enthusiasm for his work that he had felt when he first acquired his counseling position.

Brad's primary motivation now is creating and implementing effective counseling programs to serve large numbers of people. His achievements have begun earning him recognition, and he feels very good about that. Recently, however, Brad has experienced a new tension; he feels he is still not using his strongest talents for a cause that is deeply meaningful to him.

Brad's physiological, safety, and belongingness needs had been essentially satisfied in ten years at his old career. Upon receiving his termination notice, however, Brad was set back both physically and emotionally. His needs for security and belongingness suddenly became unmet needs. On the job, his primary motivation had been satisfying his need for esteem. Now he was plummeted all the way down the needs hierarchy to physiological concerns about how he was going to provide the basic necessities for himself and his family.

In counseling, Brad quickly learned that he possessed many employable skills. Although losing his job was a serious setback, his future was actually still quite secure. He was still young and employable, and he had sufficient savings to survive until he could obtain a new position. In looking at these aspects, Brad felt reassured. In fact, he really wasn't at the physiological or security level of the needs hierarchy. His primary preoccupation was at the belongingness and love level. His personal pride and esteem had suffered a great deal in his setback, but the primary motivation for his present career was with the need for affiliation, the need to feel wanted by and associated with others. Brad had chosen this career far more on the basis of his "hunger" for affiliation than out of consideration for his primary interests, talents, and personality style. And that proved to be a mistake.

Although Brad was an effective counselor, he quickly started losing his interest and enthusiasm for counseling as soon as his belongingness needs were generally satisfied. He then re-experienced the need for esteem. This occurred in the form of motivation to develop his skills and to produce significant achievements through work. In this respect, however, Brad became aware that his skills and interests were more in creative program planning and development than in personal counseling.

At the time he made his selection, Brad was unaware of how one's motivation changes when a need is satisfied. Had he been aware of this important dynamic, he would have developed plans for a career track that led more quickly to his fundamental interests and talents. Fortunately for Brad, his career choice and his organization allowed for a transfer that used his talents and fulfilled his current primary needs for esteem.

The closing statements in the case study suggest that a new shift in Brad's motivation may be occurring. His concern appears to be less in achievement for esteem and more in personal development for a worthy cause. Perhaps Brad's needs for esteem are becoming satisfied, and he is responding to inner needs for self-actualization.

EXERCISE 7-A. EXAMINING YOUR NEEDS TODAY AND IN THE FUTURE _____

Carefully peruse Tables 7.1, 7.2, and 7.3 on pages 140, 141, and 142, then answer the following questions.

1. Which of the basic needs in your life appear to be the most fully satisfied? Explain why this is so.

2. Which basic need, because it is not fully satisfied, now appears to be your primary motivator? What would have to happen for this need to be generally satisfied in your life?

3. If your current primary motivating need were generally satisfied, what need would then probably become your primary motivator? Include the possible ways your life could change.

4. How will you use the information obtained from this examination of your needs in your future career planning?

While most of the lessons to be learned from the case study are obvious, a few points warrant further elaboration. We can infer from this case study that while needs must be included in the career-choice process, they should be considered as just one part of the whole picture. People must also clarify what they have to contribute through preferred talents, interests, values, and life goals. They must also be aware that although talents and personality styles change very little after the age of eighteen, the same is not true of needs. Needs change continuously over a lifetime. In career planning, therefore, you must take into account both where you are now regarding personal needs and where you will be in the future.

NEEDS VERSUS VALUES

Clear, consciously held values are another important factor in effective career choices. The relationship between needs and values can be demonstrated by examining how each is acquired and how each influences current and future behavior.

Needs arise out of a perceived deficiency primarily physiological or social in nature. For example, the office manager whose work routine is disorderly and chaotic feels the need for a predictable sequence of work tasks. The perceived deficiency is one of structure, order, and organization. As soon as the office manager gets the safety and security of a struc-

tured and ordered work environment the need will disappear.

Unlike needs, values do not arise from perceived deficiency and do not disappear once satisfied. Values are learned and chosen from one's life experiences. For example, children whose strong interest in reading is supported and whose curiosity about natural phenomena is encouraged by understanding parents and teachers will most probably value education. As adults they may later seek out both formal and informal continuing education and encourage their children to do the same.

Both needs and values change over time, although values change to a far lesser extent than needs. Needs change as they are temporarily satisfied, while values change due to life adjustments and/or personal growth resulting from changing circumstances. As crises occur and circumstances change over time, needs emerge and re-emerge up and down the hierarchy. If what seems to be a need remains consistently strong after being satisfied, it has become a value.

Needs are the key motivators for current behavior, while values serve as guides to current and future choices of action. Your immediate behavior is strongly influenced by potent, unmet needs. Clear, consciously held values aid you in making consistent decisions about appropriate courses of action.

The interplay of needs and values can be illustrated by the following example: Your neighborhood experiences a sudden increase in theft, harassment on the streets, and other similar occurrences. The sense of safety and security in your community is threatened. You and your neighbors are motivated to take specific action to return the area to its former state. The neighborhood improvement association calls a meeting of interested parties, and suggestions are elicited from the group.

Proposed actions include initiating a Neighborhood Watch Program, increasing illumination in the neighborhood after dark, maintaining a lookout and reporting system for unfamiliar people and vehicles in the neighborhood, investing in a security system, and purchasing handguns. While you may agree and actively support most of the suggestions, the purchase of handguns you deem unacceptable. Here your values regarding the sanctity of human life guide your decision not to purchase a handgun and to dissuade your neighbors from such a purchase.

The need to restore your community to its previous safe and secure condition motivates several types of behavior. But your clear, strongly held values determine the types of actions you would support and those you would oppose. Your needs motivate the necessity of taking immediate action, but your values guide the choice of actions that you would take or support.

THE IMPORTANCE OF VALUES IN GOING FOR WHAT YOU WANT

There used to be a popular television beverage commercial that implored us to "Go for it with all the gusto you've got." "After all," it continued, "you only go around once in life." For those involved in career decision making, this is excellent advice, but going for what you want in life is not an easy task. In fact, few people really know what they want in life because they have never really taken the time and effort to determine what matters in their lives. To determine what you want, you must first know what is important in your life—the values that give your life meaning and relevance.

Values are not lofty ideals dreamed up by experts in ivory towers and held up as examples by which you ought to live. Instead, people choose, formulate, and reformulate their values as they direct their lives. Values can be seen most clearly in your everyday actions as you make decisions. You are not always consciously aware of your values, however, unless you dig deeply and search widely through your life experiences.

You will discover that values are the principles or standards upon which you make all decisions that shape the course of your life. Life in our culture is enormously complex, and each day we are bombarded by a wide array of lifestyle choices. Some are simple. For example, when you shop for groceries, do you choose nutritious foods such as grains, fresh fruits and vegetables, and low-fat dairy products? Or do you choose prepared foods that save you time? Do you look for money-saving bargains? Or do you prefer to pay more for brand-name items? Even these simple choices reflect your values.

More complex choices in your life require considerable and often difficult deliberation. Young people, for instance, face decisions such as whether to live at home where their basic needs are met or to risk moving out and fending for themselves. Young couples are often faced with the dilemma of how to balance the demands of family and career. Men and women of all ages ponder whether to terminate relationships that are not working. Men and women at midlife contemplate significant career and lifestyle changes. Older people often face the difficult choice of living alone in familiar surroundings or moving into living complexes with other senior citizens. People can best make these and other important decisions on the basis of clear, consciously held values.

DEFINING AND CLARIFYING VALUES

Directing your life in a world full of confusion and conflict is like charting a course through unknown and often dangerous waters. Values clarification provides a means of charting a course through the unknown waters of your life. Through values clarification, you can carefully examine your own experiences to discover the content and strength of your own values system. This self-assessment method will help you discover what values you actually live by or act upon rather than what you think your values should be. Values clarification is a positive, forward-looking process that focuses on both your current values and your evolving values.

Before you can clarify your values, however, you must first be clear on what constitutes a value. According to values researchers, for something to be considered a value, it must conform to seven criteria. These criteria can be summarized best by the words *prizing, choosing,* and *acting. Prizing* emphasizes the emotions or feelings, *choosing* relies on thinking and reasoning, and *acting* implies behavior. Therefore, our values are formed by a combination of our feelings, thoughts, and behavior. The seven values criteria include the following:

Prizing

1. *Prized and Cherished.* To prize and cherish something is to have an emotional attachment to it. This attachment may be to an intangible concept or to a tangible object. For example, political activists who have been imprisoned in their own countries for opposing dictatorial regimes experience strong emotional ties to free political expression. To them the concept of freedom is prized and cherished. Other people may cherish a family ring or family heirloom not for the object itself but for what it represents: a deceased parent, a loving family, a proud cultural heritage.
2. *Publicly Affirmed.* Public affirmation is simply acknowledging a belief, feeling, or attitude to others. For example, local activists who make their views known to their neighbors through a community newsletter represent one method of public affirmation. Wearing a uniform (scout, military, religious order) is another more subtle way of publicly affirming certain values.

Choosing

3. *Chosen Freely.* Freely chosen values are those you have ultimately chosen yourself rather than follow the subtle or overt influence of others. For example, choosing a religious or political affiliation of your own volition (or choosing not to affiliate) rather than merely following what your parents or family believed illustrates the idea of free choice.

4. *Chosen from Alternatives.* Without two or more alternatives, there is no choice and no true value. A true choice involves awareness of the widest variety of possible options or alternatives. For example, young people graduating from high school have a bewildering array of educational, career, and lifestyle choices available to them. Milestones such as high school graduation are critical in the lives of young people, and they are well advised to seek help from parents, friends, teachers, and counselors both in identifying and exploring their alternatives.

5. *Chosen after Consideration of Consequences.* Making the choice that is right for you first requires a careful examination of the probable consequences of each of your identified alternatives. For example, when deliberating upon a career change, factors such as job security, salary and benefits, seniority, degree of dissatisfaction, and the possibility of lateral movement, should all be weighed and considered carefully before reaching a decision.

Acting

6. *Acted Upon.* You affirm your values by acting upon them. Unless you act upon something, it is not a value but a good idea or belief. For example, if you value your role as citizen, then you would demonstrate it by voting, supporting candidates, lobbying, or publicizing officials' actions. Failure to act can prevent an idea or belief from becoming a value.

7. *Acted Upon Repeatedly and Consistently to Form a Definite Pattern.* A single act does not constitute a value. Examining your life for patterns of repeated and consistent action will help you identify your values. For example, if you consistently arrange regular physical and dental checkups, exercise three times per week, plan and eat nutritious meals, and sleep 6–8 hours per night, then you undoubtedly value healthful living. Your repeated pattern of consistent actions promotes health as one of your values.[5]

EXERCISE 7-B. LIFE VALUES ASSESSMENT[6]

DIRECTIONS

1. Place an X on the line next to each of the values below that are truly important in your life right now. For a value to be truly important in your life, it must be reflected in your behavior on a regular basis. For instance, if variety is one of your current values, then you may behave in ways that result in frequent changes in various aspects of your life, such as your job, location, friends, physical appearance, or recreation.

2. Circle the ten values that are currently most important in your life.

____ Achievement (accomplishing something important)

____ Adventure (seeking challenging new experiences)

____ Aesthetics (appreciating beauty in all its forms)

____ Affection (giving and receiving love)

____ Authenticity (genuinely being yourself)

____ Creativity (freedom to express new ideas/develop new things)

5. Louis E. Raths, Merrill Harmin, and Sidney F. Simon, *Values and Teaching* (Columbus, OH: Charles E. Merrill, 1966) 28–30.
6. Fontelle Gilbert, Seminars for Personal Growth, 6501 Inwood Drive, Springfield, VA 22150.

_____ Cultural Heritage (appreciating your ethnic background)

_____ Economic Reward (earning a high rate of compensation)

_____ Emotional Strength (managing your feelings in positive ways)

_____ Ethical Living (living morally and justly)

_____ Expertise (being good at something worthwhile)

_____ Family (having a strong bond through shared heredity and/or experience)

_____ Friendship (affiliating with others)

_____ Future Orientation (seeking to learn what the future holds)

_____ Health/Fitness (actively maintaining vitality)

_____ Inner Serenity (seeking peace within)

_____ Integrity (maintaining congruence of your words with deeds)

_____ Intellect (having a keen and lively mind)

_____ Leadership (having influence over others)

_____ Orderliness (living an organized life)

_____ Personal Development (continuing self-exploration and growth)

_____ Personal Freedom (making choices independently)

_____ Personal Safety (being safe from bodily harm)

_____ Pleasure (enjoying fun activities)

_____ Recognition (being known by others)

_____ Risk-Taking (seeking excitement via living on the edge)

_____ Satisfying Career (having meaningful and challenging work)

_____ Security (having a stable future)

_____ Self-Confidence (feeling positive about oneself)

_____ Service (contributing to the welfare of others)

_____ Spirituality (seeking the ultimate meaning in life)

_____ Variety (seeking change in activities and surroundings)

_____ Wisdom (seeking mature understanding)

3. List the ten you have selected in the space below.

ACQUIRING AND CHANGING YOUR VALUES

The predominant view about how values are acquired has been that they are transmitted from adults to children. Parents or parent substitutes articulate and model the values that they desire their children to acquire. According to this traditional view, children take the values they have been taught and make them their own.

Proponents of values clarification reject the traditional idea that values can be taught or transmitted.[7] Instead, they believe that values are learned directly from an individual's life experiences involving various influences.

---

[7] Adapted from the Intensive Course in the Crystal Life/Work Planning Process, John C. Crystal Center, Inc., 894 Plandome Rd., Manhassett, NY 11030.

As you grow and develop, you change, and so do your values. What is a value to you now may diminish in importance as you gain new information and acquire additional skills, or as your life circumstances change in significant ways. For example, in first grade, children often value their relationship with the teacher above all else, but in the upper elementary grades, children place a higher value on their relationships with peers. In adolescence, relationships with the opposite sex are usually most highly valued. Later, young adults often find that family and career values take precedence. On the other hand, some values remain relatively stable throughout your life.

DISCOVERING YOUR HIDDEN VALUES

Often you are not consciously aware of your values. Being asked to express your values directly is like asking you to count all the muscles in your body. Some are obvious and visible to you, but most are hidden from your view.

The way you choose to live your life provides clues to these hidden values. For instance, when you have free time, what do you choose to do with it? Do you read, jog, play the piano, or call a friend long distance? Other than obtaining the necessities of life, how do you choose to spend your money? What kinds of things get you riled up enough to take a stand or to take action? What do you fantasize or daydream about? When do you feel most alive and vibrant in your life? In answering these and other similar questions, you are focusing on your true values.

> ### Web Connect
>
> The University of Waterloo's Values Assessment at http://www.adm.uwaterloo.ca/infocecs/CRC/manual/values.html may also help you uncover some hidden values.

Clues to the discovery of your values constantly surround you. Everything you do or say tells something about what you value. If you find yourself living for those quiet, reflective moments when you can be alone, then you probably value time for quiet contemplation. If, on the other hand, you live for the moments of raucous, roughhouse play with your children or time with your friends, then you probably value noisy, physical activities with others.

Two good ways of discovering your hidden values are through examining past events or accomplishments in your life and by looking at your future objectives. The events or accomplishments represent choices you have made in the past and reflect what motivated you at that particular time. They tell you much about what you may still consider important in your life. Your future objectives come from the dreams and fantasies you have about the future. They, too, tell you what is important in your life right now.

 EXERCISE 7-C. UNCOVERING YOUR HIDDEN VALUES[8] _____

1. This exercise requires you to imagine that you have just been given a gift of one million dollars with only one stipulation. That stipulation is that you must use the million only on yourself.

    A. List below under Column A some of the possible ways you would like to use your gift. What would you want to do, have, or be? Some examples are provided to help start you thinking about this exercise.

---

8. Ibid.

Column A	Column B
Uses	*Possible Values*

Examples:

1. Invest in stocks and bonds	1. Financial security, challenge/risk-taking
2. Reserve season tickets to symphony, theater, and dance performances	2. Aesthetics, pleasure
3. Set aside funds for my continuing education	3. Intellect, personal development, job security
4. Start my own small business	4. Independence, risk taking, achievement

Uses	*Possible Values*

Your Selections:

B. Now that you have determined how you would use your million dollars, analyze each use for values content. In our first example, for instance, investing in stocks and bonds represents the value of financial security to those who invest in safe, low yield securities. But to those who prefer more chancy, high-return investments, it represents the value of risk-taking. The same use can represent different values to different people. Analyze each of your million dollar uses for the value(s) they represent to you and list those values in Column B. Refer to the list of Life Values from Exercise 7-C for possible values words.

2. You are the recipient of yet another million dollar gift, this time with a different stipulation. This gift is to be used only for the good of others.

A. Ask yourself what needs doing in your family, neighborhood, country, and the world. How could you best contribute? List the ways you would make a contribution under Column A. Refer to the examples below in Column A to stimulate your thinking.

Column A	Column B
Uses	*Possible Values*

Examples:

1. Establish an institute for peace studies	1. Ethical living, freedom, spirituality
2. Reform the educational system	2. Intellect, personal development, and freedom
3. Establish parenting classes for young parents	3. Affection, family, and emotional strength
4. Establish a neighborhood watch in my community	4. Service, personal safety

Uses	Possible Values

Your Selections:

B. Again analyze your list of uses in Column A for the value(s) that each represents and place them (the values) in Column B.

THE IMPORTANCE OF VALUES IN WORK

For your work to be satisfying, it must be compatible with your values. For some people, money, power, prestige, and status are what it takes for a job to be rewarding. Others may have these external rewards in their work but still find it unsatisfying. Some people must experience meaning or purpose in the work itself for a job to be satisfying.

Years from now when you reflect on your work life, will it be with a sense of satisfaction or a sense of regret? Satisfaction comes from knowing that what you did with your life was important, that your life's work had some significance and benefit for yourself and perhaps for others.

The following exercise contains a listing of values that can be derived from work. These are arranged in four categories: workplace conditions, workplace outcomes, workplace rewards, and family/personal considerations.

EXERCISE 7-D. WORK VALUES ASSESSMENT[9]

1. Read the definitions of the work values listed in four categories below. Rate each work value according to its degree of importance to you. Use the following scale in assigning your ratings:

1 = unimportant in my choice of career
2 = somewhat important in my choice of career
3 = very important in my choice of career

Place the number corresponding to your rating in the blank to the left of each work value.

A. *Workplace Conditions.* Characteristics of the workplace environment.

_____ *Safety/Security*—a work environment free from physical danger or personal harassment.

_____ *Pleasant Setting*—an aesthetically pleasing and comfortable work setting.

9. Howard E. Figler, *PATH: A Career Workbook for Liberal Arts Students* (Cranston, Rhode Island: Carroll Press, 1975) 77–79.

_____ *Caring Co-Workers*—working with people who get along and cooperate with one another.

_____ *Respectful Supervision*—having understanding supervisors who respect your wants and needs.

_____ *Competition*—a work setting where outdoing your co-workers or exceeding your own or the companies' standards is important.

_____ *Fast-Paced Work*—working rapidly to meet time or performance deadlines.

_____ *Variety/Change*—performing many different work tasks.

_____ *Travel*—work where travel is an integral part of the routine.

_____ *Inside Work*—working inside a building usually in an office setting.

_____ *Outside Work*—working outdoors exposed to the elements.

_____ *Both Inside and Outside Work*—striking a balance between both inside and outside work.

_____ *Working Alone*—doing assignments by yourself involving minimal contact with co-workers or the public.

_____ *Working on a Team*—carrying out work responsibilities as an integral part of a group of co-workers.

B. *Workplace Outcomes.* The purpose(s) that work serves in your life.

_____ *Being Competent*—striving to excel at the work that you do.

_____ *Using Abilities*—utilizing the competencies you possess to their maximum.

_____ *Making Things*—using your hands to produce or repair concrete, tangible things.

_____ *Problem Solving*—figuring our how something should be done.

_____ *Developing New Ideas*—improving upon the ways things have been done or else coming up with new ways of doing them.

_____ *Precise Work*—performing work that meets exacting standards.

_____ *Mental Challenge*—performing demanding tasks that challenge your intellect.

_____ *Social Contribution*—seeking to improve the human condition.

_____ *Influencing Others*—affecting others in ways designed to change attitudes or opinions or motivating them to take action.

_____ *Supervising/Directing Others*—being in a position to oversee and/or take responsibility for the work of others.

_____ *Aesthetic Contribution*—performing work that contributes to making the world a more beautiful place.

_____ *Spiritual Fulfillment*—doing work that contributes to the religious or spiritual fulfillment of yourself or others.

C. *Workplace Rewards*. The rewards you expect from your work.

_____ *High Salary*—choosing an occupation where the rate of compensation is in the top third (33%) for all occupations.

_____ *Good Benefits*—having health care, disability insurance, etc., as part of your compensation package.

_____ *Equitable Pay*—being compensated at a rate that is commensurate with the amount and quality of work you do.

_____ *Opportunity for Advancement*—having a good chance to advance into positions of increasing authority and responsibility.

_____ *Job Availability and Security*—working in an occupational field where you have a good opportunity to obtain and maintain a job.

_____ *Recognition/Prestige*—being perceived by others as doing important work or being an expert in your field of endeavor.

D. *Personal/Family Considerations*. Attempting to balance work and personal life.

_____ *Time Flexibility*—arranging your own work hours or working according to your own schedule.

_____ *Job Sharing*—being able to share the duties and responsibilities of a job with another person or other people.

_____ *Autonomy*—having discretion in how you complete or perform your job tasks.

_____ *Self-Employment*—being employed by and working for yourself.

_____ *Ethical/Moral Standards*—being free to act in accordance with a set of standards regarding what is the right or fair thing to do.

_____ *Regular Hours*—working a regular work schedule that allows you time for yourself and/or your family.

_____ *Easy Commute*—living close to where you work.

_____ *Acceptance*—being accepted for what you can contribute although your lifestyle may differ from your co-workers.

2. List below your 3 or 4 most important work values in each of the four categories. Add any others that are important but which were not covered above.

Workplace Conditions   *Workplace Outcomes*

_____   _____

_____   _____

_____   _____

_____   _____

_____   _____

Workplace Rewards	*Personal/Family Considerations*
_____	_____
_____	_____
_____	_____
_____	_____
_____	_____

3. Select your ten most important values from those you have listed in 2. above.

Exercise 7-E. The Core of Your Values

1. List below your top 5 to 10 values from each of the values from Exercises 7-B, 7-C, and 7-D.

7-B	7-C		7-D
	Uncovering Your Hidden Values		
Life Values Assessment	*Million/Self*	*Million/Others*	*Work Values*

2. Combine the values in the four columns above in order to come up with your top 5 values. Pay particular attention to those values that appear in more than one column.

3. Place your top 5 values in the box below.

My Top Five Prioritized Values

1.

2.

3.

4.

5.

SUMMARY

Your needs are experienced as an inner feeling that something essential for you is missing. This awareness produces a sense of acute personal discomfort or inner tension that motivates you to satisfy this need. Abraham Maslow has identified a basic needs structure comprised of five separate levels of needs: physiological, safety, belongingness and love, esteem, and self-actualization. These needs are arranged in a hierarchy, proceeding in steps from the lower level needs, which are physical, to higher level needs, which are social and spiritual. A person is motivated to progress through these needs one at a time, from the lower order to the higher order. The satisfaction of a lower level need allows a higher level need to emerge as primary motivator. This progression represents a satisfying growth process in life. For career planning, consider your needs seriously, but do not let them overshadow the importance of other personal attributes and preferences. Choose a career that will meet your currently dominating need and provide upward progression through the other needs. It is important to understand not only your current needs, but also the ways these needs are likely to change in the future.

The process of values clarification is also crucial to career/life decision making. Career choices must be based on some assessment of what is important in your life. Values clarification strategies enable you to clear up much of the confusion and conflict in your life in order to determine what gives your life meaning and purpose.

Values are not always conscious, being frequently hidden from consciousness and appearing only through the use of indirect values clarification methods. Using a variety of values clarification methods and then synthesizing the results is an effective way to derive a comprehensive listing of your top values.

People derive certain values from their jobs and careers. For some, work provides external values, such as money or material success. Others require the fulfillment of more internal values, such as helping others or seeking knowledge. You need to identify the important values you derive from voluntary or paid work before deciding on a career.

While closely related, values and needs differ in significant ways. These differences can be demonstrated best by examining how each is acquired and changed and how each influences current and future behavior. Unmet needs strongly influence your immediate behavior. Values determine the choices of action that you deem acceptable to satisfy your unmet needs.

Assignments

1. Reflect on what you choose to do when you have free time. Think of the free time you had last week. What did you choose to do with it? What, if anything, does this tell you about your values?

2. By answering the following questions, what values do you discover?

    a. Other than purchasing necessities, how do you choose to spend your money?

    b. What kinds of things get you riled up enough to take a stand?

    c. What do you daydream about?

    d. What do you find yourself doing when you feel most alive and vibrant in your life?

3. See Appendix E for further resources to clarify your values.

 Similar to small businesses that open and close, Web sites come and go. This means that some of the Web sites listed in this book will probably change during the time you are reading this material. Therefore, we have created a page on the Web where you can go to ensure you have the most up-to-date links for each of the chapters. To find these links, go to **www.CareerKiosk.org** and click on "Updated links for *Your Career*." These links will ensure that you have accurate links and access to great sites on the Web!

8

Making a Career Choice

Far too often, people tend to lay out alternatives for you. As a result, you may focus on only those alternatives. But you should always keep in mind that there may be other alternatives that haven't been mentioned by anyone. Also, you are bringing what is uniquely you to the situation, so that an alternative that may be best for most people may not be best for you.
—Gordon Porter Miller
Life Choices

Do you know people who—

☑ Make decisions without knowing what their alternatives are?
☑ Have no idea how to find information about occupational alternatives?
☑ Can only seem to identify unsatisfactory choices?
☑ Seem to ponder their alternatives endlessly without ever deciding?
☑ Just let others tell them what to do?

If so, you know people who lack the skills required to assess their available alternatives and make the best career/life decisions.

Humpty decided to go back for another session with his career counselor.

ALTERNATIVES AND DECISION MAKING

The world of work is a huge universe consisting of thousands of occupations. Statistically, picking a suitable occupation by chance or luck is inconceivable. You will need effective decision-making skills.

What is your current approach to decision making? Do you immediately want to know the "right answer?" Most people do. Good chess players, however, realize that there is seldom a single best course of action. Instead, they contemplate their full range of options, each leading to different consequences. They are likely to be asking, "What strategy do I choose to pursue? What are my alternatives right now, and how might they change depending upon the next move?" Only after surveying the whole range of alternatives and their consequences, do successful chess players decide what move to make.

Successful chess playing is similar to effective career decision making. Chess players who cannot

Web Connect

O*NET information can be found at www.onet.org. This database provides information such as skills, knowledges, abilities, interests, and work values, as well as links to other sources of data, such as census and labor market information. Through the information you find here, you can assess and compare the data for different occupations to evaluate the similarities of various fields of work. O*NET OnLine has simple user instructions on almost every page and an on-line Help section accessible from every page.

Web Connect

The Career Exploration Links provided by UC Berkeley at www.uhs.berkeley.edu/Students/CareerLibrary/links/occup.cfm is a great resource to assist you with your career research.

see the full range of alternatives available to them are unlikely to be consistent winners. People faced with career/life decisions are also unlikely to make winning decisions unless they too can see their full range of alternatives and evaluate their consequences.

At this phase of your decision-making process, try to be thorough, patient, and alert to all of your best possibilities. We have seen many people in the career planning center who, after assessing their talents and goals, became impatient with the task of identifying alternatives. They wanted to pick the first seemingly good choice they found. Some people are afraid that too many choices will just confuse them. It is true that having a lot of possibilities makes choosing more complicated. But why miss your best available option because of impatience? We urge you to take your time with this chapter's exercises as an investment in your future.

ENVISIONING THE TASK

To better understand career decision making, consider the following example. Janet, Rodney, Tim, and Cynthia all have a "CIR" Holland personality code. At this point in their career planning, each has identified the following career alternatives of interest to them:

Janet	Rodney	Tim	Cynthia
Accountant	Computer Programmer	Management Analyst	Medical Records
Computer Operator	Building Inspector	Civil Engineering	Technician
	Nurse	Technician	Management Analyst
	Elementary Teacher	Computer Programmer	Accountant
			Civil Engineering
			Technician

Which person do you think has identified the best alternatives for a "CIR" personality style? Why?

All together, these four people have identified a total of ten alternatives. These alternatives vary in suitability for a "CIR" personality style. Below, these alternatives have been separated into categories labeled "good" and "poor." These alternatives are ranked on both suitability to the "CIR" personality style and on the job-market outlook.

The Five Best Alternatives		The Five Poorest Alternatives	
B$_1$	Medical Records Technician	P$_1$	Elementary Teacher
B$_2$	Management Analyst	P$_2$	Physical Education Instructor
B$_3$	Computer Programmer	P$_3$	Nurse
B$_4$	Civil Engineering Technician	P$_4$	Building Inspector
B$_5$	Accountant	P$_5$	Computer Operator
Note:			
B$_1$ = The best alternative		P$_1$ = The poorest alternative	
B$_2$ = The second best, etc.		P$_2$ = The second poorest, etc.	

Table 8.1
Sample Occupations for the "CIR" Personality Style

Rating	Occupation	Holland Code	Comments
B$_1$	Medical Records Technician	CIR	This is the best alternative. It represents the best Holland code match and the job-market demand for medical records technicians is excellent.
B$_2$	Management Analyst	ICR	This is the second-best Holland code match, and again, job-market demand is excellent.
B$_3$	Computer Programmer	IRC	This is the third-best Holland code match with a fair employment outlook.
B$_4$	Civil Engineering Technician	RIC	This is a good Holland code match with a fair job-market prospect.
B$_5$	Accountant	CSI	While the Holland code does not exactly match the example, with two out of the three letters the same, this would be a fairly good match. The employment outlook for accountants is fair.
P$_5$	Computer Operator	CSR	While the Holland code of this alternative matches fairly well, the employment outlook for computer operators is extremely poor as this occupation is fast becoming obsolete.

P_4	Building Inspector	RCE	The Holland code here matches fairly well. The occupational outlook is tied to the highs and lows of the construction industry, which are difficult to predict.
P_3	Nurse	SIA	While the job-market for nurses is fair, this Holland code is significantly different from the example.
P_2	Physical Education Instructor	SER	While this Holland code does share one letter with the example, it is a significantly different code. The employment outlook for this occupation is fair.
P_1	Elementary Teacher	SAE	This is rated as the poorest alternative since it has no Holland code letters in common with the example.

Assessing the Sample Options

Janet has identified only two alternatives, one in the "good" column ("B_5—Accountant") and the other "poor" ("P_5—Computer Operator"). As a consequence, Janet's "best" choice is only a moderately good ("B_5") alternative. Her list does not give her much to choose from.

Rodney's three alternatives can be ranked as follows:

B_3 for Computer Programmer

P_3 for Nurse

P_4 for Building Inspector

As a consequence of his alternative selection, the best pick that Rodney could make would be only slightly better than Janet's choice.

Tim has selected alternatives that can be ranked this way:

B_2 for Management Analyst

B_4 for Civil Engineering Technician

P_1 for Elementary Teacher

P_2 for Physical Education Instructor

Tim has more and better options than either Janet or Rodney. On the other hand, his list also contains the two poorest options identified on the overall list. If Tim makes a poor decision, he could end up even more dissatisfied than either Janet or Rodney.

Cynthia, through careful alternative assessment, has identified the five best alternatives on the total list. Accordingly, with a good pick, she could choose the one alternative capable of producing the greatest amount of eventual career satisfaction. Even with a poor selection, she would still be choosing from the "good" list.

BECOMING AWARE OF YOUR ALTERNATIVES

In real life it is difficult, or even impossible, to identify all of the best career alternatives for yourself. However, you will be able to find many alternatives leading to considerable career/life satisfaction by completing the following exercises. They are designed to use both your creative and logical abilities to find a large number of alternatives. The time for narrowing down your options will come later. For now, concentrate on finding your full range of winning career alternatives.

SEEKING CAREER ALTERNATIVES FROM FUNCTIONAL SKILLS

In Chapter 3, you listed your specific functional skills and figured out your top five preferred skills groups based on personal preference and feedback from others. A good way to begin developing your career alternatives is to review your favorite functional skills, brainstorming with others to discover what kinds of careers would welcome these capabilities. Brad, our case study from Chapter 7, used this process to begin developing his list of occupational alternatives.

Brad's Top Five Skills Groups were identified as follows:

1. Inventing/Developing New Ideas

2. Communicating/Teaching

3. Planning/Organizing Data

4. Analyzing/Evaluating/Researching

5. Investigating/Observing/Experimenting

Brad gave this list of preferred skills families, along with a copy of his specific skills list, to a small group of people. He asked them to come up with a list of possible occupations where these skills would

be used extensively. In just six minutes of brainstorming, the group came up with the following list of occupations:

scientist	patent investigator
lecturer	inventor
developer of training aids	trainer
	technical writer
learning lab director	campaign manager
investigative reporter	pollster
teacher	editor
researcher	speech writer
developer of textbooks, educational materials, and programs	lobbyist

Brad was interested in most of these career ideas. Imagine the list this group might have compiled if they had spent thirty minutes or more on the task instead of just six.

 EXERCISE 8-A. ENVISIONING PROCESS _____

1. Review your specific skills from Table 3.1 on page 37 in Chapter 3. Rank the top five of these skills, based on the skills you enjoy using the most. List the top five below.

_____

Note: Be sure to prioritize your list on the basis of those functional skills you now possess and prefer using. Do not list functional skills you lack but would like to possess.

_____

My Top Five Individual Functional Skills _____

1.

2.

3.

4.

5.

2. Use the envisioning process described in Appendix D to begin developing your list of career alternatives. To do this, set aside about one hour of time in which you will be alone and undisturbed. Then do the following:

   a. Review the envisioning process described in Appendix D.

   b. Review your top five skills (Chapter 3), your thinking style profile (Chapter 4), your personality style profile (Chapter 5), and your needs and values (Chapter 7).

   c. With these skills, needs, and preferences fresh in your mind, prepare to do the envisioning process by asking yourself: What kinds of careers might enable me to use my preferred skills and have the kind of life I want?

   d. Ask yourself this question several times. Can you picture yourself in the career(s) you are thinking about? Don't worry about whether you come up with anything or not. If the process doesn't work for you, go on to the other exercises.

   e. After you complete the envisioning process, immediately list below any thoughts or images that you had and record any occupations you come up with in Appendix A.

Notes on the Envisioning Process

_____

 EXERCISE 8-B. BRAINSTORMING WITH INDIVIDUALS _____

Getting input from other people is helpful for developing your career alternatives. A good technique is to record your ranked individual skills on a piece of paper. Then give your list to someone like a career counselor, a personnel officer, a job-placement specialist, or employers of people in several different occupations. Ask them to look these skills over at their convenience and to advise you of any occupations requiring these particular skills. It is not usually a good idea to use close family or friends in this process, since they often have preconceived ideas about what is best for you. If you do use family or friends, give them your list anonymously, at least until they have provided some ideas. Record other people's career suggestions in Appendix A.

_____

EXERCISE 8-C. GROUP BRAINSTORMING

Brainstorming in a group is also a very good way to generate a list of career alternatives. Your best bet here is to get a group of four to eight people together, preferably people familiar with occupations and transferable skills. Then display your top five specific skills and top five skills groups on a large piece of paper or on a chalkboard. Next, have the group brainstorm ideas and record their suggestions on a separate piece of paper. This process will work best if you are not present in the group at the time they are brainstorming with your list. In fact, this exercise works best if the group is unaware of whose skills they are working with. Record the group's suggestions below. Then select those that interest you, and list them in Appendix A2.

EXERCISE 8-D. THE GUIDE FOR OCCUPATIONAL EXPLORATION

This exercise calls for using a Department of Labor publication called *The Guide for Occupational Exploration* (GOE) to identify occupational alternatives. The GOE can be found in most college career centers and in most public libraries. The GOE can also be purchased from the Department of Labor, or at Amazon.com.

Web Connect

The *Occupational Outlook Handbook* at **www.bls.gov/oco/** can also be helpful with your research. It is a nationally recognized source of career information, designed to provide valuable assistance to individuals making decisions about their future work lives. Revised every two years, the Handbook describes what workers do on the job, working conditions, the training and education needed, earnings, and expected job prospects in a wide range of occupations. You may want to broaden your research by visiting the *Career Guide to Industries* at **http://www.bls.gov/oco/cg/home.htm**.

This companion piece to the OOH provides information on available careers by industry, including the nature of the industry, working conditions, employment, occupations in the industry, training and advancement, earnings and benefits, employment outlook, and lists of organizations that can provide additional information.

To complete this exercise, first read the directions in the beginning of the GOE on how to use it, and then follow these steps:

1. Identify interest areas to explore by reading the descriptions for all twelve interest areas at the beginning of the GOE. Record the name and number of each interest area that appeals to you.

	Interest Areas That Appeal to Me	Interest Area Number
Example:	Artistic	1

2. Explore the work groups within each interest area that appeal to you by completing the following steps.

   a. Open the GOE to the interest areas you have identified in #1 above, and read the general statement relating to that area.

   b. After reading that statement, if you are still interested, decide which of the work groups you want to explore. Record in Table 8.1 the work group and names you find interesting.

   c. Read each of the descriptions in the GOE for the work groups you have identified above. As you read the descriptions, answer the following questions:

   • Does this appear to be the type of work I would be interested in doing?

   • Is this kind of work compatible with my most preferred families of functional skills?

   • Do the activities I have done and enjoyed in the past suggest that I would enjoy or could do this type of work?

   • Does the preparation required for doing this kind of work appear to be something I am willing to do? For example, if it requires four years of education, am I now willing to go to college for that long?

   d. After answering the questions above, if that work group remains interesting to you, explore the subgroups for that work group.

   • Record occupations of interest to you, along with the corresponding nine-digit DOT number in the space provided below.

   • List all occupations that you think you would be interested in or are unfamiliar with.

   • Omit only those familiar occupations that do not interest you.

Example:	GOE Occupations of Interest	DOT#
	Industrial Designers	142.061.026

3. Select ten occupations of most interest to you from your GOE list and record these in Appendix A2.

Table 8.2 Occupational Exploration	
Interest Area	The Work Groups and Work Group Numbers I Wish to Explore within this Interest Area
Example: Artistic 01	Literary Arts 01.01 Visual Arts 01.02

EXERCISE 8-E. COMPUTERIZED ASSISTANCE

A number of excellent computerized programs are available today to identify career possibilities. Computerized systems like DISCOVER, SIGI PLUS, CHOICES, CIS, FOCUS, etc., are available in most college career-planning centers. Some are available online for a small cost. If you have access to a computerized system, use it to identify additional career possibilities. Add these choices to your list on Appendix A2.

DECISION-MAKING TIME

Now that you have identified at least 30 to 40 alternatives, it's time to begin narrowing down the list to select your best choice. Your first step is to eliminate all but the best ten from your list. Then you will research your "top ten" to learn more about these fields to decide which one is your very best choice.

Figure 8.1 illustrates the steps in this process. Notice that the process shown here leads either to a tentative or a definite choice. Sometimes it is appropriate to make tentative choices when you have narrowed your list down to two or three choices but need more time to further explore these choices before making a final commitment.

A tentative choice, as we use it here, is different from the avoidance behavior of not deciding. A tentative choice involves allotting yourself time to explore specific options that you have identified. A tentative choice is particularly appropriate for a beginning college student who has the luxury of time to explore before needing to make a final choice.

Career changers rarely have that luxury, however, and will need to use this process to make a

> ### Web Connect
>
> *California State University* has developed a user-friendly decision-making model on its web site at **http://www.csulb.edu/~tstevens/c15-carp.htm** Once you get to this site, click on "Step 4: Make a Decision" for a different approach to help you make a career decision.

definite decision. The good news is that career changers usually have more experience and self-knowledge to draw upon for a definite choice.

Following are two case studies to illustrate definite versus tentative decision making. The first example is that of Brad, a career changer described in Chapter 6. The second is Julie, a younger college student.

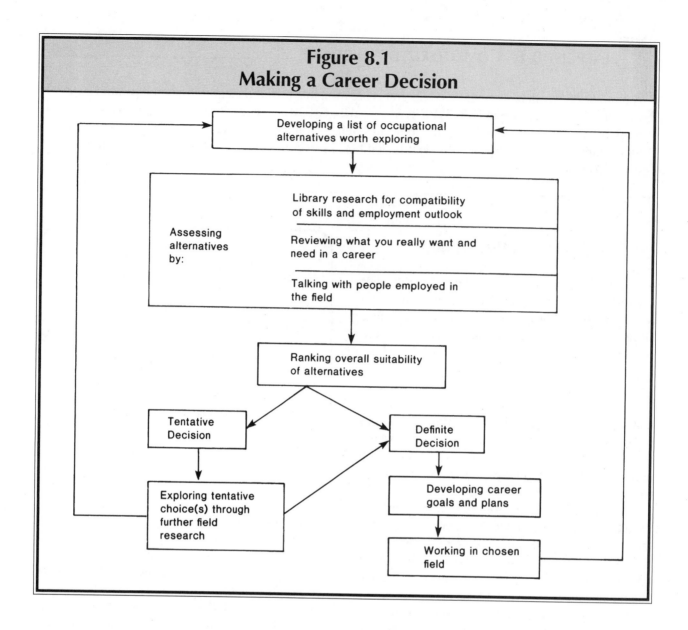

**Figure 8.1
Making a Career Decision**

Developing a list of occupational alternatives worth exploring

Assessing alternatives by:

Library research for compatibility of skills and employment outlook

Reviewing what you really want and need in a career

Talking with people employed in the field

Ranking overall suitability of alternatives

Tentative Decision

Definite Decision

Exploring tentative choice(s) through further field research

Developing career goals and plans

Working in chosen field

CASE STUDY
BRAD

Brad was confronted with a major crisis when he lost the job he had held for over ten years. With career-counseling assistance, Brad discovered that his personality style was incompatible with his previous job and career. He learned that his preferred families of skills were in the innovating, creative planning, writing, and teaching areas. Based on self-assessment, Brad developed a lengthy list of suitable alternatives and then narrowed the list down to the following:

Psychology
Counseling
Public relations/advertising
Cartooning
Journalism
College teaching

These were so appealing that Brad couldn't make any further instinctive decisions. He was advised to learn all he could about these occupations. Primarily, Brad accomplished this task through study of occupational literature and by identifying and talking with people working in fields he found interesting. He got their names from various directories and from friends and acquaintances. Initially, conducting these interviews was hard for Brad. He vividly recalls his tension and sweaty palms as he prepared to go talk with people.

Brad soon found, however, that if he called in advance, was considerate about people's time, and was straightforward about his purpose, most people really enjoyed talking with him about their work. Eventually, Brad started enjoying these information interviews. Best of all, he began learning what it would really be like to pursue a career in these kinds of occupations. At his counselor's suggestion, Brad carefully wrote down his observations and reactions from each of these information interviews immediately after conducting them. These notes were far more valuable than vague memories when he prepared to make his decision.

In conducting these interviews, Brad found that different people in the same occupation had completely different ideas and perspectives about the field. He realized how important it was to discuss the same occupation with several people. He learned, too, that there are wide ranges of differences within an occupation depending on the work setting. He also acquired a much better appreciation of what work settings were most likely to be hiring in the future, what settings offered the best advancement opportunities, and what settings had the best salary and benefits programs.

After completing these interviews, Brad reviewed what he had learned from his field research about outcomes he could expect if he pursued various careers. He also reaffirmed that what he wanted most in a career was to be associated with people he liked, to continue learning and using his knowledge, and to develop creative methods for helping adults live more satisfying lives. Based on what he had learned, Brad chose counseling in a community college as his best career alternative.

Brad recalls both the relief and exhilaration that accompanied this selection. He knew that he still had to establish his specific career goals and develop his implementation plans, but he also realized what a giant step he had taken towards creating a new and satisfying career. Later, when Brad's needs changed again, he became aware of new suitable career alternatives available to him. This placed him in a new decision situation.

His experience in the decision-making process benefited Brad in many ways. First, he learned how to make career-choice decisions more effectively and easily than ever before. Secondly, he learned to view his career as a lifelong process. As a result, he could recognize new alternatives and opportunities when they arose. He was also far more inclined to act on these opportunities.

CASE STUDY
JULIE

Julie, a gregarious young woman, graduated from high school with absolutely no idea of what she wanted to do, other than to go on to college. In high school she had acquired a large group of friends and concentrated on having fun. Julie was intelligent, attractive, and sociable, but she just had never discovered anything in school that really engaged her serious interests.

After graduating from high school, Julie decided to pursue a general studies curriculum at the local community college until she discovered a compelling career interest. After taking general elective requirements during her freshman year, she enrolled in a career planning course. In that course she discovered that she had skills, interests, and values that she had never really thought about before. She realized, for instance, that she had excellent communication skills, which enabled her to establish rapport, make excellent presentations, sell her ideas, and entertain others. She was also an excellent organizer and planner when it involved some activity that really interested her. She realized that she enjoyed helping others and that she wanted to have a balance between family and career. A job that involved performing a useful service to others, perhaps to children, was appealing.

In the course, she identified about forty career possibilities, including many she had never considered or heard of before. Eventually she narrowed this list down to three: teaching, psychology, and communications. She felt unwilling to commit to any one of these at that time. She needed more information and some related experience to eliminate alternatives from this list she felt enthusiastic about. She found out that each of these choices was a broad field in itself. What age groups did she want to work with? What types of organizations were appealing? What particular work settings did she want? If she decided on teaching, for example, what age group did she want to work with? Did she want to go into special education, elementary education, or learn a specific subject matter to teach in a high school, college, or business setting?

With the help of a career counselor, Julie worked out a plan of action that would enable her to explore all three areas and cover her bases until she was ready for a definite career commitment. She selected an arts and science major that enabled her to meet the general education requirements for each of the three fields. She also selected introductory courses in psychology, education, and communications to sample these subject areas and get a clearer idea of how her skills, interests, and energies would be useful.

In addition, Julie decided to participate in extracurricular activities that allowed her to express her interests and develop the skills she now knew she wanted to use in her career. These activities included being in a college play, working as a technical assistant in the college media department, participating in the readers' theater, taking voice lessons, and trying out for and making the college forensics team. As a team member she won numerous awards and traveled across the country.

Upon obtaining her associate-in-arts degree from the community college, Julie decided to transfer to the University of Iowa. Based on her previous activities and course work, Julie decided to major in communications. At Iowa, Julie took advantage of work/learning experiences that included working with a local radio station, where she learned marketing activities and even got to develop and record a short advertisement. During the summer, she obtained an internship with PBS, where she became familiar with the research, marketing, and management areas of a large TV and radio operation. In her senior year in college, Julie is continuing to broaden her experience by working as a production assistant with the college cable TV station. She is also refining her resume and setting up job interviews through the college career planning and placement office.

Julie still wonders sometimes whether she has made the right choice. She occasionally catches herself thinking, "Maybe I should become a child psychologist or a speech teacher." She is now content to try out her career choice in communications and to gain some experience and wisdom in the "real world." She realizes also that she is young and that she can make a career change in the future. She is not afraid of that prospect because she now knows a useful decision-making process and intends to use this process continually throughout her life. She knows that at some point in the future she will want to go on for a masters degree. For now, she wants to become financially independent and learn about herself and her possibilities on the job.

NARROWING DOWN

Throughout the course of this book you have identified a number of occupations from the various exercises and recorded these in Appendix A2. Now it is time to narrow that list down to the best ones for you. The goal is to select from this list the ten best choices for you and your unique interests, skills, and values.

Begin by crossing out those that are not particularly interesting or not practical for your situation. For example, you might aspire to be a jockey but are

6'2" and weigh 240 pounds. Or perhaps you want to become a psychiatrist but are not up to the ten years of education and training that would entail. Next, eliminate duplicate entries that have been entered with slightly different names.

Once you have cleaned up your list, reduce the number further by assigning Holland codes to the remainder and eliminating any obvious mismatches. This process will enable you to weed out not only the poor choices (the Ps) on your list, but also some seemingly appropriate choices that wouldn't work out in the long run.

HOLLAND CODING YOUR CAREER ALTERNATIVES

From your work in Chapters 5 and 6, you will recall that people have characteristic personality styles and that occupations can also be classified by 3-letter Holland codes. By comparing your own Holland code with the Holland codes of these occupations, you can determine how compatible an occupation is with your particular interests and personality style.

1. Refer now to that portion of Appendix A2 entitled *Career Possibilities*. Under the column heading *Occupations of Interest* you have listed career alternatives based on insights obtained from the assessments you completed in Chapters 3, 4, and 5 and exercises included in this chapter. Identify the Holland code, as best you can, for each of the occupations on your list and place it in the adjacent column under the heading *Holland Code*. If necessary, review the information in Chapter 5 that relates to the Holland coding of occupations. Six examples are provided below to assist you in your identification.

Occupations	Holland Code		
Examples:			
Newspaper Reporter	A	S	I
Medical Laboratory Technician	I	R	E
Architectural Drafter	R	C	I
Office Manager	E	S	R
Accountant	C	S	I
Secondary Teacher	S	A	E

In the first example, newspaper reporter, "A" is listed as the primary letter, since a reporter's primary function involves the process of creative writing. The second letter is "S" because a reporter needs to develop rapport with people in order to obtain essential information from them. Thirdly, a reporter needs to be a problem solver of the "I" kind.

Here are two additional sources of help in identifying Holland codes:

• *The Career Options Finder,* which comes with the Self-Directed Search (SDS). Look for this resource in the career library.

• *Dictionary of Holland Occupational Codes,* 3rd ed., Psychological Assessment Resources, Inc., P.O. Box 998, Odessa, Florida 33556.

2. After Holland coding each of your occupations, decide which are compatible with your personality style.

My Holland code is _____

3. If an occupation has none of the three letters that are contained in your Holland code, you may wish to delete that alternative from your list. For example, your Holland code is an ASI, and an occupation on your list has a CER code. That occupation is likely to be a very poor match for you.

• If an occupation has one letter that is the same as a letter in your Holland code, you will need to decide whether to keep that occupation on your list or not. For example, your code is ASI, and an occupation on your list is CSE. If you have no interest in the occupation, you may want to delete it. On the other hand, if you are uncertain about it, retain the alternative for further consideration.

• Be sure to retain for further exploration any occupations that share two or three letters in common with your Holland code. For example, if your code is an ASI, you should retain occupations with codes such as SAI, SIA, IAS, ISA, SEA, ASE, SIR, and IAR.

4. After completing your assessment, record the ten best occupational alternatives that are compatible with your Holland code on Table 8.2, page 168. List your alternatives under the column headed *Career Alternative,* and leave all of the remaining columns blank for now. You will learn how to fill in that information later.

EXPLORING YOUR TOP TEN

Now that you have identified your ten best career matches, you will need to apply the information you have already discovered about yourself and to acquire additional information about your ten selections. Table 8.2 on page 168 has been designed to facilitate this process and contains a numbering system to support your assessments. The following exercises will guide your assessments and information searches to find your best and most compatible alternative. The information search will help you find crucial information about the employment outlooks of your top ten matches. The process begins by assessing how each of your "top ten" will enable you to use your "most preferred" transferable skills.

 ## EXERCISE 8-F. TRANSFERABLE SKILL ASSESSMENT

Review your transferable skill assessments from Exercise 7-A and from Chapter 2, deciding which skills are essential for you to use in your work. Rank these skills below, starting with the most important.

The Individual Transferable Skills My Work Must Have
My most preferred skill is
1.
2.
3.
4.
5.

1. Study the descriptions in the *Dictionary of Occupational Titles* (DOT) and O*NET for each of the alternatives you listed on Table 8.3. Notice that the DOT provides concise descriptions of several thousand occupations. As you read the DOT descriptions pertaining to your alternatives, identify what functional skills are involved in these occupations, and record them in the appropriate subsection under the *Brief Description* column of Table 8.3. The O*NET can be accessed on the Internet at http://online.onetcenter.org/

2. After identifying the skills involved in each of your occupational alternatives, compare these with the skills you identified above as being essential in your work. Using the following scale, rate how well the skills involved in each occupation match your preferred functional skills. In the *Skills Rating* Column A of Table 8.3, list from the scale below the rating that most accurately evaluates the compatibility.

Rating

5 Would enable me to use all my preferred skills fully.

4 Would enable me to use most of my preferred skills to a considerable degree.

3 Would enable me to use some, but not all, of my preferred skills to some extent.

2 Would not enable me to use my most preferred skills, but would enable me to use my secondary skills to a considerable extent.

1 Would not enable me to use any of my preferred skills to any extent.

? Unsure how well this occupation would enable me to use my preferred skills. I need more information than the DOT provides.

3. In the *My Evaluation* column of Table 8.2, record any other information you may wish to remember about these occupations. Record any insights you discover about specific responsibilities and/or duties that are particularly appealing or unappealing to you.

Note: If you cannot locate a particular occupation in the DOT, get assistance from someone familiar with the publication. The occupation is likely to be listed under a different subject heading. If, however, your alternative is not listed in the DOT, you may need to seek other sources of occupational information.

EXERCISE 8-G. IDENTIFYING YOUR CAREER-RELATED NEEDS, WANTS, AND VALUES

Your next step in narrowing the options is to review what you really need and value in your career and life. Review your *What Motivates Me* exercises in Chapter 6 to refresh your memory about your primary values. Then consider the following:

1. Do these priorities still seem accurate? If not, what has changed, or what new insights have you acquired?

2. From your review, decide what is the single most important value in your career, and list that below. Then decide what are the second, third, fourth, and fifth most important characteristics you value in your career, and list them below as well.

   The most important thing I need, value, or want in my career is . . .

   The second most important thing . . .

   The third most . . .

   The fourth most . . .

   The fifth most . . .

After completing your employment outlook research along with your information interviews, you'll be ready to evaluate how well your occupational alternatives will satisfy these values.

ASSESSING COMPATIBILITY AND EMPLOYMENT OUTLOOK

In an age of choice, it would certainly be a mistake to select an occupation simply because it offers excellent employment prospects, especially since these can change. It would be equally a mistake, however, to select a suitable occupation without determining whether you have a reasonable chance of finding employment in that field.

To find the employment outlook of any career alternative, you can check occupational literature or obtain firsthand information from people in the field. These methods have some shortcomings, however. The job market changes so rapidly that printed occupational information quickly becomes outdated. People in the field often have more current information, but they may also have a biased view of the employment outlook. For these reasons, we strongly advocate that you use both recent occupational literature and information interviews.

A major printed source of occupational information is the *Occupational Outlook Handbook* (OOH). In addition to the print version, the OOH can be accessed on the Internet at http://stats.bls.gov/ocohome.htm. Be sure to use only the most recent issue of the OOH, which is updated every two years. Then keep its limitations in mind. OOH information is national in scope, so the situation in your local area or the area in which you wish to work may be different. Also, the OOH provides information about expected openings in an occupational field, but it does not tell you how many people may currently be preparing for a career in that field. The OOH does, however, provide an excellent general description of an occupational field and the best national employment-outlook information.

 EXERCISE 8-H. STUDYING OCCUPATIONAL LITERATURE _____

For this exercise, you will obtain information about employment outlook and your personal/occupational compatibility for each of your alternatives. The OOH will be your primary source.

1. Study each of the alternatives on your list that you can find in the OOH. You may not always be able to find information about a particular occupation you are exploring in the OOH. In such cases, you may want to go to other sources of occupational information found in most college career centers.

2. Review the self-insights you have listed on Appendix A1. With this information in mind, read the OOH. Evaluate how well each of the occupational alternatives you are exploring coincides with your own personal attributes. To what extent will each alternative fulfill what you need, want, and value?

3. In the *My Evaluation* section of Table 8.2, record what you learned about each occupation, along with your impressions of how appropriate you think it would be for you. Again, be sure to make your comments clear and complete enough to refer to later and know what you meant.

4. Note and record in the *My Evaluation* section of Table 8.2 the OOH employment outlook information for the next five years for each of the occupations you are exploring.

EXERCISE 8-I. CONDUCTING INFORMATION INTERVIEWS _____

The best sources of information you are likely to find are people working in the fields that interest you. These people can offer comments on employment outlook in their locality. They can also give you more detailed information about working conditions in their field to help you decide how well that kind of work suits you. A good way of locating these people is to ask your acquaintances if they know anyone involved in these fields. If they do not, perhaps they might know someone who might know and could give you a referral. Another good way of finding information is to call relevant companies and associations listed in the Yellow Pages of a city telephone directory. Ask for the Public Information Office and explain what information you're seeking. Another way to find people is through trade and professional associations. Many of these organizations have web sites or publications that provide an overview of the profession. Contact information for members in various geographic areas is also available. These associations can be found by using the National Trade and Professional Associations of the United States found at many career centers and libraries. The Federal Consumer Information Center also offers a list of some consumer related web sites at their site at www.pueblo.gsa.gov/crh/trade.htm

1. Use the guidelines in Appendix C to conduct your interviews. Be sure to record your impressions and thoughts immediately after conducting the interview, while it is still fresh in your mind. If you wait, you are likely to forget.

2. As you conduct your information-gathering interviews, be sure to talk to more than a single person in a field. You are likely to find that one person's views are too biased to give you an accurate reflection of that occupation. Also, as you seek out information sources, find people who have been in that field long enough to have fully experienced it. That usually takes three years or more. You will also want to ensure that you are not talking only with people who are very unhappy in their work. Remember that an unhappy person may be misplaced in the field or "burned out," having done the same job too long. Even though that person is dissatisfied, the field involved might be perfect for you.

3. After conducting your interviews, record your overall assessment of the occupational alternatives in the *Brief Description* section of Table 8.2.

EXERCISE 8-J. COMPLETING THE CAREER ASSESSMENT TABLE _____

After having obtained the data you need about occupational compatibility and employment outlook for Table 8.2, use your accumulated information to determine your best occupational alternative. To help you make this choice, we have provided an evaluation scale (Table 8.3 page 180) to assign numerical ratings to your alternatives.

1. Review the comments you have recorded in the *Brief Description* and *My Evaluation* sections of Table 8.2. Then use the evaluation scale to find suitable numerical ratings for personality style, occupational compatibility with what you want/need in a career, and employment outlook. Fill in Columns B, C, and D of Table 8.2.

2. After assigning your numerical ratings, add the scores on Table 8.2 from Columns A, B, C, and D for each of your occupations. Put the resulting score in the *Cumulative Score* column. Having computed this total for each occupational alternative, you will have a handy numerical guide for determining which of your alternatives is best.

3. Look down your *Cumulative Score* column to determine which alternative received the highest rating. Write "#1" in the *Overall Suitability* column for that alternative to indicate that this is probably your best overall choice. Write "#2" in the *Overall Suitability* column for the alternative that received the next highest score. Continue ranking all of your alternatives in this manner.

Table 8.3 Developing and Assessing Your Career Alternatives

Career Alternative	Brief Description	Compatability Ratings 1–5 scale (low–high)						My Evaluation
		A	B	C	D			
DOT, O*NET # (if available)	From Computer, DOT, Internet, Interview, O*NET, OOH	Transferable Skills	Personality Style	Needs, Wants, Values	Employment Outlook	Cumulative Score	Overall Suitability	What I like most and least
EXAMPLE: Human Resources Specialist— Training 166.227-010	Assess client training needs. Plan, organize, develop and direct training programs to meet needs. Conduct orientations and job training for new hires. Promote employee development. Evaluate training programs.	4	3	5	2	14	#5	Excellent match for my values and thinking style. Will enable me to use most of my best skills and to design programs and develop materials, which I love. Competitive job outlook. Lack interest in directing others and following detailed plans.

Table 8.3	Developing and Assessing Your Career Alternatives *(continued)*								
Career Alternative	*Brief Description*	*Compatability Ratings* *1–5 scale (low–high)*							*My Evaluation*
		A	B	C	D				
		Transferable Skills	Personality Style	Needs, Wants, Values	Employment Outlook	Cumulative Score	Overall Suitability		
DOT, O*NET# (if available)	From Computer, DOT, Internet, Interview, O*NET, OOH								What I like most and least

Table 8.3	Developing and Assessing Your Career Alternatives *(continued)*								
Career Alternative	*Brief Description*	*Compatability Ratings* *1–5 scale (low–high)*							*My Evaluation*
		A	B	C	D				
DOT, O*NET # (if available)	From Computer, DOT, Internet, Interview, O*NET, OOH	Transferable Skills	Personality Style	Needs, Wants, Values	Employment Outlook	Cumulative Score	Overall Suitability		What I like most and least

Career Alternative	Brief Description	Compatability Ratings 1–5 scale (low–high)						My Evaluation
		A	B	C	D			
		Transferable Skills	Personality Style	Needs, Wants, Values	Employment Outlook	Cumulative Score	Overall Suitability	
DOT, O*NET # (if available)	From Computer, DOT, Internet, Interview, O*NET, OOH							What I like most and least

Table 8.3   Developing and Assessing Your Career Alternatives *(continued)*

Table 8.3	Developing and Assessing Your Career Alternatives *(continued)*								
Career Alternative	*Brief Description*	*Compatability Ratings* 1–5 scale (low–high)							*My Evaluation*
		A	B	C	D			
		Transferable Skills	Personality Style	Needs, Wants, Values	Employment Outlook	Cumulative Score	Overall Suitability	
DOT, O*NET # (if available)	From Computer, DOT, Internet, Interview, O*NET, OOH							What I like most and least

Table 8.3	**Developing and Assessing Your Career Alternatives** *(continued)*								
Career Alternative	*Brief Description*	*Compatability Ratings 1–5 scale (low–high)*							*My Evaluation*
		A	B	C	D				
DOT, O*NET # (if available)	From Computer, DOT, Internet, Interview, O*NET, OOH	Transferable Skills	Personality Style	Needs, Wants, Values	Employment Outlook	Cumulative Score	Overall Suitability		What I like most and least

	Table 8.4		
	Evaluation Scale for Personal/Occupational Compatibility and Employment Outlook		
Rating Score	The likelihood that your Holland code would be compatible to the Holland code of that occupation	The likelihood of fulfilling your most important wants and needs in that occupation	The likelihood that you will be able to obtain employment in that occupation
	Column B on Table 8.2	Column C on Table 8.2	Column D on Table 8.2
5	My Holland code is a perfect match since all three letters are similar and in the same order	Better than a 75% probability	Considerably more job openings than qualified applicants in the location you've chosen
4	My Holland code is a good match since all three letters are similar but not in the same order	Less than a 75% chance, but almost certainly better than a 50% chance	More job openings than qualified applicants in the location you've chosen
3	My Holland code is a fair match since two out of three letters are similar	About a 50% probability	Number of job openings about the same as number of qualified applicants in the location you've chosen
2	My Holland code is a poor match since only one letter is similar	Less than a 50% chance	Fewer job openings than qualified applicants/stiff competition for available jobs in the location you've chosen
1	My Holland code is a very poor match with no letters in common	Highly unlikely to no chance at all	Far fewer job openings than qualified applicants in the location you've chosen and/or occupation becoming obsolete

EXERCISE 8-K. DECISION CHECK LIST

The following check list will assist you in making your decision.

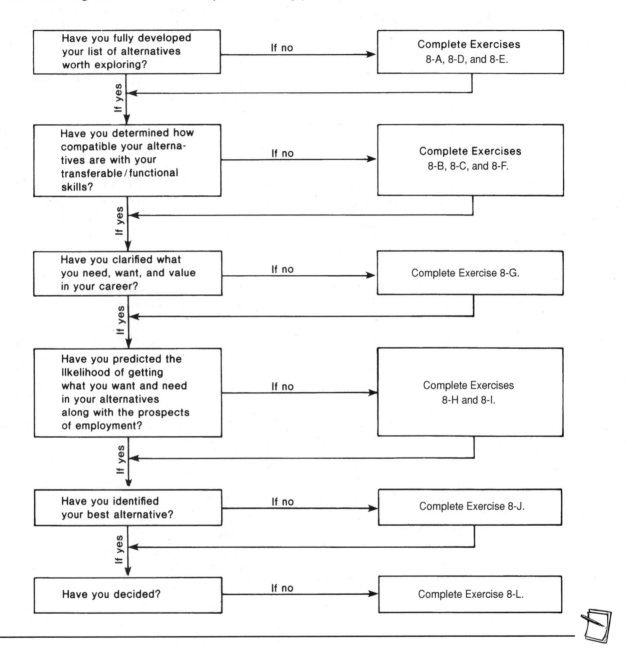

Have you fully developed your list of alternatives worth exploring?	If no →	Complete Exercises 8-A, 8-D, and 8-E.
↓ If yes		
Have you determined how compatible your alternatives are with your transferable / functional skills?	If no →	Complete Exercises 8-B, 8-C, and 8-F.
↓ If yes		
Have you clarified what you need, want, and value in your career?	If no →	Complete Exercise 8-G.
↓ If yes		
Have you predicted the likelihood of getting what you want and need in your alternatives along with the prospects of employment?	If no →	Complete Exercises 8-H and 8-I.
↓ If yes		
Have you identified your best alternative?	If no →	Complete Exercise 8-J.
↓ If yes		
Have you decided?	If no →	Complete Exercise 8-L.

MAKING A DEFINITE DECISION

Having completed Exercise 8-K, you are probably in one of the following circumstances:

1. By clearly identifying your best choice through your assessments, you have chosen a career to pursue. Go on to the section of this chapter entitled *Deciding and Taking Responsibility.*

2. Numerically you've identified your best choice, but you don't feel quite ready to decide.

3. You may have one choice with the highest numerical rating, but you're not sure that rating is accurate. Or you may have two or more choices that are so close numerically that you have a difficult time deciding which is the best option.

Note: An alternative is a good choice even if it only provided scores of 3 or better in all four columns A, B, C, and D of Table 8.2.

4. All your assessments have such low cumulative scores that you doubt that any of them are wise choices.

5. You feel frustrated because the alternative you prefer most has poor employment prospects (a low score in Column D).

If you find yourself in situation 2 above, you are probably close to selecting that alternative as your definite choice. However, it might be helpful to clarify what you would need to do in order to feel comfortable about deciding. What should you do if you find yourself in situation 3, 4, or 5 above? These are tentative decision situations. For situation 3, you need to consider the time you have available to choose. Depending upon your time, you might want to do limited or considerable field research in the occupation(s) involved to obtain sufficient firsthand information before making a definite decision.

Should you find yourself in situation 4 or 5 above, ask yourself whether you've missed an alternative or alternatives that would provide a more promising outlook. If so, it would be well worth your while to spend some more time developing additional alternatives. If you are fairly certain, however, that you have already identified the alternatives that interest you most, your task becomes somewhat more difficult. Your best bet is to look for any alternatives that provide a cumulative score of 12 or better on Table 8.2. If you have one or more alternatives in this category, decide which consideration—skills compatibility (Column A), compatibility with your personality style (Column B), wants/needs preference (Column C), or employment outlook (Column D)—is most important to you. Then pick the best alternative with this in mind.

If you decide on an alternative with a poor employment outlook, we strongly encourage you to develop your job-hunting skills by studying Chapter 11. Even in a tough job market, there are almost always jobs available somewhere. However, job openings in crowded fields are unlikely to be listed anywhere. Usually the person with the best job-hunting skills rather than the best talents gets hired for these jobs.

DEALING WITH A TENTATIVE DECISION

In some situations it is very difficult to come to a definite decision. Perhaps you lack the information, experience, and/or time needed to make a realistic decision. In such cases, it might be best to remain temporarily in your present employment situation if you are working, or to pursue a general studies curriculum if you are in college. Meanwhile, acquire further insight and experience with one of your better alternatives. You may want to explore several appealing alternatives, one at a time. Some good ways to explore a tentative decision are discussed below in *Need for Field Research.*

CASE STUDY
CAROL

Carol serves as an example of a tentative decision maker. She completed the decision-making process defined in this text, but felt that she could not make a definite career choice because of financial circumstances. She was interested in several art-related careers, but was unsure of her talent in these areas.

She was reluctant, therefore, to quit her job and go back to school full time to study. Accordingly, she decided to remain in her current secretarial job, maintaining her financial security, while exploring the art-related careers. She decided to accomplish this by enrolling in studio art courses at a nearby college. At the same time, she will be interviewing many people in art fields to obtain information about the art careers and about the job market. If Carol discovers that she does have marketable talent and finds the job market promising, she will then definitely choose an art career. In the meantime, she has the security of her present job. She also knows that if her pursuit of an art career does not work out, she still has other interesting alternatives to explore.

EXERCISE 8-L. EXPLORING TENTATIVE CHOICES

What can you learn from the previous example of Carol that you can apply to your own decision-making situation?

List those career alternatives that appear about equally suitable right now. Divide these into the following categories, according to which alternatives you find most appealing.

The Alternatives That I Am Most Interested in Right Now	*The Options I Am Less Certain about Right Now*

Once you have identified the alternatives you want to explore now, decide your best method by answering the following questions:

1. Which alternative am I inclined to investigate first?

2. How much time can I realistically give myself to explore that option?

3. Given the above time consideration, what are the best ways I can explore this alternative?

4. What will I need most to learn about myself in this exploration?

5. What will I need most to find out about the job market and the career field in this exploration?

6. Are there any other things I need to do or keep in mind while undertaking this exploration?

7. If my exploration suggests that this alternative would not be a good choice, which alternative should I explore next? Have I meanwhile discovered other interesting alternatives missing from my original list?

Further Field Research for Tentative Decision Makers

The best way to explore your options further is through firsthand experience. If you must complete your exploration in a brief time, your best bet is simply to talk to as many people as you can who are working in your fields of interest. Follow the guidelines of Appendix C for these information interviews. If, on the other hand, you have enough time to conduct a thorough exploration, consider some or all of the following methods:

1. Interning involves spending time with people working in a field you find appealing to observe directly the nature of their work, their duties, and their responsibilities. This method lets you experience a typical day of a person working in a particular career. As you can imagine, this kind of investigation can be more revealing than just asking people what their work is like. Formal internships include collegiate work/learning experiences.

2. Volunteer work is also an excellent way of both gaining realistic insight and acquiring general work experience. You can obtain valuable job references and sometimes salaried job offers in the process. Many organizations are happy to use the services of a volunteer worker, particularly when the individual has enthusiasm along with some knowledge of the area.

3. Part-time or temporary work is another excellent way to acquire firsthand experience in an occupational field. You probably

won't get a paid, part-time or temporary job in the position you really are interested in. However, you can often acquire a lower-level job in the general field. In addition to getting a job reference, you'll be in a position to find out whether you would enjoy working in that particular field.

Your main goal in any kind of field research is to find out how appropriate an occupation would be for you. It is helpful to answer relevant questions as you explore the alternatives. Among the questions to consider are:

1. What specific kinds of information will I need to learn for this field?

2. Would pursuing a career in this field get me closer to what I really want in my career?

3. What are the least appealing aspects of a career in this field?

4. What are the most appealing aspects of a career in this field?

DECIDING AND TAKING RESPONSIBILITY

If you have followed the career/life decision-making model to this point, you have made a decision. Consider for a moment what a decision is and is not.

Your decision is not:

- ☑ someone else's responsibility

- ☑ the option you fell into or had to choose because there was nothing else to choose from

- ☑ a perfect choice that will make your life wonderful forever

- ☑ likely to be the last decision you will ever have to make about your career

Your decision is:

- ☑ fully your responsibility and no one else's

- ☑ made from among alternatives that you clearly identified and investigated

- ☑ your best alternative given your self-knowledge and your available options

- ☑ likely to create new decision situations that will enable you to continue freely making choices and taking charge of your career

Congratulations! Your decision is probably the very best one that you can make at this time. If your needs change later or the outcomes of your decision do not seem to be getting you closer to what you want, remember that you can make a new decision at that time. This is the freedom associated with "taking charge."

SUMMARY

To come to a satisfactory decision about your career, you look for a match between self-insights and your identified choices. This process starts with a systematic assessment of your skills and the skills required by your occupational alternatives. Next, clarify your career needs, wants, and values to determine which of your alternatives are most likely to fulfill these. By studying the employment outlook, you can assess which of your alternatives will provide the best employment prospects. Once you have acquired and compiled this information, you are usually ready to make a realistic decision. A realistic decision offers a high probability of obtaining employment, achieving satisfaction, and being productive in your career.

Career/life decision making is a unique experience for everyone. Because no two people are the same, no two people are likely to come to the same decision after completing the same process. No two people are likely, either, to complete the process in the same amount of time. Some people complete the entire process and reach a definite decision in just a few weeks of concentrated work. Others may need many months to complete the process. It is far preferable to take the time you need to make a realistic decision than to hurry through the process and make a poor decision.

If you have completed the career/life decision-making model, you can have confidence that you have made a good decision, either tentative or definite. Having learned this process, you can use it whenever you are faced with major career/life decisions. While the model has been used in this book to make career decisions, it can be used to make other major life decisions.

ASSIGNMENT

The following situations are provided for you to consider how willing you are to make and implement a career decision in the face of typical pressures people often experience. Answer the following questions candidly, telling how you really believe you would respond in each situation.

1. You decide on a career that really interests you, but others are discouraging your plans, saying that only men/women do that kind of work. (Example: You are a woman deciding to pursue electrical engineering or a man deciding on a secretarial career.) What would you do or say?

2. After pursuing a career for many years, you decide at age forty-nine to return to college to prepare for a new career. People around you call your decision a mistake. They say you should stay with what you are doing because of your age, and besides, you're too old to go to college. How would you handle that?

3. In completing this workbook, you decide that a career in an enterprising field (E) is exactly what you want, but your parents, spouse, or friends try to pressure you into a career in an investigative (I) area. How would you respond to them?

4. You are a thirty-four-year-old housewife whose children no longer require constant personal care. You decide to return to college to begin preparing for a new career. Your spouse, friends, and/or family strongly discourage you from that, arguing that a mother and wife's role is in the home. How would you answer? What would you do?

5. Although you like your job, you decide to retire early to begin doing some of those things you have always planned but have never accomplished. Friends and associates tell you that you are foolish to quit a job you like and that people generally are not very happy in retirement. What would you do and why?

6. You have gotten into a career you dislike, but it offers good benefits and a high salary. Based on what you learned from career planning, you know you want to make a career change. But the career you want requires further education or training. Your family, friends, and/or acquaintances say you are foolish to give up your job benefits just to pursue something you are interested in. How would you respond? What would you do?

Notes

For further information on personal/occupational compatibility refer to the following web sites:

1. www.uhs.berkeley.edu/Students/CareerLibrary/links/career.cfm
   This site provides a wide range of links to other web sites highlighting occupational information and educational programs. Of particular note is information of special interest to multicultural populations.
2. http://www.review.com/career/index.cfm
   This site features occupational information presented in a creative format featuring lively descriptions. When you get to the site, click on "investigate careers" under the "learn and discover" section.

The only print form of the O*Net Dictionary of Occupational Titles is available from Jist Works, Indianapolis, Indiana, March 1998.

Setting Goals and Planning Your Career

*Control starts with planning. Planning is bringing the future into
the present so that we can do something about it now.*
—Alan Lakein
How to Get Control of Your Time and Your Life

Do you know people who—

- ☑ Have careers that suffer today because they failed to plan adequately yesterday?
- ☑ Are so focused on future goals that they neglect the present?
- ☑ Set objectives and then just expect them to happen?
- ☑ Have lives that have been made inflexible by overly detailed plans?
- ☑ Plan without realistically taking future conditions into consideration?

If so, you know people who do not effectively use goal setting and planning to take charge of their careers and lives.

THE FUTURE IN PERSPECTIVE

Futurists maintain that through collective actions, everyone participates in creating the future. Thus, the decisions made in the present will determine the shape of the future world.[1] The validity of this statement is most dramatically proved through historical examples. For instance, President Kennedy and others decided in the early 1960s to place a man on the moon by the end of that decade. This decision ushered in the space age along with such major technological advances as spacecraft design, rocket fuels, space medicine, computerized information, and communication satellites.

Today people take for granted the resulting changes in society, including instantaneous, low-cost communication with countries all over the world, immediate access to information that used to take months to compile, and simultaneous television viewing of live events, such as the Olympic Games, via space satellite.

Unfortunately, historical examples also prove society's capacity to warp the future. When the decision was made to develop and use the atomic

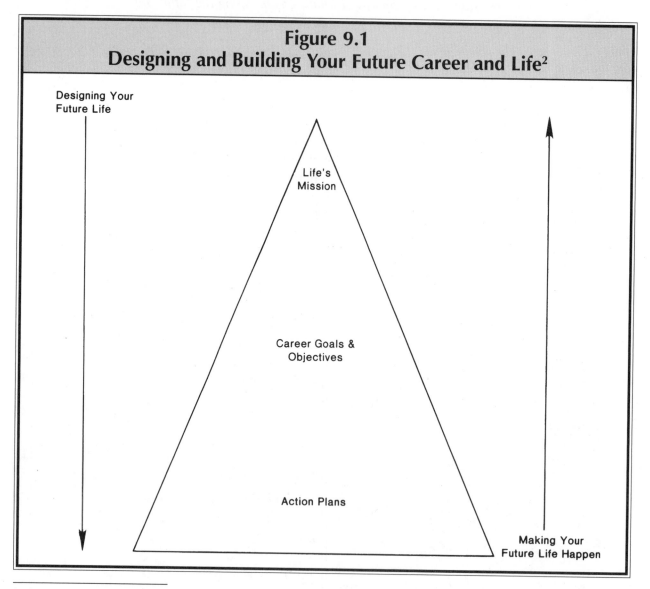

Figure 9.1
Designing and Building Your Future Career and Life[2]

Designing Your
Future Life

Life's
Mission

Career Goals &
Objectives

Action Plans

Making Your
Future Life Happen

---

1. Edward S. Cornish, *Planting Seeds for the Future*. (Stamford, CT: Champion International Corp., 0000). Copies can be obtained by writing to Champion International Corporation, Department 5360, 1 Landmark Square, Stamford, Connecticut 06921.
2. Adapted from the Intensive Course in the Crystal Life/Work Planning Process, John C. Crystal Center, Inc., 894 Plandome Road, Manhasset, New York 11030.

Bob's Internet graduation ceremony left something to be desired.

bomb, many people considered the world indestructible. Yet this decision to develop atomic weapons has resulted in the current frightening potential to destroy the human race. Previous atomic testing caused long-term damage to human health through radioactive fallout, and no adequate plans existed to cover this possibility. Nuclear accidents such as the Chernobyl disaster have also had wide-ranging world consequences. The immediate death and destruction as well as the potential long-term damage to human health and agriculture from Chernobyl signal the need for worldwide cooperation and planning in the use of nuclear energy.

INFLUENCING YOUR CAREER FUTURE

Just as collective actions shape the world's future, your individual actions shape your personal destiny. As you will see in Chapter 10, your own mindset can strongly influence your future through the power of suggestion. The term "self-fulfilling prophecy" describes this phenomenon of individual expectations

influencing future results. For example, if you approach a job interview fully prepared and expecting to perform well, you are likely to succeed. In contrast, if you expect to perform poorly ("I never do well in face-to-face contacts" or "I always choke under pressure") you are likely to fail.

Having chosen a career, you may be tempted to make minimal plans, sit back, and "let it happen." Unfortunately, what usually happens with this approach is failure. Like everyone else, you will probably experience some setbacks as you pursue a career. Lacking shorter-range goals and specific career plans, you may find these setbacks overwhelming and doubt that you can succeed. Feeling out of control, you might then reinforce your pessimism by expecting further setbacks instead of looking for other options and opportunities. Not surprisingly, a cycle of victimization develops, and few career choices are attained.

On the other hand, with comprehensive, short-range goals and plans, it is easy to view setbacks in a large perspective. You can recognize other, often better, alternatives that were not obvious before. Of course, no one can absolutely predict the future. Yet developing and following objectives and plans does give you far more control, direction, and motivation. In this way, your own self-fulfilling prophecy will be success.

CAREER GOALS/OBJECTIVES

Career goals provide you with purpose and direction for your career and life. People without goals experience more conflict and uncertainty because they just react to whatever happens instead of trying to infuse their lives with meaning. These people are likely to have far more days when they have no compelling reason for even getting out of bed. In contrast, people with carefully chosen, clearly defined goals know what they want out of their lives and careers.

Another function of clearly defined goals is that they enable people to channel their energy into meaningful activity and may even create more energy in the pursuit of life goals. The following example illustrates this point.

Denise was a conscientious and efficient secretary whose true passion was hiking and backpacking in wilderness areas. Feeling unchallenged and tied down in her office setting, she decided to attend col-

Web Connect

Office Team at **www.officeteam.com/OT/FactSheet** conducted an "Office of the Future" study, which resulted in some interesting thoughts on where careers and organizations are headed as early as 2005. You may be interested in checking out this fact sheet to spark some additional ideas on what trends may impact your career goals and objectives.

lege as a way to initiate a career change. Unmotivated and discouraged by her lack of clear direction, she dropped out her first semester. She was unable to see how her love of the outdoors had any relationship to a possible new career direction. Through the assistance of a career counselor, however, she saw that conserving natural resources for the enjoyment of everyone was the motivating force in her life.

With renewed purpose, Denise re-entered college, majored in geology, and made the Dean's List her first semester back. She joined the Appalachian Trail Conference in its mission to maintain sections of the Appalachian Trail. Currently she is collaborating with an architect friend on the development of a design for an energy-efficient home utilizing solar and geothermal power. Having a clearly defined career objective has enabled Denise to channel her energies towards results that amaze even her.

In effect, having clearly defined goals brings the future into the present. Instead of procrastinating, you can take appropriate present action because you are clear about what direction you want to go. Accordingly, you can also see what actions will move you in your chosen direction and what will not.

In this way, goals enable you to take charge of your life. Rather than just sitting back and letting things happen to you, you can use goals as catalysts for action. People who just let things happen to them are actually at the mercy of circumstances. They use up their energy fighting, denying, or rationalizing unpleasant realities.

As you create goals and act upon them, you influence your future. In other words, your mental images and attitudes about the future largely determine the shape of your future. No one can totally control the future because of unknown circumstances over which there is little control. Goal-oriented people, however, tend to be far more successful at getting what they want rather than simply taking what they can get.

DEFINING YOUR GOALS/OBJECTIVES

Goals and objectives are specific, future-oriented statements of purpose and direction accomplishable within a definite time frame. The time frame can be long-, medium-, or short-range. Although the terms *goal* and *objective* are often used interchangeably, sometimes the term *goal* is used for long-range aims while the word *objective* is used for related short-range intentions. Being well within our grasp, short-range objectives enable us to establish and reach tangible outcomes on the path towards our long-range goals. As we complete our objectives, we are then in a position to set and accomplish new ones.

Goals may be stated in a variety of ways corresponding to the strength of your commitment to complete them. The way you state your goals clearly indicates how determined you are to achieve your desired outcome. According to David Ellis, there is a hierarchy of goal-statement categories, each successively more powerful than the preceding one.

Notice that with each higher category, the language gets increasingly stronger and the likelihood that the goal will be completed gets more believable. In people's daily interactions, the strongest language (category 4) is reserved for activities requiring the highest level of commitment, such as marriage vows or promissory notes. In a court of law where the truthfulness of witnesses can mean the difference between life and death of an accused person, the most powerful language is used when swearing in witnesses: "I promise to tell the truth, the whole truth, and nothing but the truth."

Pay attention to the language you use when you state your own goals. If you state a goal in the language of category 2 (desire), "I want to get a better job," examine your willingness to make a stronger commitment to reaching that goal. Then restate your goal in the language of category 3 (intent) or category 4 (promise). "I'll do my best to get a better job," or "I will get a better job."

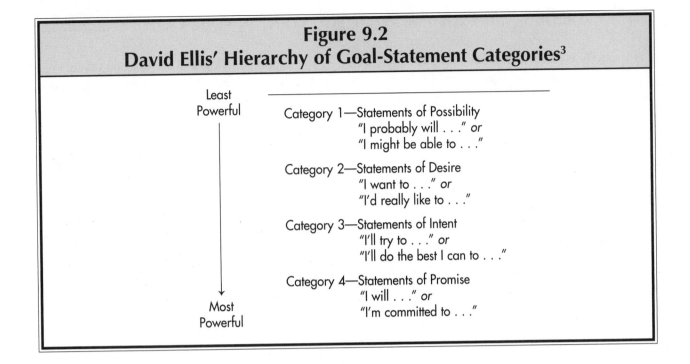

Figure 9.2
David Ellis' Hierarchy of Goal-Statement Categories[3]

Least
Powerful

Category 1—Statements of Possibility
"I probably will . . ." or
"I might be able to . . ."

Category 2—Statements of Desire
"I want to . . ." or
"I'd really like to . . ."

Category 3—Statements of Intent
"I'll try to . . ." or
"I'll do the best I can to . . ."

Category 4—Statements of Promise
"I will . . ." or
"I'm committed to . . ."

Most
Powerful

CLARIFYING WHAT YOU WANT IN A CAREER

Knowing what you really want in a career is necessary before you can develop believable career goals. Clarifying your wants, however, may not be so easy. Wants are often confused with "shoulds" that are beliefs about what you ought to do, be, or have. "Shoulds" usually are influenced strongly by the thinking of others. Your parents, social institutions, the media, public opinion, or current popular values, try to convince you of what you should do, have, or be. At your place of worship, you may be reminded of your duty to contribute your time and money to the support of the congregation. Television commercials bombard you with overt and subtle secular "should" messages: "remove unsightly hair," "take the fear out of being close," "blonds have more fun," "double your flavor, double your fun." "Should" messages from a variety of sources serve as nagging reminders of what we are "supposed" to do.

"Wants," on the other hand, are expressions of what you really desire to have, do, or be. They reflect those things that attract your interest or enthusiasm, those things that grow from your wishes, dreams, aspirations, and fantasies. They reflect the inner you—the real you.

"Shoulds" can prevent you from being in touch with your true "wants." For this reason, it is important to clearly separate your "shoulds" from your "wants." Career goals created out of "shoulds" do not work because they are too much like New Year's resolutions, full of good intentions, but in the end, usually resisted. Career goals developed out of true "wants," however, enlist our full energy and provide a winning combination. Here is an example of how to transform a "should" into a "want":

☑ I *should* lose 15 pounds.

☑ I *want* to maintain my weight at a neat and trim 130 pounds.

The following exercises are designed to assist you in identifying your "wants" and separating out your "shoulds."

3. David Ellis, *Here & Now Instructor's Newsletter* November 1986: 1, 4. This newsletter can be obtained by contacting College Survival, Inc., 2650 Jackson Boulevard, Rapid City, South Dakota 57702.

EXERCISE 9-A. IDENTIFYING WHAT YOU WANT IN YOUR CAREER _____

1. Before identifying what you do want in your career, it is important to know what you don't want or want to avoid. List below those things you have currently in your life, career and/or job that you do not want.

2. Some elements of your current life, career and/or job give you energy and pleasure. List below these current elements in your life, career and/or job that you do want to retain.

3. Now that you have more clarity about your skills, interests, and values and have made a tentative or definite career choice, what else is important for you to have in your career? List below things you truly want in your future career and/or job that you don't have now.

4. From parts 2 and 3 above, develop a list of your top 10 career wants. Eliminate those that are really "shoulds" from your list or restate them as "wants." Now prioritize your list of 10, assigning "1" to the most important and "10" to the least important.

My Top Ten Wants

1.

2.

3.

4.

5.

6.

7.

8.

9.

10.

5. Take the top five career wants from your prioritized list of 10 above, and restate each one as a specific career goal.

Examples:

a. I want to work with people who are highly committed to the customers/clients they serve.

b. I want to obtain recognition from others for the work that I do.

c. I want to make enough money to maintain the lifestyle I currently enjoy.

d. I want a job that is within walking distance of my residence.

e. I want a career that will enable me to use and develop my foreign language skills.

1.

2.

3.

4.

5.

GUIDELINES FOR EXPRESSING STATEMENTS OF CAREER GOALS AND OBJECTIVES

Career goal and objective statements follow certain guidelines to define effectively the direction you want your future to take. The most important guidelines are listed below.[4] True career goals and objectives are:

1. *Achievable*. Achievable outcomes can be completed given the physical and mental limitations of the people setting the objectives. For someone five feet tall, the goal of becoming the center of a professional basketball team is neither realistic nor achievable. Similarly, most people would not be able to achieve the objective of reading a 1,500-page book in an afternoon.

2. *Believable*. People need to feel confident that they can complete the goal or objective; that it is within the realm of possibility for them. Some people are so fervent in their belief that they will accomplish something that they actually do it despite considerable obstacles. Grandma Moses is an example of a person who defied the odds and became a recognized artist in her 80s.

3. *Specifically Stated*. Insofar as is possible, true objectives are stated in concrete terms. Short-range objectives can be stated more specifically than long-range goals because of the uncertainty of the distant future.

---

4. James D. McHolland, *Human Potential Seminar Basic Guidebook* (Evanston, Illinois: National Center for Human Potential Seminars & Services, 1976). The publisher's address is 2527 Hastings Avenue, Evanston, Illinois 60201.

4. *Presented without Alternative.* True objectives are clearly stated without any either/ or clauses. "I'm either going to buy a house or rent one" presents two opposing alternatives. The person setting up this objective may be undecided about the primary objective. In either case, objectives stated in this way simply need clarification: "I intend to buy a house, if I can find one I can afford. My second choice is to rent a house."

5. *Compatible with Your Values.* True statements of goals reflect the values that you profess. If someone values doing things together as a family unit, then that person's vacation objective would be to set a time when every family member could participate.

COMPREHENSIVE CAREER GOALS AND OBJECTIVES

Establishing reachable long-range career goals is crucial for providing future direction and perspective. But a long-range goal is less useful in clarifying what step you should take next. Long-range goals extend at least ten years into the future. It would be nearly impossible to sit down today and produce a detailed plan for the next ten years that would help you attain these goals. Even if you had the patience and perspective to do this, your plan would be foolishly rigid. Your own life will change, and the working world will present new opportunities. Accordingly, your plans and long-range goals will change.

For this reason, the easiest and most productive approach is to devise medium-range and short-range

 ## EXERCISE 9-B. REVISING YOUR STATEMENTS OF CAREER OBJECTIVES _____

Check over your top five career objectives from Exercise 9-A to see if they correspond to the guidelines listed above, then make any revisions that you feel are necessary.

1. Career Objective:

   Revision:

2. Career Objective:

   Revision:

3. Career Objective:

   Revision:

4. Career Objective:

   Revision:

5. Career Objective:

   Revision:

career objectives based on your long-range goals. A medium-range objective generally covers one to five years. As these medium-range objectives are reached, you can devise new ones to direct your progress towards the related long-range goal. Sometimes, you will want to change these medium-range objectives when they no longer are suitable. Short-range objectives cover up to one year. You will frequently revise short-range objectives.

The advantages of medium- and short-range objectives are numerous. First of all, they are totally flexible. As changes and opportunities occur, these short-range objectives can easily be revised. Also, you don't have to wait ten or more years to attain them. Successfully achieving short-range objectives keeps you motivated. If you feel discouraged because you have not yet found a suitable career choice, setting short-term objectives will provide direction for your continuing exploration. Finally, short-range objectives are specific enough to provide guidelines for making step-by-step plans. Without these plans, your future becomes a question mark—or worse.

Table 9.1 defines these three types of career objectives. Table 9.2 provides examples of all three types, illustrating the difference between vague objective statements and more effective, precise statements. Look these over carefully before devising your own short-range objective statements for Exercise 9-C.

Table 9.1
Types of Career Goals and Objectives

Long-Range Goals: These goals establish the general career direction you want to achieve over the long run or at least ten years into the future. Occasionally, you will find better alternatives and change your long-range goals.

Medium-Range Objectives: These are the career objectives you want to achieve in the next one to five years, so they are more specific. As these objectives are reached, you will establish others to progress towards related long-range goals. Medium-range objectives are frequently revised and sometimes changed completely as new options appear.

Short-Range Objectives: These are career objectives you want to achieve in one year or less, so they are very specific. These objectives are frequently revised or changed completely as new options appear.

Table 9.2
Examples of Career Goals and Objectives

| Long-Range Goals | |
Vague	More Effective
1. I want to make a good salary.	1. Within fifteen years, I will be making a salary equivalent to $75,000 in today's money.
2. I want to work with people I like.	2. I will work with people who are caring, creative, and intelligent.
3. I want to use my best talents in my work.	3. In my career, I will be using and developing my research skills, ability to organize ideas, and creative writing skills.

Medium-Range Objectives	
Vague	**More Precise**
1. I want to get a good education.	1. Within five years, I will have obtained a B.A. degree in psychology.
2. I would like to get a job in the computer field.	2. Within two years, I will be working as a computer programmer with an aerospace firm or agency such as NASA.
3. I want to be an artist.	3. Within three years, I will be working as a commercial artist for a TV station.

Short-Range Objectives	
Vague	**Precise**
1 I will finish my A.A. degree.	1. Within one year, I will have completed my A.A. degree in respiratory therapy.
2. I will get a good, first job soon.	2. In six months, I will obtain an entry-level position as a secretary with an international banking and finance firm.
3. I will attempt to learn about owning my own business.	3. Within three months, I will have researched the local opportunities for opening my own health food store.

 EXERCISE 9-C.

DEVELOPING COMPREHENSIVE STATEMENTS OF CAREER GOALS _____

For this exercise, you will further revise your long-range statements of career goals from Exercise 9-A. Using these long-range career goals as references, you will then establish related medium-range and short-range objectives. To illustrate, we will follow the example of Marlene. Initially, Marlene completed the following prioritized list of career-related life objectives:

1. I will be doing worthwhile, important work related to my math skills.

2. I will obtain professional recognition.

3. I will have opportunity for self-improvement.

4. I will have financial security.

5. I will be contributing to the solution of our inflation problems.

After Marlene's preliminary research with her work options, she decided to become an accountant. At that point, she was able to develop and refine her long-range career goals. Her revised goals are listed below:

1. I will work in a large public-service accounting firm, serving in a leadership position.

2. Within ten years, I will receive recognition for my excellent work as a C.P.A.

3. I will work for an organization that encourages personal and professional growth by sponsoring workshops and funding continued education.

4. Within twelve years, I will be earning a salary equivalent to $60,000 in today's money.

5. I will be helping to solve our economic problems by teaching sound financial management and fiscal responsibility to my clients.

Marlene then developed the following medium-range and short-range objectives related to her top long-range career goals:

Long-Range Goal #1

I will work in a large public-service accounting firm, serving in a leadership position.

Medium-Range Objectives

1. Within one year, I will obtain my A.A. degree in accounting.

2. I will graduate with a B+ average.

3. While in college, I will research fully the types of accounting business consider to be potential employers.

Short-Range Objectives

1. In one-and-a-half years, I will obtain an entry-level accounting position in a firm of my choice.

2. Within two years, I will have received my first salary raise.

3. Within three years, I will earn a major promotion.

4. Within five years, I will have earned through part-time study my M.B.A. in accounting.

Directions:

1. Revise your top five long-range career objectives from Exercise 9-A, so they are stated as precisely as possible at this point in your life. If you have made a tentative career choice in Chapter 8, your long-range career goals will be more vague. However, state them as precisely as you can, and concentrate on constructive short-range objectives to aid your career exploration. Fill in your top two long-range goals in the appropriate spaces in Table 9.3

2. After writing your long-range goals, write your related medium-range and short-range career objectives. Use Marlene's example as a guide.

3. As you complete this exercise, study Tables 9.1 and 9.2 to assist you in writing effective statements of goals and objectives.

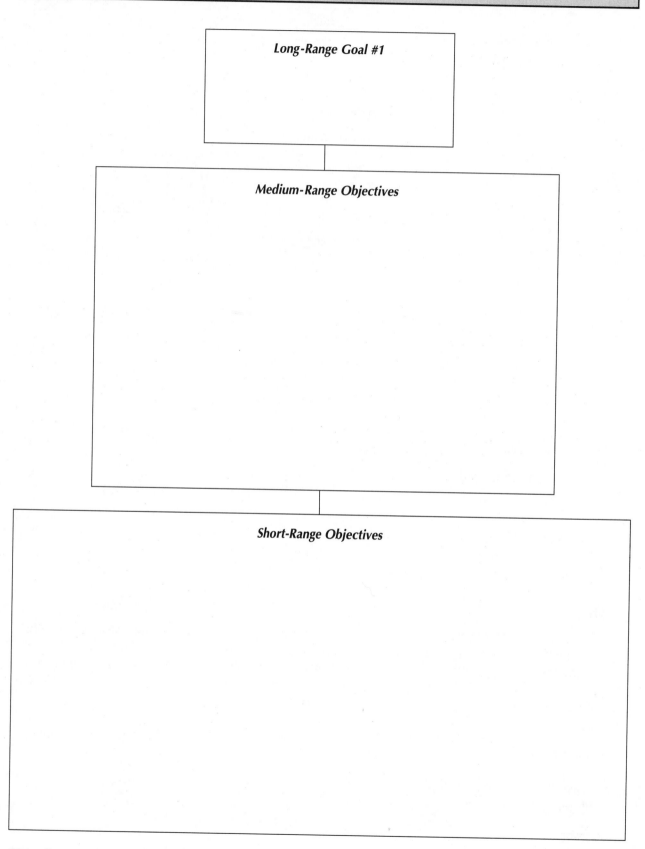

Table 9.3
Goal Planning

Long-Range Goal #1

Medium-Range Objectives

Short-Range Objectives

Table 9.3
Goal Planning (continued)

Long-Range Goal #2

Medium-Range Objectives

Short-Range Objectives

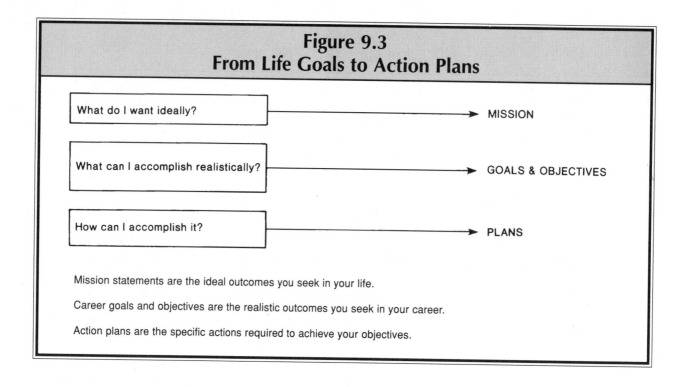

Figure 9.3
From Life Goals to Action Plans

What do I want ideally?	⟶	MISSION
What can I accomplish realistically?	⟶	GOALS & OBJECTIVES
How can I accomplish it?	⟶	PLANS

Mission statements are the ideal outcomes you seek in your life.

Career goals and objectives are the realistic outcomes you seek in your career.

Action plans are the specific actions required to achieve your objectives.

 EXERCISE 9-D. ACTION PLANNING

Figure 9.3 portrays the relationships among mission, goals, and plans. Notice that your mission is your ideal or ultimate outcome while your objectives and goals define what you can accomplish realistically within a specified time frame. Plans lay out the steps required to get what you want.

In this exercise, your task is to identify the steps necessary to accomplish the short-range objectives you listed to support your longer-range goals. Start the exercise by identifying your first significant step towards achieving your short-range objective and determining when you can complete that step. Use the following example as a guide as you develop your own action plans.

Example:

For long-range goal #1, Marlene's short-range objectives were as follows:

1. Within one year, I will obtain an A.A. degree in accounting.

2. I will graduate with a B+ average.

3. While in college, I will research fully the types of accounting businesses I consider potential employers.

From these objectives, Marlene developed the following action plans:

Steps to Take	Complete by
1. I will change my major from general studies to accounting.	May 15, 2003
2. I will talk with my academic advisor to see what courses I need to take.	June 1, 2003
3. I will investigate financial aid possibilities at the financial aid office, so I can afford to take four courses a semester.	June 1, 2003
4. I will enroll in two summer school courses.	June 15, 2003
5. I will increase my study time to 30 hours a week to improve my current grades.	July 1, 2003 to May 20, 2005
6. I will research public-service accounting firms in the area by calling the Chamber of Commerce, looking at government directories, and consulting Dun and Bradstreet directories.	Sept. 1, 2003 to May 20, 2004
7. Through the college, I will arrange for an accounting internship with one of the firms I've identified in step #6.	Jan. 1, 2004

Directions:

1. Using the above example as a guide, develop a list of action steps for the short-range objectives associated with your top two long-range goals.

2. As you review your cluster of short-range objectives for each long-range goal, think through all the related steps required to complete those objectives. List your steps on the following pages in logical sequence.

3. Indicate the approximate deadline for completing each of the steps you identify.

Action Steps for My First Short-Range Objective	Desired Completion Date

CASE STUDY
WILLIAM

William was a high school misfit. His parents took him out of public school and placed him in a private, parochial school where William did his best to prove that his parents had made a mistake. The culmination of his efforts came when he failed religion his senior year and was unable to graduate with his class.

After completing summer school to obtain his high school diploma, William jumped from one job to another, either leaving when he got bored or getting fired. He attempted to enlist in the Marine Corps but was unable to pass the physical. Angry and discouraged, William hit bottom when he was apprehended for reckless driving and placed in his parent's custody.

Given an ultimatum by his parents to "shape up" or suffer the consequences, William reluctantly agreed to try the local community college. He took just two classes his first semester, a career planning class and an art class (art was the only subject William had enjoyed in high school). Finding an environment where his creative interests and talents were recognized and encouraged, William began to believe in himself. Through the career planning process he discovered that what he really wanted to do was express himself creatively, especially through photography.

Prior to the start of his second semester, William changed from an undeclared major to a visual arts major. Filled with enthusiasm and having educational and career direction for the first time in his life, William took a full academic load his second semester, narrowly missing the Dean's List. One of his photographic collages was chosen for the student art show, and he received a second place ribbon.

This summer, William is working as a photographer's assistant. In his free time he wanders the countryside taking pictures. He is learning how to develop his pictures to obtain the special effects he wants. The best prints will be placed in a portfolio for when he transfers to the art institute in one year.

Through realistic goal setting and effective action planning, William has found direction and focus for his career journey.

Muriel waited and waited, knowing that Ralph had unrealistic long-range planning skills.

FINAL NOTES ON GOALS, OBJECTIVES, AND PLANS

Setting goals and objectives and devising action plans are skills that can be developed. Both are also ongoing processes. Many people are reluctant to set goals and objectives or make the supporting plans because they fear they will then be committed to them no matter what. Others are afraid of even positive change or afraid of failing to meet the objectives they have set. All of these emotional reactions are perfectly understandable and normal. However, consider that the only purpose of goals, objectives, and plans is to provide productive direction and motiva-

Web Connect

If you'd like to go through the decision making, goal setting and career action planning process online, the **University of Waterloo** in Canada has an outstanding site for career-decision making at **www.adm.uwaterloo.ca/infocecs/ CRC/manual-home.html** Scroll down the left column until you see the "Decision-Making" section and then work your way through the various pieces of it to result in a completed career action plan.

tion, along with the time to accommodate change. Therefore, they should never be turned into nonproductive, rigid commitments or burdens.

Since people and the working world change, goals, objectives, and plans should change whenever it is in your best interest. You will need to make these minor or major changes as you learn about new options or challenges in your career. In other words, career planning is a lifelong process. Effectiveness in this process involves skill in the interrelated activities shown in Figure 9.3. The more you practice these skills, the more effective you will become in taking charge of your career and your life.

SUMMARY

By developing a view of the future, you can build the kind of future you really want to have. No one can predict your fate exactly. However, the taking-charge method of career/life planning does allow you far more control and influence over your prospects. The career/life planning process includes clarifying what you want in your future career and life, setting prioritized goals to get what you want, and translating these into realistic objectives and planned actions.

As your personal needs and aspirations change and the working world changes, you will repeat parts of this process with increasing skill and confidence. Thus, career/life decision making becomes a lifelong process, leading you to as much fulfillment as you seek.

ASSIGNMENT

Your Future Story

For this assignment, imagine that you have been transported magically to a point ten years into the future. From this perspective, you will write an autobiography of what has happened to you over the past ten years. Thus, your autobiographic summary will cover the future as you envision it. Use your mission, career objectives, and plans along with the envisioning process described in Appendix D for help.

One purpose in completing this exercise is to become more comfortable with and enthusiastic about your future changes. Another purpose is to reaffirm what you ideally want to happen in your career and life. This way, you ensure that your self-fulfilling prophecy will be even more positive and suitable. Most students who complete this exercise find it enjoyable, revealing, and rewarding. After writing your future autobiography, why not put it away to be reviewed periodically over the next ten years? You may want to update this autobiography as you progress in your career and expand your expectations and plans.

Directions:

1. Assume you have been transported ten years into the future. From that future perspective, write your autobiography for those so-called past ten years. We recommend writing at least five to ten pages of summary.

2. Imagine that you are writing your future autobiography to send to some important person in your life whom you have not seen for ten years. Therefore, you want to tell this person all the significant aspects of your career and life over this period. To make the project seem more real, you may want to give your summary to this person, asking him/her for comments.

3. Base your future autobiography on the goals, objectives, and plans you have already created.

4. Use your imagination to envision your life having turned out the way you ideally want it.

5. Give special emphasis to:

   • some of your top and most enjoyed achievements during this period.

   • some of the high priority objectives that you accomplished.

   • some of the most satisfying experiences in your work, your leisure, and your learning.

Empowering Yourself to Succeed

Argue for your limitations and sure enough, they're yours.
—Richard Bach
Illusions

Do you know people who—

☑ Feel completely dependent upon others in making decisions?
☑ Are highly motivated to discover and investigate possible career alternatives?
☑ Blame others or circumstances for everything that happens in their lives?
☑ Believe that their career path will be determined entirely by circumstances beyond their control?
☑ Are optimistic about their ability to create a satisfying career through their own efforts?

If you do, you can observe the differences between self-victimizing and self-empowering people.

After presenting his MBA degree from the Internet, Bob wondered if being laughed at was an indicator of his chances of getting hired.

THREE KINDS OF BARRIERS

At this point, you may know what you want in your career and have some plans for achieving your goals. Unfortunately, many people come this far in the career planning process and then get bogged down. Three types of barriers or obstacles keep people from getting what they want or from even attempting to go after their goals:

☑ negative attitude pattern or mindset

☑ poor decision-making skills

☑ any external circumstance or situation that at least temporarily blocks career progress

In this chapter, you will have an opportunity to identify your own particular barriers and learn how to overcome them.

MINDSETS

Have you noticed how some people tend to be winners in life and others losers? Ask people who are consistent winners in life what their secret is, and the odds are you will receive an answer like, "I don't know why. I just expect things to go well." Losers are likely to tell you about the same thing in reverse. Patterns of winning, losing, and just getting by often correspond to the distinctive attitudes or expectations that different people have about the course of their lives.

These distinctive viewpoints that most people have about life are called mindsets. A mindset is a characteristic pattern of thinking, feeling, and believing. Some people, for example, believe that others have all the luck while they never get any breaks and remain powerless to change their lives. Other individuals expect things to turn out basically well and anticipate success. We refer to these two contrasting orientations as the self-victimizing and the self-empowering mindsets, respectively. These attitudes become ingrained, characteristically shaping a person's reactions to every situation.

The Real Victim versus the Self-Victim

A victim is defined as someone who is injured in some way or suffering from some negative act, condition, or circumstance. Unfortunately, there are many true victims in the world. Some people are impoverished, mentally retarded, or physically disabled. Other people are imprisoned for crimes they did not commit or are victims of accidents they didn't cause. People like these do live with limitations or restrictions, and they truly lack some of the options that you may take for granted. Yet many of these individuals remain optimistic, gaining strength from dealing constructively with their obstacles to create better lives and careers for themselves. They don't consider their disabilities real barriers and often refer to themselves as simply having "*different* abilities."

In fact, most people who feel like victims are not really victims of external circumstances or fate. These imagined victims are called self-victimizers.

The Self-Victimizing Mindset

Self-victimizing people are inclined to be uninvolved, dependent, and inflexible in the career-choice process. They rarely generate much energy or enthusiasm for the process of career choosing or career changing. They may underestimate their potential capability for making good choices. Typically, self-victimizers will rely on others to decide for them or wait for circumstances to determine what happens. Self-victimizers are unlikely to explore the full range of available career alternatives out of the rigid conviction that it doesn't make much difference anyway.

Self-victimizing people often feel harmed by circumstances, agencies, or people whom they perceive as hostile. They may say things like "I just can't get ahead because I am a member of a minority, a member of the majority suffering from reverse discrimination, short, tall, fat, thin, ugly, pretty, too smart, too dumb, too poor, too rich, too unskilled, too skilled, too old, or too young."

The legitimate victim is someone who qualifies for a job but doesn't get it because of race, sex, religion, etc. Self-victims are those who do not qualify for a job, but maintain that they were denied because of their age, ethnic background, social class or whatever. Self-victimizers use circumstances such as these to justify their belief that they are essentially helpless in the career-planning and job-hunting process.

Jack obtained a job that he wanted very much. Yet he knew that the job didn't pay well and was a temporary position funded by a grant. Nevertheless, he hoped that the position would somehow continue, that his salary would somehow be increased, and that the job would somehow lead to a promotion within that organization.

Since the job had temporary funding, Jack's boss repeatedly advised him to begin searching and preparing for a more secure position. His boss also advised that their organization had no plans to create any new positions or hire additional staff for the foreseeable future. Jack chose not to act on this advice, however, feeling that things would somehow turn out all right.

Three years later, the funding ran out, and Jack's job was terminated. He expressed shock and anger. Jack accused the organization of callous unconcern considering his years of service. Just as he was about to leave, a vacancy did open up. Jack applied for that position but was not hired, losing out to a better qualified woman employed by the same organization.

Upon learning this, Jack threatened to bring an affirmative action suit against the organization, claiming reverse discrimination. Jack could not admit that this particular woman was better qualified for the position and that the selection had been carefully made by a committee of both men and women. Even if this hadn't been the case, Jack's negative behavior had ruined his reputation at the organization.

Jack clearly exhibits numerous self-victimizing traits. He was unwilling to even consider the future seriously, let alone explore career alternatives. He felt so strongly dependent upon the organization that he expected "them" to take care of him. He was uncompromising in his attitude about considering other options, stating that he was just not interested in working somewhere else and wanted to stay on.

Jack's surprise and anger after his inevitable layoff shows his dependency and lack of responsibility for his career and life progress. When problems arose, Jack blamed others for what happened. Several months after this incident occurred, Jack remained unemployed and was making no progress towards another employment goal. Instead, Jack's energy was tied up in feeling wronged by the organization and complaining about his "unjust" treatment.

The Self-Empowering Mindset

"Empowering" means giving someone permission to exercise some type of strength, influence, or power. Self-empowering people give themselves internal permission for exercising power. People with "self-empowering mindsets" feel free to engage in activity geared to getting what they want, and they are optimistic about getting it.

Self-empowering people take responsibility for creating the conditions they want in their lives, while self-victimizing people take whatever comes their way. Both groups may begin in exactly the same conditions and circumstances. Because self-victimiz-ing people conclude that they are powerless to change or create, they passively take what they get in life, perhaps hoping for the best. In this sense, they make themselves total victims of chance and circumstance. Self-empowering people, in contrast, will be actively inclined to create and implement desired goals. What happens in the life of the self-empowering person is likely to occur more as a result of self-motivation than external circumstances and conditions.

Self-Empowerment and Career Choice

Self-empowering people go about choosing and implementing their careers far more actively and ef-

The board was having second thoughts about appointing Cecilia as public relations director.

fectively than self-victimizers. They are also more involved, independent, and flexible in the career-choice and implementation process than are the self-victimizers. Although the self-empowerers are more likely to achieve satisfying careers, they, too, will end up in some unsuitable situations. However, unlike self-victimizers, they actively initiate career changes that will provide greater satisfaction.

Self-empowerers take the time and effort to learn what they need and want in a career and then go ahead and do whatever is required to achieve it. Once they have established career goals, they are inclined to pursue these optimistically and enthusiastically. But self-empowerers recognize that no career decision is likely to produce perfect results. For this reason, they remain flexible and strive to obtain the best results, given their unique situation.

CASE STUDY
ANNE

At the age of 37, Anne gave up a successful and fulfilling career in teaching to become a full-time mother and housewife. She put her whole energy, enthusiasm, and creativity into this job, just as she had done with teaching. Years later, after her kids had grown up, Anne decided it was time for her to return to an outside career. Since she had been out of the job market for a long time, Anne decided to enhance her credentials by obtaining a masters degree in education. While working on her M.A., Anne began establishing contacts. Through her networking, Anne obtained a part-time educational research job at a community college. She obtained the job even though other candidates had educational backgrounds far better suited to the position than her own.

Soon this job experience, her new M.A. degree, and her networking efforts paid off, and Anne landed an excellent full-time position as an educational researcher with the American Association of Junior Colleges. Through her energy and positive thinking, Anne had created a new career for herself when many were advising her that she was too old to start over again. However, Anne realized that this career was not her final step. While she got outstanding evaluations, Anne was just not energized by her work.

At this stage most people would probably have said something like, "Oh well, I'm just lucky to have such a good job. At my age, I'd better just keep what I have." But not Anne. Anne had far too much to contribute to simply hang in there and wait it out. She didn't know what kind of work would enable her to use her talents more fully. But Anne knew how to ask questions and then seek out answers. She found out that Richard Bolles, the author of *What Color Is Your Parachute?*, conducted workshops to help people identify their top skills and interests and set goals aimed at self-realization. Anne went to his two-week course and came away determined to use her talents as a career/life planning specialist.

Once again Anne was faced with a barrier. Her educational background was in high school education and college administration areas. What she wanted to do now involved counseling and teaching in a college setting. The difficulty of making that kind of transition would stop most people. Anne was determined, however. She would either make it on her own as a consultant in private practice or get a job at a college that was looking for talent above "the right" credentials. Anne did the latter through networking. She identified what colleges within commuting distance had strong career/life planning programs and targeted her first choice.

At the time, however, Anne's potential employer had no immediate or anticipated positions. But the people at that organization were impressed with Anne, and she was a patient and persistent problem solver. As a result, within six months she was teaching a career decision-making course there and working in a part-time career/life planning specialist position. Within one year, she had been hired as a full-time professor of career/life planning. Over the past ten years, she has helped hundreds of individuals find themselves, clarify their career/life goals, and move into careers that utilize their skills and engage their interests. At this point she has established a reputation for herself within the career/life planning field and is a very popular instructor, guest speaker, and well-paid consultant. Her success has clearly not come through luck. Anne is where she is today because she knew what she wanted, went after it, and didn't let her barriers stop her.

Table 10.1	
Traits of the Self-Victimizing and the Self-Empowering Mindsets	
The Self-Victimizing Mindset	**The Self-Empowering Mindset**
• sees little or no choice available	• sees life full of choices
• sees problems as hopeless barriers	• sees problems as challenges to be solved
• believes people who get ahead are just lucky	• feels that people get ahead primarily out of their own efforts and preparation
• is resistant to change and unwilling to seriously consider other options	• is open to change and willing to change for a good reason
• feels career is determined by external circumstances beyond control	• feels career is determined by personal efforts
• feels unable to influence own career	• feels empowered to influence own career
• is uninvolved in own career development	• is totally involved in own career development
• gives little consideration to personal desires in career and life	• gives serious consideration to personal desires in career and life
• does not know or investigate the career options available	• thoroughly investigates the career options available
• allows others and events to make personal decisions	• actively makes personal decisions
• has either no career objectives or sets unrealistic goals	• sets realistic and achievable career objectives
• avoids future career planning	• carefully plans career future

 EXERCISE 10-A. ASSESSING YOUR MINDSET TENDENCIES _____

1. After reviewing the material on the two mindsets, including Table 10.1, determine your self-victimizing and self-empowering traits.

    I am like self-victimizers in that:

    I am like self-empowerers in that:

2. Rate yourself on the scale below by placing an "X" at the place that best describes your assessment now. Make this assessment based on your current general attitudes rather than your particular mood at this moment.

The Self-Victimizing versus Self-Empowering Scale										
0	**1**	**2**	**3**	**4**	**5**	**6**	**7**	**8**	**9**	**10**
Totally Self-Victimizing		Somewhat Self-Victimizing			A Little of Both		Somewhat Self-Empowering		Highly Self-Empowering	

3. a. What are the main things you learned about yourself in doing this assessment?

   b. How do you feel about your assessment?

4. After you have decided where you are currently on the self-victimizing versus the self-empowering scale, decide where you want to be. Go back to the scale now and place a large "G" (for goal) at the point where you really want to be.

5. a. What would you have to change in order to become as self-empowering as you really want to be?

   b. Are you willing to make the effort to change?

How to Become Self-Empowering

Fortunately, your place on the self-victimizing versus self-empowering scale results far more from the way you perceive the world currently than the way the world actually is. Your attitudes were not acquired at birth. Instead, they were developed over the years through learning a certain style or bias that continues to influence your thinking and behavior today. Just as your attitudes were acquired through learning, they can also be productively changed through learning.

To become more self-empowering, start changing your self-victimizing attitudes now by working on the following steps:

1. Become aware of your actual attitudes and beliefs involving career choice.

2. Don't allow your behavior to be controlled by your ineffective attitudes. You can accomplish this through good decision making. Make carefully considered decisions. Then carry them out, even though your traditional biases may cause you some initial difficulty.

Priscilla learned to be a risk taker after becoming self-empowered.

3. Set productive and accomplishable goals, and complete them. By accumulating minor accomplishments over a period of time, you make a habit of success. In this process, your old self-victimizing attitudes will fade.

4. Acknowledge your successes. Whenever you have a successful experience (big or small), reward yourself. Most people get a perverse kind of payoff in some way from their old self-defeating habits. Acknowledging your successes can help you trade in your negative payoffs for positive ones.

5. Create affirmation statements. Write them out, and place them where you will see them. Repeat them to yourself a number of times. An affirmation statement might be like this: "I am a powerful and effective person. I learn from and am successful in all I do."

THE FIVE COMPETENCIES INVOLVED IN CAREER/LIFE DECISION MAKING

How effective you are as a career/life decision maker is determined both by your mindset and your competencies. A competency is a special skill, expertise, or facility that you have developed through practice over a period of time. For career planning, you will need to have the following five basic competencies:

1. *Self-Assessment.* This competency is the ability to analyze your career-related attributes, such as your personality style, interest patterns, potentials, needs, and values. It also involves objectively assessing your strengths and weaknesses and being able to see how these influence your career. Knowing yourself is an ongoing life process. The better you come to know yourself, the better able you are to make realistic and satisfying career choices. With poor self-assessment skills, you are unlikely to be able to make realistic career choices.

2. *Identification of Options.* This competency is the ability to identify available career options. It is one of the biggest problem areas in the career decision process because of the large number of available choices

and the scattered sources of information. There are over 20,000 occupations to choose from and over 40,000 different job titles. First you need to become proficient at acquiring information and data about occupations, including knowing what resources are available and what information-gathering methods work best. Then you need to get information about the particular jobs available in your chosen field as well as information about the job market in your chosen work location.

3. *Goal Selecting.* This competency is the ability to select goals or targets that are likely to produce a sense of satisfaction, achievement, and direction. People who have selected meaningful goals experience a sense of purpose, and their goals provide guidance for their careers. If you lack meaningful goals, you are likely to experience frustration and indecision in your life.

4. *Planning.* Planning involves the ability to translate goals into action plans. Meaningful goals have little value unless you set up realistic action plans to accomplish these ideals. Poor planners avoid planning because it is easier to just dream about reaching certain goals. Good planners envision their desired career goals and devise specific steps to accomplish them.

5. *Problem Solving.* Problem solving is the capability of handling obstacles that arise in any phase of your career. While you might hope to avoid career problems, this is unrealistic. Incompetent problem solvers will be stopped whenever problems arise. They may give up in such circumstances, look to others to solve the problems, or just wait for things to work out of their own accord. In contrast, competent problem solvers expect such obstacles and develop a facility for approaching problems as challenges and opportunities to use their skills and to learn.

 ## EXERCISE 10-B. ASSESSING YOUR CAREER-CHOICE COMPETENCIES _____

Use the following graphs to assess your current effectiveness in these five career-planning competencies. Base your assessment on where you actually see yourself at this point in life, rather than where you would like to be or think you should be.

1. Rate your decision-making effectiveness below by placing an "X" at the point on each of the five scales that most accurately describes your current level of effectiveness. Use the "clues for assessment" to help you decide.

   a. *Self-Assessment (Knowing Yourself)*

   Clues for Assessment:
   - How effectively can you describe your best and most enjoyed talents?
   - How effective are you in describing your career-related interests and values?
   - How effective are you in pinpointing what you really want in a job and in a career?
   - How effective are you in describing the working conditions that most appeal to you?

0	1	2	3	4	5	6	7	8	9	10
Very Ineffective		Somewhat Ineffective			A Little of Both		Somewhat Effective		Very Effective	

b. *Identification of Options*

Clues for Assessment:

- How effectively can you identify kinds of occupations that best match your interest and ability patterns?
- How effective are you in finding occupational information and using it in your career decision making?
- How capable are you of developing possible options from your imagination?
- How familiar are you with current job-market conditions in your field of interest?
- How effectively can you analyze occupational outlooks for the future?

0	1	2	3	4	5	6	7	8	9	10
Very Ineffective		Somewhat Ineffective			A Little of Both		Somewhat Effective		Very Effective	

c. *Goal Selecting (Knowing What You Want for the Future)*

Clues for Assessment:

- How effectively can you define what you want in a career in the form of specific goal statements?
- How effectively can you define what you want to accomplish in your life?
- How effectively can you use self-knowledge and knowledge of the world of work to develop meaningful goals for yourself?

0	1	2	3	4	5	6	7	8	9	10
Very Ineffective		Somewhat Ineffective			A Little of Both		Somewhat Effective		Very Effective	

d. *Planning (Knowing How to Get What You Want)*

Clues for Assessment:

- How effectively can you identify specific actions or steps that need to be accomplished to achieve your ideal goals?
- How effectively can you predict possible outcomes of specific actions over a long period of time?
- How effectively do you manage your resources (money, time, energy)?
- How effective are you at regularly getting the things done that you really need to accomplish?

0	1	2	3	4	5	6	7	8	9	10
Very Ineffective		Somewhat Ineffective			A Little of Both		Somewhat Effective		Very Effective	

e. *Problem Solving (Creating Alternatives as Possible Solutions)*

Clues for Assessment:

- How effectively can you identify the problems that could keep you from accomplishing your objectives or goals?

- How effective are you at foreseeing possible alternatives when obstacles keep you from achieving what you want?
- How effectively can you select those alternatives that make the best sense for you?
- How effective are you at seeing problems as challenges to be solved?

0	1	2	3	4	5	6	7	8	9	10
Very Ineffective		Somewhat Ineffective			A Little of Both		Somewhat Effective		Very Effective	

2. After you have decided where you are currently on the five competencies, decide where you want to be. Go back to each of the five scales and place a large "G" (for goal) at the point where you want to be.

3. a. From completing the preceding scales, what did you learn about your current effectiveness level in making career/life decisions?

   b. What do you see as your main strengths as a career/life decision maker?

   c. What do you see as primary problem areas in your current ability to make effective career/life decisions?

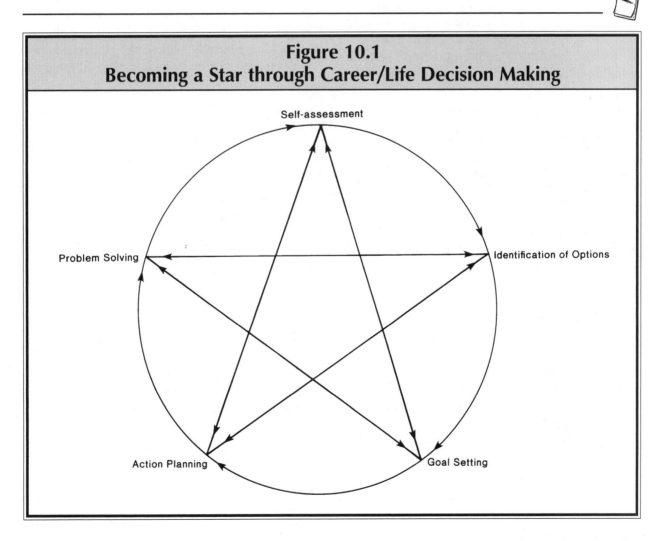

Figure 10.1
Becoming a Star through Career/Life Decision Making

COMMON SITUATIONAL BARRIERS

A joke floating around the computer field, where huge projects are commonplace, goes like this. Question: "How do you eat an elephant?" Answer: "One byte (bite) at a time." For most people the process of selecting and reaching a career goal seems as overwhelming as the huge challenge of "eating an elephant." The computer programmer approaches this challenge by acknowledging the whole elephant (goal/design phase) and then programming one byte at a time. Having set your own general career goal, you should now approach the goal one step (or bite, using the elephant analogy) at a time. You can no more get a new career going in "one bite" than you can gulp down an elephant in a single mouthful.

By now, you have already taken several big bites out of your career-development elephant. You have selected the kind of occupation you want and developed goals to give definition and direction to your career and your life. That is impressive progress. There are still a number of big bites remaining to make that choice a reality. You have problems to solve, barriers to get over, and actions to take.

By clearly identifying these barriers, you can devise a series of appropriate steps to navigate over, under or around them. Without this kind of awareness, however, your barriers may remain insurmountable roadblocks, leaving your career/life goals in the realm of dreams rather than reality. The previous sections of this chapter have discussed overcoming barriers involving negative mindsets and faulty decision-making skills. This section will focus on overcoming career barriers common to situations faced by college students without significant job experience and by career changers.

Barriers Facing College Students

The barriers facing college students are often related to a lack of working experience. As a member of this group, you may be feeling some fear and concern about getting that first, entry-level job within your career field. Welcome to the club. This is a common "anxiety" with most college students, particularly for liberal arts majors and increasingly for general business majors.

A common response to fear is procrastination, putting off those things you need to do to find out what jobs are available within your new field and then making yourself "marketable." Procrastination has left many students with a college diploma but

Table 10.2 Common Barriers to Getting Started in a New Career	
College Student Preparing for a Career	**Career Changer**
1. Fear of beginning a career	1. Fear of change
2. Procrastination	2. Procrastination
3. Undefined career identity	3. Lack of support
4. Lack of experience	4. Feeling boxed in by current job stereotypes
5. Establishing competencies for initial job in a chosen career field	5. Establishing credibility and competencies for a job change within a new career field
6. Not knowing what entry-level jobs are available	6. Not knowing what is available
7. Shyness about networking with contacts in the field	7. Shyness about networking with contacts in the field
8. Lack of trust in own ability to make and follow through on personal decisions	8. Relationship conflict about change
9. Inability to visualize job specifics within new field	9. Inability to visualize self working in a new career
10. Lack of job hunting know-how, experience, and tools	10. Lack of an ongoing plan and time frame for making change
11. Lack of self-confidence	11. Poor self-concept or lack of self-confidence
12. Unassertiveness	12. Unassertiveness

Web Connect

To help identify some barriers that you may be facing, check out the **Barriers to Employment** site at www.geocities.com/Athens/Academy/5450/3main.html. The barriers covered in this site include personal, career decision-making, job search, lack of experience, language, training and educational, financial, emotional, physical, personality, technological, and self-imposed. After reviewing the different kinds of barriers, read the section on Breaking Through the Barriers.

without the foggiest notion of what to do about an entry-level job. Many students decide to go on to graduate school, not with any clear career goal, but mostly to avoid entering that big, strange world of work. But what do you do after getting a masters degree with no specific career goal? Get a doctorate?

Lack of job and career experience can be a real barrier. A crucial part of career implementation is being able to visualize or mentally picture yourself doing what you want in a work setting suited to your tastes. That can be hard to do if you lack work experience. Yet a clear career image of yourself gives you the kind of self-confidence needed to take the next step and to sell yourself effectively to prospective employers. Lack of a clearly defined career identity, however, can fill you with uncertainty and render you unassertive. The "taking charge process" advocated in this book is incompatible with unassertive behavior.

How do college students demonstrate that they have the capabilities needed to perform effectively in an entry-level career position? Employers have businesses and organizations to run, and they need to hire people whom they can trust to get the job done. That means you are going to have to demonstrate clearly your superior strengths and capabilities for doing the job. If you can't, you are not going to get hired. That may sound harsh—but competition and no-nonsense qualifications are a reality. How to es-

tablish your credibility is a problem you must solve if you really want to obtain gainful employment in your field.

If you are a young college student, you should start implementing your own life and career plans now, step by step, to gain more confidence and competence. Unless you are a very unusual student, you have probably been depending upon the help and support of parents or other adults in making your decisions. It's a new ball game now. On the one hand, you can no longer rely on others to make and follow through on your most personal career/life decisions. On the other hand, as an inexperienced career and life decision maker, you are afraid to trust your own guidance.

You might be inclined either to avoid decision making or to be reluctant to move ahead with your decision until after graduation. The problem is that unless you start taking effective action on your decision now, it will remain a fantasy.

Another major hurdle to overcome is finding out what kind of entry-level jobs are available and how to prepare yourself for getting hired. This requires researching publications and getting out to talk with people in the field. Finding the necessary time can be difficult when you're struggling to find time to prepare your college assignments, do term papers, prepare for exams, and have a social life. In addition, talking with people in your potential or chosen career field can be scary. It's all too easy, therefore, to put off these activities until tomorrow and tomorrow and tomorrow. The problem with tomorrow is that one of those tomorrows will be graduation. At that point, suddenly getting a decent job and implementing a career will seem like eating that elephant in one gulp.

If this section seems depressing, we're sorry. We wouldn't be doing you a favor, however, by avoiding those "hard realities." The good news is that you can hurdle these barriers if you confront them head on with a realistic plan of action. That will leave you with far more confidence and competence than many other people in your same situation. Remember, everyone who has ever been employed had to start somewhere. The point is that you want to target your entry-level position, not be grateful for anything you can get.

Start clearly identifying your own barriers now by completing Exercise 10-C on next page. Then read further for ideas and suggestions on "hurdling your barriers" by developing an appropriate plan of action.

EXERCISE 10-C. COLLEGE STUDENT BARRIERS

Review Table 10.2 for the list of common barriers faced by college students. Circle any barriers that you believe are particularly pertinent to you, and add others, if necessary. Then list the five barriers below that you are the most concerned about:

1.

2.

3.

4.

5.

Strategies for College Students

Now that you have considered the bad news, the good news is that most barriers can be overcome. In fact, almost every barrier you will ever face is not so much a "bad condition" that exists in the world as it is a "mental state" that exists in your head. The way to overcome barriers is with positive thinking from which you develop a unique, workable plan of action. The following ideas and suggestions are offered to help you get started.

Web Connect

If you're interested in reading about how others have created self-empowering lives, visit ThriveNet's site at **www.thrivenet.com** and go through some of the articles.

1. Visualize the kind of entry-level job you want to have and mentally rehearse being in that role. Use the visualization technique described in Appendix D of this book. Give yourself about 20 minutes of quiet relaxed time for this process once a week. The visualization technique is a way to bring the future into the present and reduce fear of the unknown. You can then create a clear picture of what you want so that you know what you are going after. This will decrease your fear and procrastination while increasing your confidence.

2. Gain more confidence about your decision-making capabilities by reviewing the steps outlined in Chapter 8 or in additional books on decision making that your librarian can recommend. Your college counseling center may even offer workshops in decision making. Start practicing decision making by looking for all the opportunities available to make decisions and evaluate your performance. When you're in a decision-making situation, follow the steps in a conscious way, making sure that you both gather and analyze the available facts and draw upon your intuitive powers. Keep in mind that only you have the inner knowledge necessary for making effective decisions. Call on other people for information, ideas and reactions, but don't let anyone else make your decisions for you.

3. Complete your short-term plan from Chapter 9 to achieve your visualized entry-level job. Your plan will probably include information research at a local library, college career center, business or government library, or personnel offices. Your plan might include visits to the college career planning and placement center to discuss job-getting strategies with a career counselor. It might also include activi-

ties like networking (conducting information interviews) with people working in your field of interest to learn what those jobs are really like, to see what differences exist in jobs within different settings, to become familiar with businesses and organizations hiring people in that field, and to get tips on getting hired. Your plan could also call for summer work associated with your field, internships, volunteer work, related club and organization activities, and class projects or assignments that help you learn more about your field.

Setting goals, developing a plan, and following that plan is a strategy for career success. Post your plan in a place where you will see it daily—try a piece of newsprint over your desk. Make notations on your plan, indicating what you did and when you did it as a record of your progress. Discuss your plan and your progress with counselors, faculty, friends, and network contacts. Ask them for ideas and suggestions on steps for achieving your goal, and revise your plan whenever necessary. Your plan will be both your tool for success and antifear and antiprocrastination assurance.

Here are some ideas for clarifying your career goals while in college and gaining job-related experience and skills:

1. Use class projects to focus on personal career issues. Term papers can be an excellent way to research subject areas related to your chosen career field and to establish your writing, thinking, and communicating competencies. Consult with your professors about ideas for such projects. A useful research project would involve visiting and communicating with companies and organizations that you want to learn more about and talking with people who are performing work of interest to you. Keep some of your best papers as examples of some work-related skills that can be applied on the job.

2. Visit the college career center to investigate summer jobs, volunteer work, internships, and cooperative education experiences. Summer jobs are excellent opportunities to gain work-related experience in your field and to establish your

competencies. Don't take summer jobs just to earn money. Be creative and look for ways to gain experience, self-information, job possibilities, and job recommendations.

Cooperative educational experience and internships are wonderful opportunities to acquire job-related experiences and to develop your own career identity further. Volunteer work with businesses and organizations related to your field can also be an excellent source of exposure. Perhaps you can include a volunteer work experience as part of a class project or a special study project. You might develop a volunteer project on a career-related activity with a favorite professor. Be sure to ask any employers you have worked for and professors in your field for letters of recommendation. Add these to your job credential file.

3. Take advantage of the numerous clubs, organizations, student government, and work activities available on almost every college campus. If you are thinking about a career in writing, look into opportunities with the college paper. Interested in communications? Check into possibilities with college radio and cable TV stations. Want to become a manager? Investigate possibilities with the college governance board or involvement in a leadership activity with a campus organization. Considering psychology, philosophy, or anthropology? Become active in the clubs associated with these disciplines.

4. Develop your job-hunting skills and your awareness of what's available in the job market by reading Chapter 11 carefully. Don't wait until graduation to begin the job-hunting process. If you are visionary and creative, you can move through entry-level job preparation in an organized way and even have fun with it. Since the job market is vast, there are always openings available. Start with the career planning and placement office to find out what is available.

Networking is often the most valuable source of job information. How does the shy or unaggressive personality handle networking? Remember that assertiveness can be learned. To become a more confident speaker, take speech classes, practice speaking out in class, and join activities that involve improving your skills. Drama classes and psychology workshops teach assertiveness skills and help you improve your self-confidence. Remember also that you can "feel" unassertive but act in an assertive way.

CASE STUDY
DICK

Dick is a big amiable guy with a ready grin and a "laid-back" appearance. You soon learn from talking with Dick that he loves to discuss ideas and is a diversified reader, particularly in science-related areas.

Dick comes from a family of professionals. His father is a biologist with a Ph.D., and his mother is a chemist. Dick is the youngest child with a brother and sister who have also gone on to become practicing scientists. In comparing himself to his family, Dick always felt intellectually inferior. He was pretty much a "C" student in high school and a bit of a loner. He tried college for a while after high school, but dropped out before finishing his freshman year. He just hadn't discovered anything of interest, and he failed math to further confirm that he wasn't much of a student.

Dick bummed around for a couple of years trying odd jobs here and there, but generally was just drifting along with his life. Eventually, he learned about a career planning class being offered at the local community college and decided to give it a try. In the course, Dick decided that he wanted to be a science writer. He was still concerned, however, about his ability to do college-level work.

Dick's counselor helped him see that his barrier wasn't lack of intelligence, but lack of self-confidence. Fortunately, finding a career goal had already given him a big boost over that barrier. This really was the first time Dick had ever felt energized about any kind of goal in his life.

Dick started back to college and was amazed at how well he was doing now that he was motivated by his career goal. He worked diligently, and his efforts paid off. He even found that he could "get" math. He obtained a tutor and worked hard. To his amazement, he now got straight As, even in math.

Dick still had some questions about his ability to be a successful student and a science writer. He knew that he had enjoyed creative writing in high school and that he loved reading science fiction. He had some doubts, however, about whether his family would accept him as a "writer," since he assumed they wanted him to follow the family tradition of becoming a scientist.

Dick began talking with his professor about his science writing goal and obtained names of local science writers to contact for information interviews. Dick set up some interesting research papers to do, including one that involved spending a weekend with a yogi who claimed that he could levitate. Dick's eyes really gleam when he talks about this project and what he learned from the yogi, though he didn't actually observe him levitate. Dick's instructor regarded his paper highly and suggested he share it with others. Dick did, and received validating feedback on his developing skills. Dick also arranged to take an anthropology course and write a paper on an archeological dig taking place at the site of an old home in the southern part of the county.

Dick has now completed his A.A. degree at the community college and enrolled in the journalism program at the state university. After his first semester there, he arranged to be a summer research assistant with a university biologist conducting research on bats in southern rural Ohio. Dick was optimistic that the results of this project might produce a significant breakthrough in improving intelligence in human beings. Dick maintained a journal for this project to use either in a course project or a feature story in the college paper or alumni journal.

Dick is now serving as a writer on one of the university's numerous publications. He also plans to continue conducting information interviews with science writers and to develop his job-hunting network during his last year in college. Through his networking so far, he has learned that his chances of getting an initial job with a major paper like the *Washington Post* right out of college are slim, but he has several ideas about getting an entry-level position with a smaller paper. Dick continues to check in with the folks in the career planning and placement office on a regular basis. He is in the process now of adding to his credentials file, refining his resume, and feeling good about himself as a learner, a writer, and a person.

EXERCISE 10-D. A COLLEGE STUDENT'S PLAN OF ACTION

Using the ideas and suggestions above, develop a plan for how you intend to overcome the specific hurdles you identified in Exercise 10-C. Be as specific as you can. Identify real activities that you can and will do to move yourself through your barriers and onto the road to a satisfying entry-level job in your chosen career field.

I plan to take the following actions to hurdle the five barriers I have identified:

Barrier	Action
1.	
2.	
3.	
4.	
5.	

Barriers Facing Career Changers

Have you noticed how many people talk about career change but never do it? By career change, we mean a shift to a different kind of work, often in a totally different field. We know people who are desperately unhappy or bored with their jobs or even on the verge of losing their jobs and yet make no move to improve their situation. Why? Fear of change seems to be the biggest culprit. You may not like the situation you're in, but at least you know what you've got. This fear of change is often disguised with concerns like: "I'm too old to change" or "I've got my family, kids, parents, dog to support" or "I've been a widget technician, lion tamer, tank driver all my life. Who would want to hire one of those?" Procrastination usually goes hand in hand with fear. It's hard to get started on a task you fear. It's much easier to complain about the current situation or to engage in "if only I had done it differently" daydreams.

What is frightening about career change? If you have been at a job for a while, you are probably making a stable salary, with some benefits. Even a bad job provides some structure for your life. Changing careers certainly can involve a significant reduction in income and lost benefits. A career change situa-tion also usually involves uncertainty about one's marketable skills and what they may be worth. People under stress tend to discount their worth and ability to make productive changes. It's unusual for people to be positive, realistic, and optimistic about themselves under such circumstances.

Career changers often find it difficult to obtain much support for making big changes in their life from mates, family, friends, and colleagues. That's particularly true the longer you have been in a career, the older you are, and the bigger your salary and/or benefits. It's often difficult to support yourself without the nurturing support of at least one other significant and trusted person. Career change talk has been known to produce serious conflict in relationships.

Another common barrier faced by the person in a career transition is feeling so boxed in by current work that it is difficult to visualize doing something very different. A person's current job title also makes it difficult for others, particularly prospective employers, to see an employee performing in a very different role. How do you develop a belief that you can do something very different from your current work? How do you establish your credibility and competence for doing a different kind of work?

Next, how do you find out what positions are available, where your prospects are best, and how to make the change? Most people have fallen into their careers as a result of circumstances. Few people really know how to make a career switch and job hunt effectively.

With all of these barriers to career change, it's no wonder that most people feel trapped in their current situation. But does it have to be that way? We think not. Are you feeling so unhappy with your current career that it is hurting your emotional and physical health or your personal development? Unless your distress is connected only with your current job, it's worth making either a career change or career redirection. A career redirection involves remaining in your line of work but negotiating some satisfying changes in your job, such as moving out of supervision and into technical applications, for example. To begin resolving your barriers, however, you first need to know what they are so you can take appropriate action. Take a few minutes now to clarify your specific barriers to career change by doing Exercise 10-E. Next, read further for suggestions and ideas to overcome these obstacles.

 ## EXERCISE 10-E. BARRIERS TO CAREER CHANGE

Review Table 10.2 for the list of barriers to career change. Circle any barriers that might keep you from making a career change. Add any additional barriers to the list that affect your situation. Then list below the five barriers that you feel are most likely to keep you from getting what you want in your career.

1.

2.

3.

4.

5.

Strategies for Career Changers

Here are some ways to overcome negative mindsets and other psychological or emotional barriers:

1. Overcome the barriers of fear and procrastination by making your vision of what you want more vivid than your vision of what you fear. It is impossible to achieve what you really want without knowing clearly what that is. We are not advocating here that you develop some utopian vision, but a realistic picture of where you could use your actual talents more happily. At least twice a week use the visualization process described in Appendix D to imagine the kind of job you want to be doing and to mentally rehearse doing it. The clearer you can make that picture, the more likely you are to actually achieve it. You will be shifting your energy from fear and avoidance of an unknown future into enthusiasm for where you are going.

2. Conquer the lack of support barrier by establishing a support group to help motivate you. Look for people who can really support you, listen to you and provide suggestions, ideas, and feedback. You want the kind of support that will be both honest and constructive. Avoid both pure critics and well-intentioned, but inexperienced supporters who might lead you down a blind alley with naive ideas. Check in with people in your support structure on a regular basis. We highly rec-

ommend that you seek out the assistance of a professional career counselor to include in your support structure.

3. Prepare in advance for the possibility of conflicts with your spouse, partner, or family over career change. Communication is the key here. Share your vision with your mate and include him/her in the planning as much as possible. Remember also that you have more to bring to a relationship when you are fulfilled in your work than you do when you're unhappy, bored, depressed or feeling blocked, trapped and helpless.

   What do you do if your mate simply is unable to support your change? Some individuals have found it necessary to leave their spouse in order to make the kind of career change needed for a better, fuller life. Their spouse simply could not support the change. Only you know what your situation really is, what your possibilities are, and what decision to make.

4. Make an action plan that becomes your "antiprocrastination" program of specific steps required to transform your vision into reality. See the previous section for college students to get more details on sources of information for this plan. As you clarify your visualized future, make any necessary changes. Post your plan in a spot you will look at often. A prominent spot over your desk is a good place.

To find out about specific job alternatives and market yourself effectively, read Chapter 11. Then consider the suggestions below:

1. Clarify what you really can do in a new career by giving up your current job labels and focusing on your transferable skills along with a vision of what you want.

Your goal is to identify specific accomplishments you have achieved in your paid or voluntary jobs that are related to your new career goals. Using the guidance provided in Chapter 11, capture these in concrete terms on your resume.

Developing your resume in this manner will help you build up your credibility and your competency for your career change both on paper and in your mind. You must do that for yourself before you can ever hope to convince prospective employers of your suitability for a job within a new career field. Also consider approaching prospective employers with a two-page marketing or resume letter instead of a standard resume with cover letter. These letters are often a better strategy for career changers because you can emphasize relevant achievements without calling so much attention to the job titles you have held that are outside the occupation you are targeting.

2. Networking and job-hunting effectiveness are vital skills and activities in a career change. Networking is how you find out what's actually available, where you want to work, and how to get hired there. To overcome shyness or unassertiveness barriers that most people experience about networking, consult a career counselor for guidance. Perhaps all you need is a few names to begin your networking, along with a little encouragement. If your confidence is still lacking, practice information interviewing with your friends first. Remember that you can learn to be more assertive, even if you feel shy. Don't use shyness as a reason to avoid getting out and talking to people.

After a dozen years as a professional hockey player, age caught up with Nels. It was time to look for a different kind of work, but what does an ex-jock do? Nels hadn't been a superstar, so he considered that his days in the limelight were over for good. He had no career preparation, and, as far as he knew, no skills or personal contacts that would qualify him for anything more than a physical labor job. Based on that assumption, Nels felt fortunate to obtain a job as a forklift operator in a food chain warehouse.

After a couple of years of hoisting boxes, Nels decided there had to be more to life than this. The switch from the roar of the crowd to the endless boxes of the warehouse was too great a change for him. But the dilemma remained: what could he do? After an acquaintance told him about a career planning course available at a nearby college, Nels enrolled.

In the course, Nels discovered that he had in fact a number of valuable skills and that his strongest interests were in science and technology. He thought it would be wonderful to be a geologist or a petroleum engineer and search for oil wells. At first Nels rejected the idea flat out. He just couldn't picture an "ex-jock" who had never taken a college course doing that. How could he do all that math? Nels wasn't even sure he could spell thermodynamics, let alone understand it.

Little by little, however, the idea began to shape into a clear vision in his mind. After numerous sessions with his career counselor and considerable self-assessment, Nels reluctantly did a couple of information interviews with a geologist and an engineer. After these interviews Nels was hooked. He knew he wanted to be an engineer. While he wasn't sure if he could do the college work, he decided to "give it a whack."

A year after taking the course, Nels stopped in to visit his career counselor to ask if there was a follow-up course he could take to verify his career decision. The counselor learned that Nels was getting As in his college course work. His self-doubts came from the lack of support his wife and friends had for his new career decision. They were incredulous that the "ex-jock" was considering something so different like engineering. His counselor was able to reassure him on that score and assist him in finding a way to get the support he needed from his wife and friends.

Nels' career counselor saw him again a year later, when he stopped by the office to share a "breakthrough" success he had achieved. From the contacts established over the past two years, Nels had landed a job as an engineering technician with a petroleum exploration firm. He would be working with and assisting a team of geologists and engineers in the kind of work he had dreamed about. Nels confided that it was only because of his interests, his good grades, and most of all the contacts he had established that he had obtained the job. In fact, he really didn't have the A.A. degree yet that was listed as a job requirement.

Best of all, the company would pay Nels' way to a bachelors degree in engineering after he had been with the firm for one year. Nels was elated. He realized that if he hadn't been willing to visualize himself in this role and then check out the realistic possibilities, he would still be hoisting boxes in the warehouse. True, he would never be in the "limelight" again, but for him, this would be just as good. Nels would be doing interesting work and developing himself in a direction that appeared right for his skills and interests.

Cheryl came to the "Career Direction" workshop looking for promising alternatives to her career as a nurse. It was not so much that Cheryl disliked nursing, but rather that she was just "burned out" after ten years in the profession. She was tired of waiting on patients and taking orders from doctors. Cheryl just didn't want to do that any more.

In reviewing the data from her career surveys, the career counselor saw that the problem was more than just a career burnout situation. Cheryl's thinking-style profile showed her to be a left-brain oriented, logical, and controlling thinker. While Cheryl could be empathetic and feeling, that was just not her strongest suit. She liked technical activities and was good at planning and organizing. Cheryl was introverted and liked to think things through on her own more than to interact with people. She particularly resented following the directives of doctors rather than deciding on her own.

Cheryl discussed alternatives with her career counselor. The problem was that Cheryl had some rigid requirements. She had to maintain her current income level, did not want to lose her benefits, and definitely did not want to go back to college for years as part of a career change program. Based on her situation and the information available, the counselor suggested that Cheryl consider redirecting her career within the health field rather than starting a totally new career.

The health field has enough variety and occupational possibilities to enable one to move away from the service-delivery side of nursing and into a more technical specialty. As a technical specialist, Cheryl would be able to utilize her top strengths much more fully and would not have to carry out doctors' directives. There were a number of possibilities in the area: computer diagnostics, medical technology, technical consultant. By selecting a career track that would count much of her previous job experience and by taking selected courses, Cheryl could probably maintain her current income while making the switch.

Cheryl was not in a career change situation, but rather a career redirection. The career center could only provide limited information on what kinds of jobs within the health area would best utilize her skills, where these jobs were, and how to get them. Cheryl needed to learn specifics and get more strategic advice by conducting information interviews and establishing a network of contacts. She was excited about the redirection possibilities, but discouraged about the need for establishing personal contacts with other health professionals, since she tended to be a loner.

But Cheryl went ahead anyway by talking to some of the nursing instructors at the college and a nurse who had held a variety of interesting jobs in the field. Cheryl began to engage herself more fully in the networking task and developed her career redirection plan. She realized that she could not make an immediate change, but at least now she had a goal to follow and was identifying what steps to take to get there. As a side benefit, Cheryl's new goal gave her hope and energy. She was no longer "burned out" as she took charge of developing her career in a more self-fulfilling direction.

EXERCISE 10-F. A CAREER CHANGER'S PLAN OF ACTION _____

Using the foregoing ideas and suggestions, develop your plan to overcome the specific hurdles you identified in Exercise 10-E. Identify specific activities that you can take to move yourself through your barriers. Whenever you can, specify dates for when you intend to accomplish a specific activity.

I plan to take the following actions to hurdle my five major barriers to career change:

Barrier	Action
1.	
2.	
3.	
4.	
5.	

SUMMARY

Successful career/life decision making requires effective attitudes and decision-making skills along with methods to overcome situational barriers. Your attitudes largely determine how effective you can and will be in implementing your career choices. People develop characteristic outlooks, some inclining to pessimism and others to optimism. Self-victimizing people are characteristically uninvolved, dependent, and inflexible in the career-choice process.

In contrast, a self-empowering mindset gives you permission to think, feel, and know that what you do makes a difference in the outcomes of your life. Self-empowerers tend to be involved in the career-choice process, independent in decision making,

and open to compromise in order to achieve the best outcome possible in a particular situation. While it is no simple task to transform a self-victimizing mindset to a more self-empowering inclination, the time and energy involved in making this shift are well worth it.

Career competencies are skills that can be enhanced through learning and practice. Five specific competencies are involved in career/life decision making: self-assessment, identification of options, goal selection, planning, and problem solving.

To overcome situational barriers, such as being a college student with no professional work experience or being an older career changer, you will need current information sources, realistic self-assessments, support groups, action plans, and personal contacts.

ASSIGNMENTS

1. Interview three or four people such as your spouse, parents, friends, acquaintances, colleagues, banker, or service people, to find out such things as: what kind of work they do, what turns them on and off about their work, how they got into that type of work, whether they would advise anyone else to get into their line of work. As you interview these people, attempt to discover whether they tend to be more self-victimizing or self-empowering about their work. Note: If they are self-victimizing, don't volunteer this opinion. Remember that change has to be initiated by each individual.

2. Think about the following questions:

   a. In what ways might a person with a self-victimizing mindset go about the career-choice process differently from a person with a self-empowering mindset?

   b. In choosing a career, is it more effective to be uncompromising or willing to compromise? Why?

   c. Is it preferable to make your own career-related decisions or to have an expert or knowledgeable person decide for you?

   d. Why might some people prefer to be uninvolved in the selection and implementation of their careers?

   e. In what ways is a person with a self-empowering mindset more likely to have a more satisfactory career than a person with a self-victimizing mindset?

 Similar to small businesses that open and close, Web sites come and go. This means that some of the Web sites listed in this book will probably change during the time you are reading this material. Therefore, we have created a page on the Web where you can go to ensure you have the most up-to-date links for each of the chapters. To find these links, go to **www.CareerKiosk.org** and click on "Updated links for *Your Career*." These links will ensure that you have accurate links and access to great sites on the Web!

REFERENCES

Waitley, Dennis E. *The Psychology of Winning*, a cassette tape series. Chicago: Nightingale-Conant Corporation, (n.d.). Contact the publisher at 3730 West Devon Avenue, Chicago, IL 60659. Telephone: 1-800-323-5552.

Searching for a Job to Fit Your Talents

. . . there is always someone in the market place who wants to buy your special talents. All you have to do is to let enough people know about the merchandise that is available.
—Carl R. Boll
Executive Jobs Unlimited

Do you know people who—

☑ Need a job but are so anxious about job hunting that they just can't seem to get started?

☑ Can get a job any time they want because they know what they have to offer and are self-confident and assertive?

☑ Just don't know how to get a job or make a job change?

☑ Stay with a job they hate or have outgrown for "security"?

☑ Find security by remaining open-minded and flexible enough to make successful job changes when necessary?

If so, you have seen the difference between self-victimizing, reluctant job seekers and self-empowered, effective job seekers.

Watching "Cops" on TV does not count as experience in law enforcement.

GREAT JOBS AND BARRIERS

This chapter assumes that you have developed a clear career goal, obtained whatever education or training you need, and are now ready to find and obtain a great job. Incidentally, we define a great job as one that lets you fully use your top interests and skills to perform a valuable service and rewards you with both personal satisfaction and a good income.

Most of us find getting the right job one of life's most difficult challenges. Perhaps the main reason is that we aren't sure how to conduct an effective job hunt. It's also true that after hearing so much about employment problems, we're afraid there isn't much available out there. We feel inclined just to keep what we have or take any available job. Fear about job hunting limits our effectiveness and may keep us from going after those really great jobs.

This chapter is designed to help you break through your own job barriers and those created by our country's incredibly rapid change. Thousands of traditional jobs in manufacturing are disappearing while thousands of new service and high-tech jobs are being created and added to the job market. You are likely to be changing jobs and careers many times in your lifetime. By reading this chapter carefully and doing the work involved, you will become an effective, confident job hunter. Even better, you'll discover that getting a good job becomes a problem-solving game. Playing the "getting-hired" game can actually be fun—and can be far more rewarding than Monopoly!

UNDERSTANDING THE GETTING-A-JOB GAME

To play the game effectively, you need to understand the game board—that is, the job world. Picture this world as a market and yourself as a product. William Cohen sums it up well in the statement, "Job hunting is a sales situation. You are the product. Your prospective employer is your customer."[1] You are in great shape, however, because you have mastered the most important task in the game of salesmanship—you understand the product. The work you have accomplished in self-understanding gives you a tremendous advantage over the competition. Most other job searchers out there don't know what they are selling to whom, or even that they are in a sales game.

It's helpful to think of the job world as being two markets—the visible and the hidden. Job openings in the visible job market are listed in places like classified ads and on college placement office job lists. In contrast, the hidden job market is a whole world of jobs and potential jobs that are never listed anywhere.

Outside of knowing the product (you), knowing the difference between these two markets is the second most important piece of information you need to become an expert in the "getting-hired" game. Job-hunting experts like Richard Bolles (*What Color Is Your Parachute?*) and Tom Jackson (*Guerrilla Tactics in the Job Market*) tell us that only about 10 to 25 percent of the available jobs at any one time are ever listed anywhere. In other words, fully 75 to 90 percent of the jobs are hidden!

While you shouldn't ignore advertised openings in the visible job market, we advise most job hunters to focus on this hidden job market. Why? First, the hidden job market is where the greatest number of opportunities lie. And second, you will encounter less competition and less rejection in the hidden job market. Since most of our nation's job seekers are going after ten to twenty-five percent of the jobs, there are usually huge numbers of applicants for every listed job. So to play the "getting-hired" game effectively, you need to address all those opportunities awaiting you in the hidden job market.

In his book, *Guerrilla Tactics in the Job Market*, job-hunting specialist Tom Jackson provides us with a good idea of just how big the hidden job market is. Jackson informs us that over 400,000 employers in the United States employ more than 50 workers.[2] Almost every employer this size has current or potential openings caused by people quitting, about to quit, being asked to resign, retiring, or expiring. Additionally, millions of new jobs are created every year in this country—even in times of recession, downsizing, and corporate re-engineering. What this means is that in almost any area of the country, there are thousands of job opportunities awaiting you right now. But you are going to have to be creative in finding them because the great majority of them are not readily apparent.

---

[1] William A. Cohen, *The Executive's Guide to Finding a Superior Job* (New York: AMACOM) 7.

[2] Tom Jackson, *Guerrilla Tactics in the Job Market* (New York: Bantam Books, 1978) 120.

As a 58-year-old career changer, Ralph had learned how to network with a younger crowd.

At first, tapping the visible or traditional job market may seem like the easiest way to get a good job. You would answer a few classified ads each week, check in with one or two employment agencies, and perhaps mail out your resume to a list of employers you find in the *Yellow Pages*. Unfortunately, if you are a recent college graduate, a returning worker, or a career changer, you're not likely to get many acceptable job offers from these traditional approaches.

The visible job market best accommodates job seekers with training and experience in "high-demand" job slots and those with special skills for which there is an urgent need. For example, the traditional approach can be effective for an experienced nurse, a computer systems analyst, or fundraiser who wants to make a job change (but not a career change). Otherwise, the visible job market offers you few alternatives, heavy competition, and a distorted, negative view of available opportunities. In a large organization a classified job ad typically gets several hundred responses, including responses from highly experienced people. A job ad placed on an online job site, such as Monster.com, may receive even more

responses than classified ads. Thus, this is not a viable strategy for the great majority of normal job seekers at this time.

Employment agencies can be another dead end. Private employment agencies stay in business by charging a high fee, even though their service is often just handing packets of resumes to prospective employers. If the employer pays the fee, he or she expects a well-qualified candidate with significant experience. Many employers won't use state employment agencies because they don't want to be inundated by massive numbers of job seekers, nor fee-based agencies because they can find people easily enough in today's highly competitive job market. If, however, you do consider using a fee-based agency, see whether they will guarantee to find you a job that fits your qualifications and meets your salary requirements. We haven't found one yet that does this. But again, if you have high demand skills, you may wish to consult with a service that specializes in placing individuals with your specific competencies.

For most people, a job-hunting strategy that concentrates primarily on the hidden job market improves the odds of being successful at the "getting-hired" game—both online and offline!

CHOOSING YOUR STRATEGY

Here is the situation as you prepare to engage in the "getting-hired" game. There are dozens, perhaps hundreds, or even thousands of employment opportunities in the vast playing grounds of the hidden job market that are well matched to your skills and motivations. They need people who can and want to perform the work necessary for the success of their business or organization. Their profits, the quality of their goods or service, the attainment of their "bottom lines," their future viability are dependent upon hiring people with the right match of skills, knowledge, personal attributes, and motivation. But the employers with these great jobs don't know that you are out there or what you can do for them. They would often welcome potential employees coming forward and identifying themselves. This saves them the expense of agencies or advertising and time lost in the job listing, interviewing, and hiring process. The bad news, of course, is that unless you assertively play the game with the right players, you won't find these unadvertised positions.

So your task in the game is to decide which employers you might really want to work for and to show them directly that you are the right person for the job. The great thing about this game is that every player can win. All you have to do is follow the steps and play the game assertively and skillfully. Figure 11.1 outlines the steps involved in the game. Whenever you are ready, start the game—it's your move!

First Move—Know Your Product

Effective salespeople realize that to be successful they have to know and really like their product or service. Imagine trying to sell a car to someone when you can't quickly and accurately tick off a list of its best features or answer the customer's questions. Can you see yourself attempting to sell a product you don't believe in or personally care about? How convincing will you be, and how likely are you to make a sale?

Like it or not, when you're in the job hunting game, you're in a sales situation. What's true in selling a product or a service is equally true in selling yourself. By completing the earlier exercises in this book, you have already learned about yourself, the product in the "getting-hired" game. You know your unique features, your skills, interests, needs, and values. Now you need to verbalize, summarize, promote, and answer questions about them—with enthusiasm! Your customers (potential employers) need to understand what your product/service can do for them. In this regard, imagine yourself as a highly desirable product/service that customers are anxious to buy and can benefit from. When you can do this you will be much more effective in selling your talents to the right customers, for a fair price (we're talking salary here!).

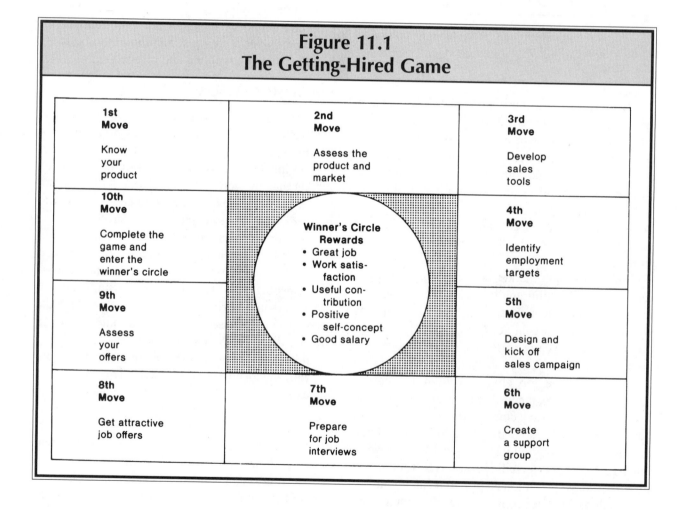

Figure 11.1
The Getting-Hired Game

1st Move Know your product	2nd Move Assess the product and market	3rd Move Develop sales tools
10th Move Complete the game and enter the winner's circle	**Winner's Circle Rewards** • Great job • Work satisfaction • Useful contribution • Positive self-concept • Good salary	4th Move Identify employment targets
9th Move Assess your offers		5th Move Design and kick off sales campaign
8th Move Get attractive job offers	7th Move Prepare for job interviews	6th Move Create a support group

EXERCISE 11-A. SELLING YOUR PRODUCT

1. Review your preferred functional skills, your top self-management skills, and interests along with your needs, values, and goals.

2. Make a list of your best attributes as if you were a service you were preparing to sell for a profit. Decide what things are most unique about your service. Why would a customer (employer) want to purchase your service?

3. Gather a few friends or acquaintances together and assign them the role of potential customers (employers) for the product you're selling. Practice your selling skills with them by relating your career sales pitch to your top personal attributes. Wherever possible, point to selected personal accomplishments that demonstrate the kinds of skills and motivations you are selling. Have your friends and acquaintances ask searching questions about what you can do for their organization and why you would want to work at such an activity. Practice really liking your product/service and learn to sell what you can do for an organization with genuine enthusiasm. Ask for honest feedback from the group and use their evaluations to improve your product knowledge and salesmanship. Switch roles after one session to get a dual perspective. Ask questions, observe their responses, and adopt anything of value.

Second Move—Assess the Product and Market

For your next step in the "getting-hired" game, remember this critical point—*don't sell your product/service to the wrong customer*. Think of the mistake it would be to sell an elegant car to someone who just wants any old car as long as it will perform. This valuable car would soon deteriorate into junk. You want to sell yourself to the employer who values what you have to offer, uses your services appropriately, and treats you with the respect you deserve. In doing this, we do not advise the kind of misplaced self-confidence that translates as cocky or obnoxious behavior. We do advise that you present yourself as someone special—because you are! However, it's up to you to clearly and specifically show how you are special and to do that in job-related terms.

As a self-empowered job seeker, the responsibility of getting your product/service to the right customer is up to you. In contrast, self-victimizers take any job they can get and then gripe about being neither appreciated nor satisfied. Your second move is to decide what kind of customers (employers) you want to sell your services to and what you are best equipped to do for them. You'll also want to begin assessing what your product/service is worth in the current job market. Begin by posing these questions:

1. What markets (employers) have the greatest need for your services? (See Exercise 11-A)

2. What are the most valuable benefits you can bring to each type of employer? What past accomplishments prove that those benefits are real?

3. What should your product sell for (reasonable market salary for the service you can deliver)?

When you've found answers to these questions, you will be able to decide which kind of employers to target in your job sales campaign. Think of this as exactly the same kind of task that successful businesspeople perform when they have a product or service to sell.

To help with your product/market assessment, here are some more specific questions to consider:

1. What kinds of people would benefit the most from your service (young or old, uneducated or well educated, male or female, majority or minority)? Note: All employers, including the government, are in business to sell or provide a service to certain kinds of people. Identifying the people you are most interested in serving

and best prepared to serve could help you target those employers who cater to these populations.

2. What kinds of employers (businesses and organizations) would find your services most useful? (If, for example, you are a gifted idea person, then companies who need bright, innovative people could best use your skills—advertising agencies, political campaign offices, sales and marketing departments, fundraising organizations).

3. What causes might your product (your talents, energies, values, and interests) best serve? Do you have a strong desire to improve the efficiency of the transportation system, clean up the environment, conserve energy, improve people's health and longevity, create more beautiful cities? What kinds of organizations deal in some way with the cause you most want to serve? (If, for example, your cause is to improve people's health, you might consider the opportunities available with health food stores, hospitals, wellness centers, government and world health organizations, athletic coaching staffs, or sports programs).

To help you define characteristics of target employers further, answer these questions.

1. In what geographic location (city, locality) do you most want to work? What area might have the greatest demand for your services?

2. What size of business or organization do you want to work for? What size of organization is most likely to need your services? Do you want to work with a business with interests and concerns that are local, national, or international? Do you

have foreign language skills that might be of service in an international firm, or computer competencies to bring to an employer in need of enhancing their capabilities? Examples: A young college graduate sold his computing knowledge to a printing company in the process of transitioning from a manual to an automated operation. A midlife career changer sold his computing expertise to a travel agency in need of enhancing its data accessing and reporting capabilities.

3. What kinds of products or services do you want your employer to be associated with (potato chips, computers, plumbing repair, counseling, electronic equipment, bakery goods, day-care centers, toys, family therapy, financial information)? Suggestion: Review the index or table of contents to the Yellow Pages of a city telephone directory for product and service ideas.

4. Do you have a preference for working with a profit or nonprofit business or organization? Would you get a greater sense of satisfaction working for an organization or business that was committed to maximizing profits or one devoted to providing valuable service to people or the environment?

5. What kinds of activities do you want your work associates to be doing? What people would find your skills and interests most useful? What kinds of businesses or organizations would employ those people? (For example, a high Holland code "C" person with wonderful organizing skills who enjoys being around creative people might be able to create order out of chaos for a growing electronics firm, a group of architects, or artists.)

EXERCISE 11-B. DEFINING IDEAL EMPLOYERS _____

1. After considering the above questions, make two lists to help you assess where your job-related skills and attributes can best be marketed. Entitle the first list *Types of Organizations* and the second, *Characteristics of an Ideal Organization.*

   Under the first heading, develop a list of at least ten (preferably 20 or more) types of organizations that you would both enjoy working for and where your abilities could be in demand. Use the index of a city *Yellow Pages* directory for general ideas, but be sure to make the categories as specific as possible. Entries like electronic sales companies or educational institutions are too general to be useful.

   Under *Characteristics of an Ideal Organization,* list those things that are important to you in an ideal job setting. List ten or more items under this heading.

   Sample entries might look like the following:

What I'm Looking for in an Ideal Employment Situation

Types of Organizations	*Characteristics of an Ideal Organization*
• an accounting firm • a computer software sales company • a conservation consulting firm • a men's clothing factory • a public broadcasting company • an arts dealership • a dude ranch • a children's toy sales company • a sports outfitting firm • a primary day-care center	• medium-sized city in NW, USA • company size of 50–100 employees • community-involved business • associates knowledgeable about science and high technology • equal opportunity employer • team-oriented leadership • company with Asian operations • location under a ten-mile commute • profit-making organization

---

   a. After completing your two lists, prioritize the first one to identify your top three employer types. That narrows down the employers you're targeting to a manageable few categories. You will use these categories later to compile a list of specific employment targets.

   b. Rank your *Characteristics of an Ideal Organization* list, identifying the top five preferred traits. These specific characteristics will also help you find appropriate employment targets.

   c. Print your two prioritized lists and post them near your work or "thinking space" as an ongoing reminder of what you are aiming for.

2. After developing your two prioritized lists, create a mental picture of your ideal employment site through the envisioning process described in Appendix D. The purpose of this part of the game is to create a mental picture of the kind of work setting that fits your career objectives. Repeat this envisioning process once or twice each day until you get a clear mental picture of yourself working in your ideal job site. This will give you an intuitive sense of what to look for and where to look for it.

Third Move—Develop Your Sales Tools

Your sales tools are the means by which you make potential employers aware of and interested in your product. You will need to develop four different tools to play the "getting-hired" game. They are your resume, your personal sales letter, your networking skills, and your job-interviewing skills.

The personal sales letter, networking, and job-interviewing skills will be discussed later in the chapter. For now we will concentrate on the first sales tool you should develop—your resume. Your resume serves two important functions. First, preparing your resume causes you to clarify your career goal and your best and most salable attributes. A good resume also identifies selected accomplishments and relates these to the type of work you are seeking. Here your transferable skills need to be clearly and concisely revealed.

Keep in mind that your resume serves first and foremost as a tool of *career self-definition* and secondly to help potential employers assess how closely your qualifications match their needs. But—a resume alone won't get you a job. Jobs are obtained through interviews! Usually it's your networking efforts, sales letters, and telephone calls that produce interviews. A well-prepared resume can help get job interviews by assisting your "targeted" employers in summarizing pertinent information about you. And,

conversely, a poorly done resume will sabotage a job-search campaign.

Because there is so much information, good and bad, readily available on resume writing, we will not go into detail here. A number of excellent resume-writing resources are listed at the end of this chapter, and we also encourage you to consult with your local library or bookstore.

As you develop your resume, we recommend that you keep these five guidelines in mind:

1. Be clear and organized. Write your resume with the knowledge that an employer is likely to take just a few seconds to review it! Your resume therefore needs to be concise but "hard-hitting."

Web Connect

To find helpful examples of resumes for more than 20 different career fields, check out College Grad's collection at **www.collegegrad.com/resumes/ index.shtml** This site also has an interesting section called Best College Resumes. This site should help you get a great start with your resume.

2. List those top skills and accomplishments that are relevant to your career objective. Don't be repetitive, and don't put any information on the resume that doesn't relate directly to the job you want. Don't sell yourself to the wrong job!

3. Be ready to revise and customize your resume for specific employers. Do not have just one resume printed and mass mailed.

4. Make your resume look great—it represents you! Print it out on a laser or letter-quality printer and use only top-quality paper (heavy bond with rag content) and traditional colors (white, off-white, gray). Be creative in the way you play the job-hunting game—but not in your resume presentation.

5. Use your resume as a tool in your getting-hired campaign rather than your sole tactic. Often it's best to send a specially prepared resume to networking sources and/or a potential employer *after* an initial meeting rather than handing them a mass-produced, general resume that is likely to hit the trash bucket before you're out the door.

 ## EXERCISE 11-C. DEVELOPING YOUR RESUME

1. Remember, first and foremost, that your resume must clearly state exactly what you're selling! Begin by developing a clear and concise career summary. This summary should include these three elements:

   - An opening line that defines you career-wise. For example: "An articulate leader-manager with six years experience creating, organizing, and implementing educational and recreational programs for children and young adults."

   - A second line that identifies those skill areas you are promoting. For example: "Top skills include human resource training, educational and recreational program development, and leadership training."

   - A final line that defines your top personality traits or personal assets (those aspects that most work about you). For example: "A creative, outgoing, and supportive facilitator with a proven track record of inspiring initiative, responsibility, and team work in others." You may find it helpful here to review those self-defining attributes you identified from the assessment activities in Chapters 3 and 4.

2. Your resume should go on to list carefully selected achievements that reveal how you have successfully used those transferable skills that you are "showcasing" in your career summary. In writing up your achievements, it's a good idea to identify:

   - specific tasks or problems you tackled

   - definite actions you took

   - concrete results you achieved

   In this regard, remember two things: first, it's not enough simply to list your top skills; you need to show how you have used them. And, second, in today's job market—*results count*! Your resume, therefore, must show both that you are skilled and results oriented. Later in the chapter we will look at resume samples that pertain more specifically to career changers. Here are some typical examples a college student might use:

- As assistant camp director and head counselor: developed, organized, conducted, and evaluated a week-long training course for over fifty counselors, which significantly increased staff professionalism, enhanced client morale, and reduced staff turnover by over fifty percent.

- Organized, implemented, and managed a creative and unique monthly activities program for a youth social club. The program became so successful that paid group memberships doubled over a two-year period.

- As an academic tutor, helped dozens of students clarify their personal goals and develop and implement self-motivating new plans.

- As a fundraiser for the college newspaper, identified sponsors and communicated to them the value of advertising in and/or supporting the paper. Sold advertisements and generated fund donations that produced over $150,000 in an eighteen-month period.

3. You'll need to decide whether a functional or chronological resume is the best format for your purposes. Generally, employers prefer the chronological because it's easier to follow work history in that format. An exception might be where particular types of expertise, skills, or personal attributes are more important than work history. In such cases, a well-written functional resume might better lay out your expertise. If you are a job seeker with a work history of experience that directly relates to the kind of work employers might be looking for, you may be well advised to use the chronological format. If, on the other hand, you are just graduating from college with little relevant work experience but a great deal of knowledge and skill to sell, or if you are making a career change, you may be better advised to develop a functional resume.

In making your choice about which format to use, keep in mind that a chronological resume tends to focus on your past work history while a functional resume addresses those skills and knowledge bases you intend to concentrate upon in the future. In fact, we recommend that you develop both kinds of resumes, beginning with a functional. The reason is that the process of developing a functional resume forces you to clearly define yourself in terms of what you are selling (knowledge, skills, motivations, personal attributes) and to highlight them with relevant achievements.

4. Study the examples for ideas and consult one or more resume-writing guides for additional help. See if your local college career planning and placement office offers resume-writing assistance and take full advantage of it. We strongly recommend that you personally write your resume. While most people find this difficult, the process of self-defining is critical to the whole job campaign. You can't play a winning game without engaging in this critical step!

5. Try out your resume with a number of people to obtain feedback and suggestions. Ask friends, faculty members, administrators, work associates, acquaintances, and networking contacts to critique your resume. And don't be afraid to make changes. Think of your resume as a dynamic and ongoing process of career self-definition, rather than as a finished product.

Resume Writing for the Electronic Age

Increasing numbers of organizations are converting to computerized tracking of applicants and resumes. This goes for recruiting firms and state employment services as well. If you can create a computer-friendly resume, you'll have a competitive edge over someone who is not up on the technology and whose resume can't be added to a database.

Computers look for different key words. While people scan for action verbs and related accomplishments, computers scan primarily for nouns, the words that identify the job requirements and responsibilities. As you prepare your computer-friendly resume, keep in mind a specific job so that you can incorporate as many key words, from the job description, as possible into your resume. This should increase your chances of having your resume 'pop up' from the data base when the human resource staff are searching for potential applicants to fill a vacant position.

In addition, e-resumes are becoming the resume of choice by employers. E-resumes vary in design, depending upon the employer's request. Often, however, an employer will request an e-mailed version of your resume. Or, an employer will ask you to submit your resume through the company's web site. In any case, you need to know how to develop an e-resume for your job search.

Web Connect

Computer-friendly and electronic resumes are written differently than the traditional paper resume. For an e-course on how to write electronic resumes, we recommend two different sites: **ProvenResumes** at **www.provenresumes.com/reswkshps/electronic/electrespg1.html** offers tips on how to write an e-resume and **eResumes** at **www.eresumes.com/tut_keyresume.html** will help you find lists of key words by job category and key words for personal traits for scannable resumes.

Figure 11.2
Sample Resume

Example: One-page functional resume, graduate student applying to a trade association for a training and development position.

ELLEN H. LAWSON
554 South Road, Queens, New York 10578
(212) 533-1208; elawson@hotmail.com

SUMMARY An experienced professional development trainer with multicultural experience. Top skills include training needs analysis, program design and delivery, and communications. An energetic, creative, self-initiating, results-oriented, highly responsive and responsible individual.

EDUCATION ASTD Certificate Program, New York University, 2001
M.S. Queens College, in Spanish, 1999
B.A. in Education, 1990. NY State Regents Scholarship, 1994

RELATED ACCOMPLISHMENTS

Training
- Trained and supervised ten professionals in educational methodology.
- Organized and conducted training program in elementary English for Hispanic garment workers. Doubled the enrollment by second year.
- Planned and taught college literature to 300 students, primarily adult. Received top evaluation scores.

Needs Analysis
- Initiated, organized, and expanded field work for language majors to meet community needs. Received special Mayoral commendation in 1993.
- Researched, analyzed, and evaluated effects of the open classroom on motivation and achievement. Study resulted in program revision by James Madison High School.

Design and Communication
- Designed program for incorporating audiovisual material into existing courses at Queens Community College. Recommendations were followed by professional staff for three years.
- Organized and supervised overseas study program in England for twenty participants.
- Organized peer-tutoring program, resulting in twenty-five percent increase in standardized test scores.

PROFESSIONAL EXPERIENCE
1999–Present Spanish and Special Education Instructor, Queens Community College.
1997–1999 Spanish Teacher, James Madison High School, Queens, NY.

Adapted from Anne Miller, *Finding Career Alternatives for Teachers* (New York: Apple Publishing Company, 1979) 53f.

Figure 11.3
Sample Resume

Example: Functional resume, 29-year-old elementary education teacher seeking a media or public relations position.

SHAWN MEDLINGER
1791 Sparrow Lane, Shimmering Springs, MD 20908,
(301) 774-7464, smedlinger@yahoo.com

SUMMARY

An experienced "up-front" communicator with experience in education and public relations that includes working with students grades K–12; teachers; and media personalities, such as journalists, disk jockeys, and television broadcasters. Top skills include public speaking, creative writing, innovative presenting, and acting as a media liaison. A dynamic, creative, well-rounded individual who delights in entertaining and influencing.

ACCOMPLISHMENTS

Innovative Presenting
Taught Montessori education for sixth grade students for three years. Developed innovative teaching materials and programs, including subjects like Greek and Roman mythology, Arthurian legend, and basic Latin, which had never been taught in the school before. Used creativity, teaching skills, and love of interacting with youth to successfully prepare sixth graders for junior high. Created and developed Humane Education program for the Montgomery County Humane Society. Taught students grade K–12 and their teachers about proper animal care, wildlife rehabilitation, and animal-related medicine and legislation.

Public Speaking
Currently serving as Public Relations Director for Montgomery County Humane Society. As the official spokesperson, participate in weekly television interviews and have a permanent time slot on Channel 23 news. Engage in weekly radio interviews to promote animal shelter and animal care. Speak to students, youth groups, and civic organizations on requested topics. Frequently affirmed by broadcasters and television producers to be "a natural" in conducting broadcast interviews.

Creative Writing
Gained valuable writing experience in college as an English major and taught English for three years at the Barrie School. Used writing skills to publish school newsletters and write proposals. Currently serve as chief writer/editor for MCHS: write newsletter ANIMAIL; prepare all correspondence—letters to students, Congressional representatives, sponsors, and celebrities; editor of a biweekly column for the *Montgomery Journal;* and prepare all media public service announcements.

Media Liaison
Skilled in working with various forms of media, including radio, television, and print journalism. Track record of success in proposing stories, conducting interviews, and providing public information. Often acknowledged for being "cool under pressure" and diplomatic in handling stressful "on the spot" situations.

EMPLOYMENT HISTORY
Director, Humane Education and Public Relations, Montgomery County Humane Society, 1999–present
Teacher, 6th Grade, Barrie School, Silver Spring, MD, 1994–1999
Program Director, Summer Work Program, Barrie Day Camp, Silver Spring, MD, 1990–1994
Technical Publications Intern, IBM Inc., Rockville, MD, 1989–1990

EDUCATION
B.A. English, University of Maryland, 1989

This edited version, used by permission, name and address changed

Figure 11.4
Sample Resume

Example: Functional resume for career changer—U.S. Naval officer seeking a college counseling/teaching position.

Donald S. Mayport
4401 Anchor Avenue
Annapolis, Maryland 21403
(410) 749-0220; dmayport@aol.com

Summary
A seasoned counselor/educator with ten years of experience working with diversified populations in a variety of work places and academic settings. Top skills include educational development, creative problem solving, and personal motivation counseling. Support skills include writing, conceptualizing, and academic research. A personable and resourceful team player with vision and facility for inspiring individuals and groups to achieve top performance.

Accomplishments
Educational Development
- As a history and government professor at the U.S. Naval Academy, researched and developed course materials, and delivered four different courses for junior- and senior-year students during a two-year period. Received strong student evaluations in all classes, totaling over 500 individuals, in spite of teaching new offerings each semester.
- Developed projects and course assignments that resulted in a "love-of-sea" feeling in college students enrolled in a naval operations course that had been considered to be a "dreaded requirement."

Creative Problem Solving
- Located and discovered how to use complex training aids and visual graphics to motivate students enrolled in a college navigation course. Result was that while previous classes disliked celestial navigation and acquired techniques through rote memorization of formulas, these students became intrigued with content that they could visualize and mastered techniques through "in-depth" understanding.
- Led a team of ten in undertaking a seemingly impossible job to be accomplished within an intolerably short time frame. The task was achieved with sterling results within the allotted time through implementing a number of novel solutions, which in the process significantly boosted team morale and confidence.

Personal Motivation Counseling
- In a one-year period, enhanced the morale of a 25-person team through individual counseling, publicly affirming individual successes, and establishing a sense of team identity. Resulted in a significant reduction in disciplinary cases and increased utilization of educational development benefits.
- Through extensive personal counseling and concerned attention, helped dozens of young men with low self-esteem and job performance problems become conscientious self-developers and productive performers.

EMPLOYMENT HISTORY:
U.S. Naval Academy, Political Science Instructor, Annapolis, MD, 1996–Present
U.S. Navy, Manager of 65-man division, 1994–1996
University of Minnesota, Navigation Instructor and NROTC counselor, 1991–1994
Division Officer, U.S. Navy, Team leadership and general management, 1988–1991

EDUCATION & TRAINING
B.S. in Geology, Colorado State University, Fort Collins, CO, 1985.
M.A. in Education, University of Minnesota, Minneapolis, MN, 1994.
- Three graduate level courses in human relations training at The George Washington University, Washington, D.C., 1997–1998.
- One week intensive instructor-training institute, 1990.

Figure 11.5
Sample Resume

Example: Chronological resume for career changer—U.S. Naval officer seeking an educational administrative and/or counseling position.

Donald S. Mayport
4401 Anchor Avenue
Annapolis, Maryland 21403
(410) 749-0220; dmayport@aol.com

SUMMARY
A seasoned counselor/educator with ten years of experience working with diversified populations in a variety of work places and academic settings. Top skills include human resource development management, educational development, creative problem solving, and personal motivation counseling. Support skills include writing, conceptualizing, and academic research. A personable and resourceful team player with vision and facility for inspiring individuals and groups to achieve best performance.

PROFESSIONAL EXPERIENCE
Political Science Instructor, U.S. Naval Academy, Annapolis, MD   1996–Present
Teach courses in U.S. government, foreign affairs, history and international relations. Serve as academic advisor for midshipmen.
- As a history and government professor at the U.S. Naval Academy, researched and developed course materials, and delivered four different courses for junior- and senior-year students during a two-year period. Received strong student evaluations in all classes, totaling over 500 individuals, in spite of teaching new offerings each semester.
- Developed reading projects and course assignments that resulted in a "love-of-sea" feeling in junior college students enrolled in a naval operations course that had been considered to be a "dreaded requirement."

U.S. Naval Shipboard Division Officer   1994–1996
Managed a 65-person division onboard a U.S. Naval aircraft carrier. Responsibilities included training, evaluating, and directing all activities of a complex and rapidly changing operation.
- Continuously solved complex problems involving the maneuvering of aircraft and equipment on the hangar deck, managing five crews of men, to support flight operations by supplying the aircraft needed, at the time and place needed, and garaging aircraft being removed from the flight deck.
- Safely completed all scheduled operations under duress of intensive operating conditions, while maintaining high crew morale through ongoing personalized attention to the personal and professional development needs of individuals.

Naval ROTC Instructor, University of Minnesota   1991–1994
Taught semester-long, college-credit courses in navigation and naval operations. Served as the academic and military advisor to 60 junior-class NROTC students.
- Located and discovered how to use complex training aids and visual graphics to motivate students enrolled in a college navigation course. Result was that while previous classes disliked celestial navigation and acquired techniques through rote memorization of formulas, these students became intrigued with content they could visualize and mastered techniques through real understanding.
- Counseled over 100 college students, assisting them with academic decision making within the context of long-term career perspectives.

EDUCATION
B.S. in Geology, Colorado State University, Fort Collins, CO, 1984.
M.A. in Education University of Minnesota, Minneapolis, MN, 1994.

Additional training:
- Three graduate level courses in human relations training at The George Washington University, Washington, D.C., 1997–1998.
- One-week intensive instructor-training institute, 1990.

Figure 11.6
Sample Resume

Example: Computer-friendly resume that can be scanned into a database. Note that there is no bolding, underlining, or other graphical design on this resume. The identations are **not** made with the tab key, but with the spacing bar.

Jenny Q. Public
Home Address:
458 Suffolk Avenue
Olney, MD 20006

OBJECTIVE:
To obtain a position utilizing my computer skills as a Web page designer and programmer.

EMPLOYMENT HISTORY:
8/00–present, HTML Programmer at Conor Associates
    HTML code for all Web pages designed by Conor Associates public relations firm.
    Developed client Web sites including flow charts, Perl scripts, and web-to-data base applications.

2/00–8/00, Graphic Designer at Conor Associates
    Created multimedia presentations, four-color brochures, and magazine ads.
    Product manager for client creative projects.
    Network integration assistant for the art department.

1/99–1/00, Assistant Graphic Designer at Prince George's Community College
    Assisted in development of advertising/promotional materials for director's presentations.
    Designed posters and flyers for promotional events.
    Assisted in producing mechanicals.

7/99–1/99, Assistant Computer Operator at the Quatro Corporation
    Entered client data into financial data base.
    Managed client files.
    Generated financial reports in response to account inquiries.

EDUCATION:
BA in Communications, University of Maryland; College Park, MD, 1990, GPA: 3.55

ADDITIONAL SKILLS:
Programming/Scripting Languages: C++, HTML, Perl, JAVA, and UNIX
Systems: MacOS, Win95, Solaris
Software: Aldus Pagemaker, Adobe Photoshop, Corel Photopaint, EXCEL, Microsoft Word, QuarkXPress

Web Connect

As mentioned in Chapter 2 *Virtual Career Planning,* we recommend that you read the 70+ page article titled *Networking on the Internet* at **http://dlis.gseis.ucla.edu/people/pagre/network.html** by Phil Agre. It is updated regularly and provides details on how to network effectively online.

Fourth Move—Identifying Your List of Employment Targets (ETs)

Now you're ready to begin the action stage of the game. To do that, you'll need to decide who you're playing the game with—that translates into developing your list of employment targets. We refer to these as your ETs; they are the specific employers you want to contact for a job. Here are a few good resources for developing your ET list.

People: Do you have friends, associates, or acquaintances who might know of employers or employment sites that meet your envisioned job setting and job objective? (Remember, you're looking for employer names for your list rather than known job openings.) Perhaps your acquaintances don't know of specific ETs but know of someone who does.

Information Interviewing/Networking: You've probably already obtained names of ETs while you were doing the information interviews

described earlier in the book. When you begin talking with your ETs, if they don't have any potential openings, ask if they can provide additional names for your list.

Yellow Pages Telephone Directories: Although the *Yellow Pages* are limited by incomplete index headings and incomplete listings, they are a useful directory. Most libraries have *Yellow Pages* directories for other cities if you're searching for ETs outside your area. Just remember that the size of the ad does not necessarily reflect the size of the employer. In fact, many large organizations do not bother listing themselves in the *Yellow Pages.*

Internet Job Banks and Classified Advertisements: The Internet job banks and the classified ads appearing over a period of months are a good source of specific ET names. Look for the organizations that fall into your employment target categories. (They may not be advertising for the position you want, but don't worry about this. You are just compiling an employer list. Many companies never advertise positions they can fill by word of mouth.) For a national or international job search, check the classified ads in appropriate city newspapers or in magazines like *The Economist.*

Web Connect

The Internet has made it incredibly easy to find people for whom you don't have contact information. One site called **Telephone Directories on the Web** at **www.teldir.com/eng** will link you to over 350 directories for businesses, individuals, fax numbers, and e-mail addresses in the United States as well as more than 150 countries.

Web Connect

Classified ads are traditionally found in periodicals, but as you know, the Internet is exploding with job listings. To find jobs that are relevant to your career, check out the career-specific pages with links to these job banks on the **Riley Guide** at **www.rileyguide.com/jobs.html.** If you don't find anything that matches your career interests at this site, then check out the job boards on **My Job Search** at **www.myjobsearch.com/career.html.** Also, more than 1,000 schools participate in Monster Trak at **www2.monster trak.com/trak2000/schools/index.html,** which is an online jobs database mostly for entry-level positions. Check out this site to see if your school participates.

Web Connect

You can look up your local Chamber of Commerce, or the one located where you plan to live at **www.uschamber.com/Chambers/Chamber+Directory/default.htm**

Chamber of Commerce Offices: Most local Chamber of Commerce offices have listings of employers in their county. Often these lists categorize the employers, list the number of employees, and sometimes include annual sales revenue. Choose the size of employer you seek by consulting such lists.

Magazines, Trade, and Professional Journals: Look through the business news sections of these resources for businesses and organizations engaged in activities of particular interest to you. *Time, Fortune, Newsweek, Business Week,* the *Wall Street Journal,* and the *New York Times* are all excellent sources for career-related topics of national scope. Almost every type of business, occupation, trade, profession, or interest area has some kind of a regular publication—professional journal, newsletter, magazine. These are excellent sources of information for ETs. If you aren't familiar with the magazines and journals related to your job interest, look up your field in indexes like *Magazine Index, Reader's Guide to Periodical Literature,* and *Business Periodicals Index,* to find relevant articles. *The Encyclopedia of Associations* (published by Gale Research Corporation) describes activities and publications of all associations. It provides names, addresses, and phone numbers.

Specialized Directories: These directories provide basic information on business organizations. They include: *Dun and Bradstreet Million Dollar Directory* and *Dun and Bradstreet Middle Market Directory.* The *U.S. Government Manual* describes agencies, programs, and basic job positions. Top managers' names are included, but be careful to assure that you are taking these names from a recently published reference.

College Career Planning and Placement Offices (CPPs): Many of these contain a wealth of information about ETs. University and college CPPs will have information on employers of a national scope, while the community college should have an excellent listing of ETs in the local area. Remember that it doesn't matter whether these ETs have listed current, relevant job openings.

Web Connect

Many of the business directories are now available in an online format. The best site to learn about researching companies online is, in fact, called **Researching Companies Online** and can be found at **http://home.sprintmail.com/~debflanagan/index.html** This site will also help you find the most appropriate online business directory for your job search needs.

Web Connect

Many trade journals are now available online through an association's web site. To find an association that represents your professional interests, search the more than 6,500 associations that have web sites and are searchable at the American Society for Association Executives at **http://info.asaenet.org/gateway OnlineAssocSlist.html**

Web Connect

To find the web site for the career office at your university or college, go to **JobWeb's** site at **www.jobweb.com/catapult/homepage.htm** and use their data base of links to explore what information is available to you both at the physical location of the career office as well as through the web site. This site is provided by the National Association of Colleges and Employers.

EXERCISE 11-D. RECORDING YOUR EMPLOYMENT TARGETS

1. Use the resources mentioned in the previous section to identify an initial list of 50 to 100 ETs.

2. You will have far more success in your job campaign if you are organized. Begin your organization by obtaining 3 x 5 cards and a file box with alphabetical separators. Be sure to record the name, address, telephone number, and potential contact persons for each ET on a separate 3 x 5 card. File your cards in alphabetical order.

Fifth Move—Designing Your Sales Campaign

Dozens of current books offer their own no-fail variation on the best ways to get a job. If you are perusing these resources, keep this fact in mind—you get most job offers only one way, and, like it or not, that way is through effective personal, face-to-face contact. The effectiveness is measured by your ability to sell potential employers on your value to their company or organization. You don't get a job offer through your resume or the "just right" personal appearance, though poor appearance on either may certainly prevent you from getting an offer! And, worst of all, hardly anyone ever gets a good job by being "discovered." The chances of that happening to you are about the same as winning the million dollar lottery. So you might as well concentrate your efforts and energy on kicking off your job campaign, regardless of whether you choose to target the hidden job market or open job market. You might find it worthwhile to enroll in a sales class if you're having difficulty defining yourself as a marketable product or if your feeling awkward about the process of "self-marketing."

The next step in your "getting-hired" campaign is to design your sales approach. In addition to the traditional approach of sending a resume with a custom cover letter, consider the following three nontraditional methods for getting job interviews:

Personal Sales Letter. Send out your personal sales letter to selected employment targets, preferably to a manager with the authority to hire you. This sales letter replaces your resume with cover letter as the initial communication. You present your resume during any interview produced from this approach only if the employer asks for further materials.

Telephoning for Interviews. Call an appropriate hiring manager with each ET to arrange for information interviews or actual job interviews.

Networking and Job Proposals. Design a proposal for the job you want to have with a particularly appealing ET. You present your proposal, verbally or in writing, to the person with the authority to hire you for that position. This method is normally used during or after one or more general information-gathering sessions or informal interviews, often in combination with other approaches.

In designing your sales campaign, we recommend that you experiment with both traditional and nontraditional methods and then concentrate on a combination of those activities that best fit you. If you are targeting a long-range job campaign to other localities, are a career changer, or are answering a classified ad, you may wish to concentrate your efforts on the personal sales letter and/or telephone methods. If you have developed your telephone skills, you might put most of your effort into this method. If you have narrowed down your employment targets and have significant background information on them, any method can be effective. The job proposal method requires having considerable background information. Become more familiar with the three methods by reading the following descriptions. Then design and kick off your own sales campaign.

Your Personal Sales Letter

In writing the sales letter, remember that you will be sending it out to your ETs and that you are writing the letter to show how your skills and qualifications will meet their needs. You want to show in your letter, through your previous accomplishments, in what ways you have the skills, attributes, and experience needed to help solve your ETs' employment problems. However, you don't want to come on too strong or in an arrogant manner by presuming to have instant solutions. Just represent yourself as a motivated candidate with useful, relevant skills and

Web Connect

To find samples of letters that address a variety of job and career-related situations, check out *Career Lab's* collection at

www.careerlab.com/letters

experience. William Cohen identifies these five components of the sales letter.[3]

1. *Opening Attention-Getter.* The task here is to get your ETs' attention and motivate them to read on to discover why you are writing. Examples: (1) (Recent graduate in the communications field) "If your Marketing Department could use award-winning writing and speaking skills, you may be interested in my background." (2) (Recent community college computer programming graduate with volunteer experience but no salaried job experience) "Having worked on professional systems development since my sophomore year in high school, I am ready for a challenging computer-programming position." (3) (Housewife applying for administrative assistant position) "Through fifteen years of experience, I've become an expert on organization, time management, administrative support, and motivation."

2. *Explanation.* Here you answer the question of why you are writing. Example: "I am writing to you directly in case you need someone with my expertise as a computer programmer (administrative assistant, marketing specialist)." Be specific in your explanation here. A general statement that implies you are looking for anything or that you can do anything will almost inevitably rule you out.

3. *Motivation.* The task here is to create a strong desire for your service. Cite accomplishments that directly relate to the type of job you are seeking. Examples: (From a homemaker with no previous paid work

experience) (1) "In less than two months, I mastered complex IBM and Microsoft word-processing systems through my own self-study and practice. I am now training colleagues in these systems." (2) "In just two weeks of neighborhood canvassing, I collected over $1,500 in contributions to the United Fund." (3) "Over the past five years, I have organized and managed five record-breaking fund raising events for The Sacred Heart Church. My responsibilities included designing a concept; collecting, organizing, and motivating volunteers; promoting the events; and accounting for cash receipts."

4. *Credibility.* The task here is to convince the employer that everything you have said in your letter is true. Incidentally, it is crucial to be honest in your sales letter, just as it is in your resume. The trick is to find the terminology that powerfully reflects what you actually have done and can do. Present facts about your attributes in short, action-packed sentences. Cite only things that relate positively to the kind of job you want, and omit anything else. Find some specific facts of relevance to report. Examples: (1) "I have a B.A. in Business Administration from Ohio State University (1987) specializing in financial management." (2) "I have successfully completed courses at Prince George's Community College and the University of Maryland in Pascal, C++, and Systems Analysis." (3) "I was on the Dean's List for two consecutive years in my Business Administration Program." (List awards, but only if they are relevant.)

5. *Call to Action.* The last part of your sales letter tells the employer what you want him/her to do (invite you in for a meeting/interview). Phrase this in terms of the employer's best interests. Examples: (1) "If you would like a personal meeting to discuss how my background and skills could assist you, please call me at (telephone #) between 9 A.M. and 5 P.M." (2) "I would be happy to demonstrate how I

---

[3]. William A. Cohen, *The Executive's Guide to Finding a Superior Job* (New York: Amacom) 36–37.

could assist your company. I will call your office within the next two weeks to discuss meeting for that purpose."

Addressing Your Personal Sales Letter.

Figure 11.7 shows a sample sales letter. Address these letters to a particular individual and include an accurate title, whenever possible. For impact, send your letter directly to the manager with authority to hire you. You can get this name by calling the organization and asking for the name of the manager who handles the department you are targeting. Just ask the receptionist for the name of the person in charge of marketing, communications, training, computer services, or whatever division fits your job objective best. If you aren't sure, get the name of the general manager of that office. Be sure to get his/her correctly spelled name, title, and address. As standard procedure, you may be transferred to Personnel or asked why you need the information. Just say you're mailing in a proposal, and retain a relaxed, friendly tone. Avoid mailing your letter to the Personnel Department unless you seek work in that division. Since the Personnel staff screens out candidates lacking standard credentials, the career changer or recent graduate is often ignored.

Telephoning for Interviews

The objective here is to obtain the name of the person with the power to hire at each ET and then call him/her to arrange a personal meeting (job interview). Your task is to communicate the following: (1) You are interested in that company and the particular mission of this manager's work. (2) You feel you have something of real value to contribute to the organization/company and to this mission. (3) You would like to arrange a short meeting to discuss current or future job opportunities. If you get a positive response, arrange a meeting time and place. Record it in your schedule book.

Conducting this kind of telephone campaign is difficult for most people. To prepare for it, you may want to practice making these calls to your career counselor or to friends. Or you may want to use a tape recorder to hear how you sound before actually making the real telephone calls. Then get out your ET contact cards and start calling. You can expect to hear "no" far more often than "yes" during your telephone requests for meetings. But don't let that discourage you because you will also hear "yes" sooner than in letter writing or resume selling, assuming, of course, that you have genuine qualifications and are able to present yourself with confidence and tact. As a motivator in making these calls, you might wish to remember the following:

The Getting-Hired Reality

1. You get jobs through interviews.

2. The more calls you make, the more interviews you obtain.

3. The more interviews you have, the better your chances of job offers.

4. The more job offers you receive, the better your chances of a great job.

Example of a Telephone Approach. Begin by finding out the name of the person with the power to hire for the kind of position you want (obtain his/her title, and phone number). Often you will be able to get this information by calling the organization and asking the receptionist the right questions. You may want to call at a busy time such as a lunch hour when you're less likely to be asked the purpose of your call. (By the way, some employers screen out these calls because they assume you are an executive search specialist trying to offer their managers an-

other job!) If you're asked the purpose of your call, tell them you have a personal matter to discuss.

Your conversation might go something like this: "Hello, my name is Marlene Berg, and I need to get in touch with the person responsible for your radio advertisements. May I have that person's name and title please? . . . Thank you, and how can I get in touch with him?" (Have your ET index card and pen handy to write down the information as you get it.)

Once you get the right name, decide what you want to say and what action you want as a result of

---

Figure 11.7
Sample Sales Letter

From Marlene Berg, who is campaigning for a media copywriter's job at a large advertising company.

822 Malone Drive
Bethesda, Maryland 20815
March 30, 2002

Mr. Robert Blake
Director of Media Sales
Highlights Advertising Agency
1400 Marlow Avenue
Cincinnati, Ohio 54082

Dear Mr. Blake:

As a copywriter I created an advertisement for radio station WTYK that resulted in a 12 percent product sales increase for the sponsoring agency. This was the greatest response the station had ever had from one of its ads.

Your company may need a creative media copywriter with demonstrated ability to influence through the use of language. If so, you may be interested in some of my other achievements:

- I have a Bachelor of Arts degree in Communications from the University of Ohio (1999).

- I completed 63 hours of course work in marketing and communications, maintaining an "A" average.

- This educational background is supplemented by 14 months of experience writing advertisements for a university and a large advertising firm. During this time I wrote over 50 successful advertisements for the print and broadcast media, including the one described in my opening paragraph.

- I wrote two papers on the art of persuasive writing. Both papers were published by well-known journals in the communications/advertisement fields.

I would like to meet you personally to discuss putting my experience to work for Highlights Advertising Agency. You can reach me at (301) 986-5666 between 9 a.m. and 5 p.m.

Sincerely,

Marlene Berg

---

your call. Let's assume that you get the information you need and put your call through to Robert Blake, Director of Media Sales. Your first task will be to get the secretary to let you talk with Mr. Blake. You might say something like, "Hello, this is Marlene Berg calling for Robert Blake."

If the secretary puts you through immediately, consider yourself lucky. Most likely the secretary will ask for your company name and the reason you're calling. In response be prepared to say something like, "I have a business proposal that I want to discuss with him." Should she ask if she may help, tell her why you are calling, briefly stressing that you have some useful experience to offer, and ask for the most convenient time to call. Take your ET's secretary into your confidence rather than being terse or hostile. Secretaries are typically asked by busy managers to screen calls, but if they think you are sincere, motivated, and qualified, they just might help. Be positive and gracious.

Once you get through to Mr. Blake, your conversation might proceed something like the following: "Hello, Mr. Blake, this is Marlene Berg. Do you have a moment?" If he says "no," respond, "Fine, when would be a good time to call back. I'd like to talk with you about your new contract with WTYK." If he says "yes," begin with a statement that will get his interest, such as, "I believe that you do all of radio station WTYK's advertisements. Is that correct?" Once you have his attention, be prepared to communicate something about yourself that relates directly to the challenges he has, such as, "You may be needing creative copywriters with expertise in promoting commercial products to WTYK's younger listeners. I have had excellent results in similar kinds of work and am very familiar with the preferences of WTYK's listening audience. I would like to meet with you to discuss how I could be of service."

At this point, listen to his response and be prepared to add specific facts about your relevant skills and experience. For example, "I worked for two years with one of the best media experts in Maryland and have substantial knowledge of ad writing and experience with radio advertisements." Close the conversation with a request for a meeting (avoid the use of the word "interview") to talk further. You might say something like, "I think it would make sense to show you some of my work and discuss this in more detail. Are you free tomorrow afternoon or Wednesday morning?"

If Mr. Blake says "okay," then prepare for your meeting (interview). If he indicates that he has nothing available now, say that you understand and would still like to meet him to discuss future opportunities if he anticipates openings within the next six months.

Don't let an ET's initial resistance deter you. Resistance is a natural and expected reaction to a cold telephone call of any kind. Continue communicating enthusiastically the value you can contribute to the company. Your assurance can break through objections and get you an interview.

Once you're in the office, if Mr. Blake likes you, he'll remember you. He may have an opening in a few days or weeks. If he's sufficiently impressed by you, he just might create a position for you. On the other hand, if he says "no" to the meeting, don't take it personally. Just call the next person on your list.

The Job Proposal

The job proposal approach involves using the information-interview process to meet three goals:

1. Identify and become familiar with potential organizations where you might like to work.

2. Determine current needs and problems of these employers, and match these with your skills and experience.

3. Determine the name of the person who has the power to hire someone for the type of job you want.

Accomplishing these goals involves first conducting numerous information interviews with well-qualified people who are doing the kind of work that interests you. As you talk with these individuals, ask them questions designed to acquaint you with how one gets hired for a job like theirs, what they like and don't like about this organization, and what the organization's primary strengths and problem areas are. After you have conducted a sufficient number of these job research interviews, you should know which organizations you prefer, who has the power to hire you for the type of job you want, the organization's unique needs, and how your strengths and assets can be of particular assistance there.

With this knowledge, you then design a specific proposal of how you can be of assistance to that organization. Next, arrange for a personal meeting with the person with actual hiring power. At this meeting, you convincingly present your proposal. With this method, you can effectively promote yourself for current or future job openings. You might even find that an employer is so impressed by you that he/she develops a special position for you—it happens! This method is more fully described in Richard Bolles' best-selling book, *What Color Is Your Parachute?* (available in most bookstores and college career-planning offices).

EXERCISE 11-E. KICKING OFF YOUR SALES CAMPAIGN _____

1. Conduct 10 to 20 information interviews with people who are working in a job similar to the kind you think you would like to have. Your task here is to get a better sense of their job and their company. Note: These are to be information interviews and not job interviews. Focus on four areas of inquiry:

   • What is it like to do that job and what the career opportunities are at that organization? Where could an entry-level position lead in the years ahead?

   • What is that particular organization like. What business is it in? What are its strengths and what are its major problems? What kinds of employees succeed at this organization? Who has the power to hire people in that particular field within that company (name of person, title, what he/she is like, a good way to get to meet them).

   • What other types of related jobs does this person know about that might possibly interest you? You're looking for new job possibilities, too.

   • Can this person refer you to other individuals for information interviews or recommend other organizations as ETs?

2. Out of the companies you have visited for information interviews, pick three you like the best. Develop a two-page written proposal to present to the person with the power to hire at each of these ETs. In your proposal indicate how you could serve that organization/business by helping them capitalize on their strengths and solve their problems. Be sure to show how your service will provide more value to the organization than the cost of your salary.

   Arrange for a meeting with the person with the power to hire you. Your previous information interviews (contacts) within that organization should be of great assistance here. Use your proposal as interview preparation, and be prepared to discuss your ideas, if appropriate. If you get positive response, you may want to leave your written proposal. Ask whether an appropriate job opening will be available during the following few months. Be sure to send a thank-you letter as a follow-up to these proposal presentation meetings and include any details you were asked about but didn't have available at the time.

3. Refine your personal sales letter, and send it out to 25 ETs or modify it as a response to current classified ads that appeal to you. (A well-written and targeted sales letter often has a better chance against the classified ad competition just because it stands out.) You are trying to get at least one interview. The experience you have acquired in conducting information interviews and presenting your proposals should help you improve your sales letter. If you get no interviews, you need to assess and revise your letter and your techniques. If you get more than five interviews from this mailing, you have done a terrific job!

4. Select 30 to 50 ETs and telephone for interviews to the people with the power to hire. If this produces three to five job interviews, you're doing great. If less than that, you need to evaluate and revise your approach. Should you obtain ten or more interviews—hire out as a consultant!

Getting-Hired Guide

Many factors influence the number of contacts required to get one job interview. These include: your qualifications for the job, availability of the job type in the locality you are exploring, the degree of your assertiveness and salesmanship, and the time of year. Nevertheless, here are some rough guidelines to help establish your sales campaign. Use these to play the getting-hired game:

10–20 contacts	= 1 job interview
5–10 interviews	= 1 job offer
1–5 job offers	= 1 great job

Evaluating Your Results. Keep assessing the progress of your "getting-hired" campaign, and revise your game plan as needed. Use your ET index cards to keep track of your actions and results. Here are some sample entries:

Date	Action Taken/Results Produced	Action Party
4/20/01	Conducted information interview. Harry Owens, Vice President for Sales and Contracts, has the power to hire. Phone: (421) 397-2888. His secretary is Sue Hawkins.	Mel Downs, Exec. Dir. for Marketing Phone: (421) 397-2801
4/21/01	Sent Mel a thank-you letter.	
4/29/01	Received letter of no openings now/will keep you on file. Note: Still some promise here. Call Doug P. back about 5/15/01 with a new issue.	Doug Powell, Dir. of Public Relations, Phone: (875) 101-1542
4/30/01	Telephoned for interview. Arranged meeting for 5/3/01 8 A.M. in her office (Rm. 307)	Marge Tower, Managing Editor (310) 572-0893

As you review your entries, stop and take stock of how you're doing. What seems to work the best and why? What causes problems and why? It's always worth the effort to redesign your sales campaign, if needed.

Sixth Move—Creating a Support Group

The next step in your "getting-hired" game is to identify your needs for personal and financial assistance and to set up a support group to help meet these needs, if necessary. Finding the right job may take anywhere from two to six months of full-time, concentrated work. Even if it doesn't take that long, it's a good idea to prepare yourself emotionally and financially for that contingency.

If unemployed, you may need financial help sometime in your job campaign. Plan for it now by developing a realistic estimate of money needed and a list of possible sources. Too many job seekers make abrupt, destructive career decisions because they feel trapped financially. If your ETs and information interview network are substantial, getting a loan from credit card/bank sources or friends may be your best alternative. Otherwise, consider part-time or temporary work to provide some financial security. Career planning offices, classified ads, and state employment services and temporary agencies can assist you here. Just keep enough time and energy free to attain the award you've strived for—a fulfilling job with good pay.

Because the job campaign is psychologically stressful for most people, it's also a good idea to establish a personal support group. Enlist the support of friends, acquaintances, your college counseling staff, or a professional career counselor, if you need it and can afford it. If there is a job club in your area, join it. Inquire at your college career-planning office and/or employment service office to see if there is one available.

You seem really stressed out lately Howard . . . let me give you some advice . . .

Try turning down the vibrator level on your pager.

Once you have obtained your support group, check in with them on a regular basis. Also, call upon them when you are feeling low and need support or when things look promising and you want to celebrate. You will need to be prepared for rejection, even if you are a strong job candidate. By sharing your feelings of disappointment, your support group can help you recharge your energy and motivation.

Seventh Move—Prepare for Job Interviews

You can expect your personal visits, sales letters, and telephone calls to begin paying off in the form of formal and/or informal job interviews about two to three weeks after your "kick-off campaign." You need to prepare for this in several ways. First, de-

 EXERCISE 11-F. ESTABLISHING A SUPPORT STRUCTURE _____

1. Using the guidelines described above, estimate how long your job campaign may take and determine your financial needs for that period of time. If you will need money, make a list of people who might be able to help. Decide on your best approach and then contact them for assistance. Keep trying until you know your financial needs are adequately addressed.

2. Arrange for personal support from acquaintances, a college career planning and placement office, job club, or professional counselor. Schedule regular times to meet (at least once per week) and make agreements to check in when you need encouragement or have good news to share.

Web Connect

Monster.com at http://content.monster.com/jobinfo/interview will help you practice your interview skills and provide feedback to help you improve. Cabrillo College in California also put together excellent guidance for different aspects of the interview on their web site at www.cabrillo.cc.ca.us/studserv/career/intguide.html.

velop interviewing skills well before you reach the job interview stage of the game. If you are not experienced with interviews, seek the help of a career counselor, and/or visit your library and read up on the subject, and/or enroll in an interviewing course.

Second, be prepared for the kinds of questions that you are likely to be asked. Below are some examples. Practice answering these until you have concise, confident, enthusiastic responses that are always well-targeted to the job you seek:

1. Tell us something about yourself.

2. What are you looking for in a job?

3. Why do you want to leave your current job?

4. Why are you interested in working with this organization?

5. What background and experience do you have to bring?

6. What are your top strengths?

7. What are your weaknesses?

(Answer by explaining how you are transforming a former minor weakness into a strength. Don't say that your only weakness is that you work too hard. Employers don't like baloney.)

8. What are your future goals and plans?

9. What salary are you asking for? What did you earn in your last job?

10. What would you like to know about us? What questions do you have for us? (Be prepared to ask at least three questions that show you know something about the organization and want to know where it's heading.)

Third, have a wardrobe that is appropriate for the interview. Your personal appearance is very important. Ask your friends and/or support group to check you out and give honest feedback. Get into proper attire, and be at the right place at the right time!

Fourth, prepare for the interview. Learn as much as possible about your ET's business. You can usually get information by visiting your ET's personnel office well before the interview. Explain that you're interviewing for a position there and would like to see an annual report, company newsletter, brochures, or any other available information.

Be prepared to ask questions as well as to answer them. Remember, interviews are a two-way proposition: you'll be deciding whether a company is the right place for you, just as they assess whether you are the right person for them. Employers are rarely impressed by job candidates who are so passive that they have no questions to ask. On the other hand, don't try to take over the interview. Finally, review the job interviewing "dos and don'ts" listed in Table 11.1 on the next page several times to keep an overall perspective.

Table 11.1
Job Interviewing Tips

What to Do	What Not to Do
• Prepare for the interview. • Know the organization's purpose, strengths, and problems. • Know how you can be of value. • Dress appropriately (the way people dress at that organization). • Bring samples of your work. • Know what points you want to make. • Be prepared to ask insightful questions. • Sell your skills, interest, energy, and achievements. • Relate your career goals, skills and achievements to the mission of the organization. • Listen closely to questions, and respond only to what is asked. • Know your field's salary ranges (the "going rate") for the type of position you want and the minimum salary you're willing to accept. • Answer the real question—Why should they hire you?	• Arrive late. • Forget your interviewer's name(s). • Ask what the company does. • Bring and read notes. • Get lost in your own thoughts. • Focus on your need for the job. • Pretend to know things you don't. • Indicate that you have all the organization's answers. • Just sit and wait for the interviewer(s) to ask questions. • Answer a question not asked. • Give long meandering responses. • Indicate that your main interests are in salary and benefits. • Monopolize the conversation. • Be overly concerned about time off. • Be defensive. • Be dogmatic. • Avoid eye contact.

Eighth Move—Get Attractive Job Offers

Your goal in each job interview is to discover whether you really want the job, and if so to lead your interviewer(s) to making an attractive offer. To do that, you need to come to each interview prepared to help direct the outcome. That doesn't mean that you aggressively take over the interview. It does mean, however, that you come prepared with information, the right attitude, and a clear goal. A successful interview usually follows these five steps:

1. Personal introductions and small talk.

2. Short introduction of yourself and your interest in a job with that organization.

3. Questions and answers to establish your qualifications and interest in the job and to assess how well you would fit in with that organization.

4. Your questions to obtain additional information about the organization, the job, and the career possibilities.

Henderson realized that he had chosen the wrong clothes for the interview.

EXERCISE 11-G. INTERVIEW PREPARATION _____

Prepare for each interview by answering questions like these:

1. What business is the employer in?

   - What products/services do they sell and to whom?
   - What is their history?
   - Where are they heading in the future?
   - What thing is the organization noted for and proudest of?

2. What are the three major problems this organization now confronts or will confront?

3. What specific value can you be to the company in solving these problems?

4. Which of your top skills would be most valuable to this company?

5. How do your past achievements and current goals relate to the goals and mission of this company?

6. If you were the interviewer, why would you hire you for the job you want? List ten reasons, but use only the top three or so. Blasting the employer with too many reasons on the spot may make you look over- or underconfident.

7. What is the salary range the company pays for a job like this? (Find this out through information interviews.)

8. What is the minimum salary you will accept and your realistic ideal salary?

_____

5. Closure involving either a job offer and salary negotiation or clarification of the steps remaining to a job offer.

To get into the right frame of mind for the interview, we recommend that you mentally rehearse an ideal interview two or three times before the actual meeting. Use the envisioning exercise described in Appendix D. Relax, close your eyes, and then run through the whole interview in your mind. See yourself meeting your interviewer(s), knowing his/her/their name(s), and feeling relaxed and assured. Envision yourself doing well and fully enjoying the interview game. Imagine your interviewer(s) asking questions and your responding to them with assurance and enthusiasm. In your mind, establish good eye contact with your interviewer(s), and ask questions that will give you needed information and demonstrate your knowledge and interest in the organization.

Envision your interviewers moving from asking you questions to convincing you of the benefits of working at that organization. Picture the interview coming to a close with the interviewers offering you the job at a fair salary and your thanking them and asking for a couple of days to think it over. This envisioning process will help you prepare for the interview and generate the personal confidence you'll need to do a terrific job.

Be honest, assured, prepared, and energetic during the interview, but most of all, be your best self. During the interview, you will want to stress how your skills/experience relate to the job. Express enthusiasm for the opportunity to provide a valuable service for the organization. Of course, you don't want to be overbearing about your knowledge and skills. Don't pretend to have all of the answers to the organization's needs. That could be a real turnoff to an interviewer. Instead, let your personal confidence in your abilities and your enthusiasm for the job shine through.

Be prepared to answer questions honestly, and don't pretend to know something you don't. Be goal oriented during the interview so you and the interviewer stay on track. Remember, you want to get a positive job offer and not just have a nice conversation.

At appropriate times during the interview, be prepared to ask questions like these:

1. What kind of person would you consider an ideal candidate for this job?

2. What kind of challenges does this job offer?

3. What are the organization's primary goals and plans for the future?

4. What achievements in your division make you the proudest?

5. What kinds of people would I be working with here?

6. How would you describe the management style here?

7. What kind of advancement would be possible for anyone performing this job well?

8. What traits do you appreciate most in an employee?

9. What are the major strengths of the organization?

If you are seriously interested in the position, begin moving the interview towards a job offer. Think of yourself as a salesperson closing the deal. Don't leave the interview without offering your interviewer(s) ample opportunity to purchase your services. Ask questions like: "What do you think? Do we have a possible match here between your requirements and my qualifications?"

If your interviewers show some reluctance, try to discover their real objections. If they have some reservations about a particular aspect of your experience or skill, respond with positive facts and examples to resolve any false concerns. If their objections are legitimate, reconsider whether the position is suitable for you.

Salary Negotiation

If you are asked salary-related questions early in the interview, answer generally. Just say that your

Web Connect

You can get a head start on salary negotiations by researching salaries through one of the 300+ salary guides on JobStar at http://jobstar.org/tools/salary/index.htm

salary requirements are negotiable and depend upon the job description. Once there is strong mutual interest, go ahead and discuss salary. Ask the interviewer what salary range they have for the position. If the range is acceptable, decide what your worth is and why you think so. Base that on your experience and skills and not that you need the money.

However, if the top of their salary range is below the going rate for this position and below your minimum requirements, express some concern. If your qualifications and experience are limited, it may be fair. But if you are well qualified, don't sell yourself short. You may want to stress again the value you bring to the organization. Ask about additional bonuses, special benefits, or significant salary increases after a three- to six-month trial. When you have a firm offer, express your serious interest. Ask the interviewer to put the offer, including any special agreements, in writing. Finally, inquire when they would like your answer.

Interview Follow-up

Immediately after each interview (one to three days), send a typed letter thanking the interviewer for meeting with you. Also, use the letter to indicate any additional points to support your value to the organization. If you are seriously interested in the position, say so and express your hope for a favorable agreement. Include your telephone number so they can reach you for further information or discussion.

If you haven't heard anything from your ET within a reasonable amount of time (two weeks), pursue the matter with him/her by telephone. Also, call a company when you have another job offer, but are still interested in them. This confirmation that you are valuable to another employer often results in action. Be sure to express the confidence that you could make a valuable contribution to the company. If you have acquired any new information, skills, or insights related to the position, mention them. Close by asking whether you are still a candidate. If so, ask whether they have any questions that you could answer or if there is anything else that you might do to support your candidacy. This kind of follow-up can increase your chances of success considerably.

Ninth Move—Assess Your Offers

At some point, after conducting a number of interviews, your efforts will begin paying off in the form of job offers. The ideal situation, of course, is to have several job offers. If you have done a thorough and assertive job campaign, that is very likely to happen.

As you reach this final stage of the job campaign, there are a few important things to consider. The first issue is what to do after you get a job offer. Do you take it? Do you try for others? What if it's close to what you want but not exactly? These, of course, are questions that only you will be able to answer, and they warrant discussion with your support group. Consider the advancement opportunities, management style, work environment, and your gut feelings.

If you have a tentative offer or are being seriously considered for a job you really want, resist the temptation to halt your job campaign. Tentative job offers often do not pan out. Continue your interviewing process until you get a firm, written job offer that really appeals to you.

Tenth and Final Move—Complete the Game

When you get the right job, it's time to complete the game and enter the winner's circle. An understandable sense of elation goes along with getting a great job and from the desire to get moving with your career. However, it's a good idea to pause and reflect upon what you have done for yourself and what others have done for you. Completing the game means acknowledging yourself and those who contributed to your successful job campaign.

Entering the winner's circle is symbolic of beginning your new job and experiencing the rewards it offers. A great job offers three major rewards: opportunities for contribution, growth, and income. Research studies consistently show that the main reward people want from a job is the opportunity to make a worthwhile contribution. We're unlikely to experience a sense of meaning or purpose in life un-

less we know that our skills and energies are being used productively.

The second most important reward your job can offer is the chance to grow. Growing means using and developing your skills along with learning and applying new knowledge. Growing means being stimulated to do and be your best. That is far more important than having a comfortable job. You're likely to become bored and unmotivated in a comfortable job.

The third reward, usually overemphasized, is salary. A good salary is important both for a healthy self-concept and as compensation for worthwhile service performed. Being paid a good salary alone, however, is insufficient to provide job satisfaction. It takes all three rewards for that. Surprisingly, your income is likely to be the least important reward unless it is considerably lower than average. That observation comes as a result of our work with numerous career changers who were earning a good salary but hated their jobs because they lacked the first two greater rewards.

As you enter the winner's circle with your new job, we encourage you to keep your career and life goals in mind. Remember that career development is a lifelong process. Your job is the vehicle that enables you to carry out your worthy life goals. Your job, however, is not the end of the line: it's only the beginning. If you have a job where you're performing useful service and growing, you're sure to reach a point where you'll be ready to make a bigger contribution. Then it will be time for you to revise your career goals and get ready to play a bigger game in your life. And as you do, your valuable service will command a greater income. So play the game well, give it all you've got, and exercise your self-empowering skills to the fullest. Go for it! Enjoy being a winner.

JOB-SEARCH CASE STUDY

This chapter has covered most of the available job search methods in a competitive job market, stressing nontraditional methods. Career changers will find many of these methods helpful to meet the challenges of their job search. However, if you are about to graduate from college and look for your first entry-level career position, following every step of the "getting-hired" game will be overwhelming and probably unnecessary. Consider using a simplified version of these methods, sending out a standard resume and custom cover letter to both advertised openings and prospects uncovered by following the methods of this chapter. Use contacts to bolster these traditional written materials, so they get to the right people. Revise your materials when necessary to fit the particular job. Ara, the case study for this chapter, completed a typical job search for a recent college graduate, including both traditional and nontraditional approaches.

CASE STUDY
ARA

Ara graduated from the University of Maryland with a B.A. in radio and television production. Ready to charge out and land his first full-time career position, Ara combed through the classified sections of the *Washington Post*, *New York Times*, and *Baltimore Sun* newspapers. He had decided he wouldn't limit himself to just the Washington, D.C., metropolitan area. Ara followed up on five ads for production technicians by sending his resume with appropriately enthusiastic cover letters. (At this stage of his search, he was using a standard resume with a customized cover letter.)

While Ara waited for results from this traditional approach, he followed a friend's suggestion to look in trade magazines as well as contact cable organizations for more prospective employers. After doing just that, and making a list of some thirty possibilities, he drafted a general all-purpose cover letter and sent it off with his standard resume to the list of possibilities. By now, a couple of months had passed, and Ara had received his first of what would be five rejection letters for the production technician positions. He was discouraged.

Ara's family and close friends encouraged him to continue looking for the kind of job he really wanted. In fact, his father gave Ara the name and phone number of a colleague at work who knew someone at the local cable commission. Before Ara had a chance to make contact with his father's friend, he received one letter expressing mild interest in his resume but lacking the type of position he wanted. Would he come for an interview for a floor manager's position instead? Ara decided to go for the interview. Since this was the first positive step in his job search, Ara went to the interview for practice. Although this interview didn't have any positive ending, Ara soon got another lead from his applications and interviewed for a set designer position and an audio technician position with local county cable stations. Both interviews went better than his first one, and Ara held out some hope for the audio technician position especially.

By now Ara had called his contact at the local cable commission, introduced himself to the woman, told how he had gotten her name, and explained briefly his relevant interests, experience, and degree. Ara was in luck. The woman told him that he had contacted her just two weeks before a production technician position opening was going to be advertised. She encouraged him to watch for the ad and then submit his resume and letter of interest. Most important, his contact told him how to revise his resume so that his skills would focus on the job description.

Now Ara felt he was getting somewhere. Ara's revisions of his resume were more time-consuming than he had anticipated, but through his contact, he had gotten a head start. While he was working on his resume, he received a few more "thanks, but no thanks" letters. He did get two more calls for interviews but turned one down, since it was for a part-time position in New York City. Ara wisely decided to go on the other interview for set design and construction, instead of counting on the cable commission job. Meanwhile, he got another rejection from the earlier interview for audio technician.

Ara finally finished redoing his resume to "fit" the cable commission position of production technician. This position seemed tailor-made for Ara. It called for some writing and producing, even directing some small projects. These were skills Ara excelled in and enjoyed using in his college TV classes. He sent in his resume along with a cover letter and kept his fingers crossed. In just five days, he was invited to come in for an interview with the same contact he had originally reached on the phone. What an interview it was! Ara was relaxed from his previous interview experience. He felt very good about the way he answered and asked questions. The woman told Ara he would hear from her in two days. On the second day, Ara received a phone call from the cable commission offering him the job. Although he wanted to shout "yes" into the phone, he kept his composure and said he would like to think it over and let them know in twenty-four hours.

Ara did accept the job offer and is still excited about his work after being on the job for six months. As he reflects back over the five months of ups and downs, raised hopes and rejections, he feels it was all worth it.

Similar to small businesses that open and close, Web sites come and go. This means that some of the Web sites listed in this book will probably change during the time you are reading this material. Therefore, we have created a page on the Web where you can go to ensure you have the most up-to-date links for each of the chapters. To find these links, go to **www.CareerKiosk.org** and click on "Updated links for *Your Career*." These links will ensure that you have accurate links and access to great sites on the Web!

REFERENCES

Beatly, Richard. *The Perfect Cover Letter*. New York: John Wiley and Sons, 1989.

Boe, Anne and Bettie B. Youngs. *Is Your "Net" Working: A Complete Guide to Building Contacts and Career Visibility*. New York: John Wiley and Sons, 1989.

Kaplan, Robbie Miller. *Sure-Hire Resumes*. American Management Association, 1989.

Kennedy, Joyce Lane and Thomas J. Marrow. *Electronic Resume Revolution: Creating a Winning Resume for the New World of Job Seeking*. New York: John Wiley and Sons, 1994.

Medley, H. Anthony. *Sweaty Palms: The Neglected Art of Being Interviewed*. Revised ed. Ten Speed Press, 1992.

Washington, Tom. *Resume Power: Selling Yourself On Paper*. Revised ed. Mount Vernon Press, 1993.

Yate, Martin. *Knock Em Dead: The Ultimate Job Seeker's Handbook*. Holbrook, MA: Bob Adam's, Inc., 1994.

APPENDIX A1 SELF-INSIGHTS

Self-Insights	Acquired from Chapter #

APPENDIX A2 CAREER POSSIBILITIES

Occupations of Interest	Holland Code	Occupations of Interest	Holland Code

APPENDIX A3 SELF-PROFILE SUMMARY

A puzzle is composed of many pieces. As each piece is fitted together in its proper place, a picture of the whole puzzle begins to emerge. Similarly, the self-assessment phase of the career decision-making process includes many pieces in the form of independent assessments. Each assessment you complete is a piece of the personal puzzle that becomes a self-profile of your career-related attributes. A graphic display of your self profile, together with a completed example, is included in the following pages of this appendix. The directions for completing your self-profile are outlined below.

After completing your functional skills assessment in Chapter 3, place your top individual functional skills in priority order under the *Information, People,* and *Things* categories. To round out the skills piece of your self-profile, add your top three special knowledge skills and your top five self-management skills listed in priority order.

The next assessment is Ned Herrmann's Thinking Style Assessment included in Chapter 4. After completing your thinking-style profile, place the number of your preference code (1, 2, or 3) for each quadrant of the Herrmann pictorial above the line provided in each square.

From Chapter 5, place the letters representing your Holland code in the boxes provided. Under each letter of your code include three characteristics that best describe you from those listed on page 108 of Chapter 5.

The final pieces of your self-profile come from Chapter 7. List your top five values in priority order in the space provided. Complete your life goal/mission statement and place it in the rectangle at the bottom of the page.

The result is a profile of your most important career-related attributes.

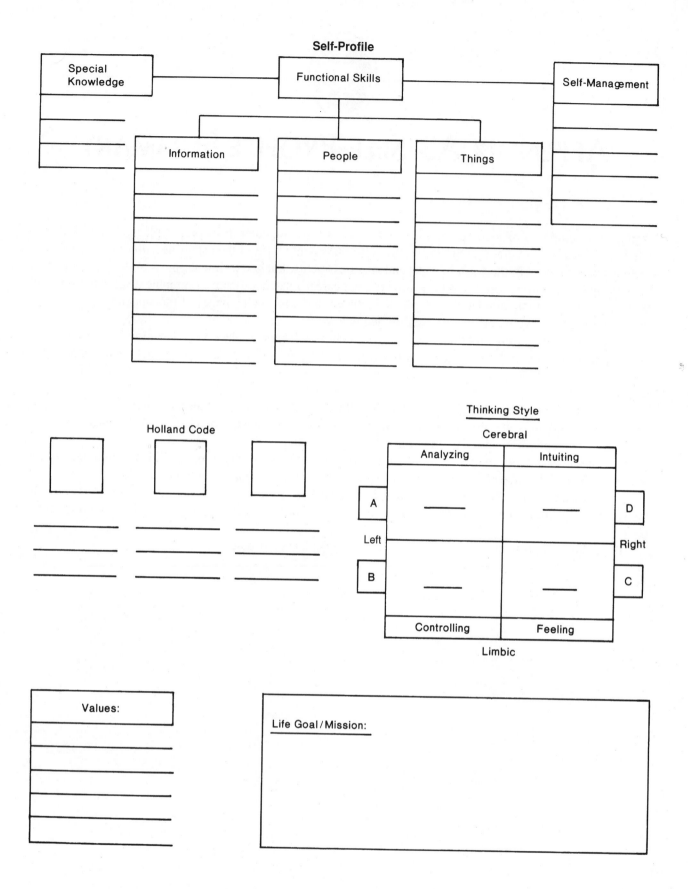

Self-Profile

Special Knowledge	Functional Skills	Self-Management

Information	People	Things

Holland Code

Thinking Style

Cerebral

Analyzing	Intuiting
Controlling	Feeling

A B — Left — Right — D C

Limbic

Values:

Life Goal / Mission:

Self-Profile Example

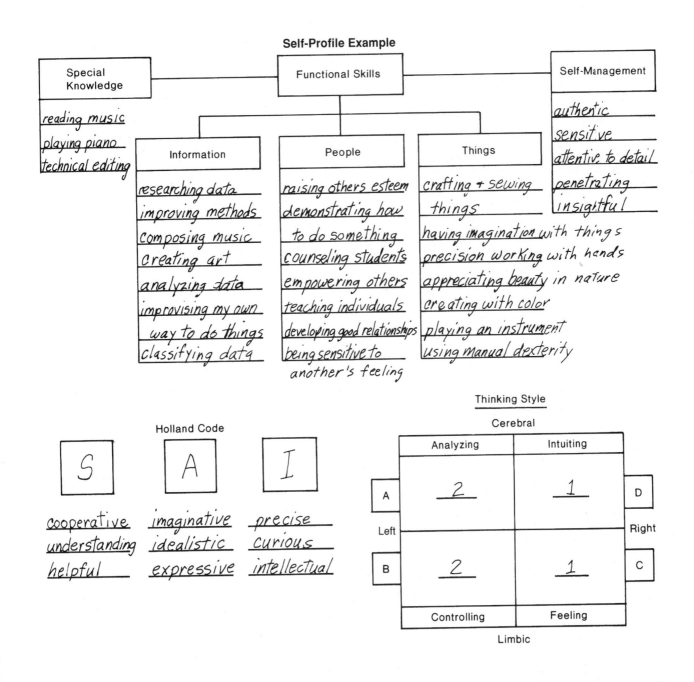

Special Knowledge	Functional Skills			Self-Management

Special Knowledge:
reading music
playing piano
technical editing

Functional Skills:

Information:
researching data
improving methods
composing music
creating art
analyzing data
improvising my own way to do things
classifying data

People:
raising others esteem
demonstrating how to do something
counseling students
empowering others
teaching individuals
developing good relationships
being sensitive to another's feeling

Things:
crafting + sewing things
having imagination with things
precision working with hands
appreciating beauty in nature
creating with color
playing an instrument
using manual dexterity

Self-Management:
authentic
sensitive
attentive to detail
penetrating
insightful

Holland Code

S
cooperative
understanding
helpful

A
imaginative
idealistic
expressive

I
precise
curious
intellectual

Thinking Style

Cerebral

	Analyzing	Intuiting	
A	2	1	D
Left			Right
B	2	1	C
	Controlling	Feeling	

Limbic

Values:
personal development
close relationships
mental challenge
appreciating beauty
empowering others

Life Goal/Mission: By exploring truth and beauty in the arts and physical world, I will strive to grow and find meaning in my own life that I can experience with friends and use to improve the lives of others.

APPENDIX B PERSONALITY-STYLE COMPATIBILITY ANSWERS

Authors' Answers to Exercise 5-B

1. Since biology is primarily an "I" curriculum and is opposite "E," the "E"-type person is likely to be very dissatisfied. Types that are opposite each other on the hexagon are very dissimilar. The "E" type here would probably drop out, flunk out, or wisely change to an academic program that would be compatible with the primary "E." The "E" type, persisting in the "I" curriculum, would be likely to experience a very low energy level, a tendency to be ill frequently, and a general lack of interest in academics and probably life in general.

2. Here again, the "I" type is going into an occupation that is just the opposite. Both salesperson and warehouse manager are "E" types. The "I" type is likely to be very dissatisfied on the job and search for ways to experience satisfaction outside of work, if not look for a more compatible occupation.

3. An "A" person who enrolls in an "A" curriculum is likely to experience satisfaction. Both personality type and curriculum are compatible. The "A" person is likely to be very energetic, and enthusiastic about and attentive to his/her studies.

4. The "C" person is not likely to last very long in an "A" occupation. The "C" and "A" types are opposite on the hexagon. The "A" environment would be too flexible and frustrating for the "C" person, who would want structure and a schedule of activities to follow. The "C" person in this situation would be most likely to channel energy into looking for a new, compatible occupation.

5. The energy level of an "S" person in an "R" job would be very low. The chances for success and stability would be extremely low, since these types are opposite, and characteristics are very dissimilar. The "S" person might experience a high absentee rate from work due to illness or lack of interest. Here again, any energy might be directed into seeking a compatible occupation.

APPENDIX C CONDUCTING CAREER INFORMATION INTERVIEWS

Talking to people about their work is an effective way to gather information in your occupational exploration. Initially, to get comfortable with the idea of interviewing people, talk to family, friends, or anybody you know well. This should help minimize your anxiety about interviewing.

Conduct information-gathering interviews to find answers to the following questions:

1. How did the person get started in that kind of work?

2. What does the person enjoy about his/her work?

3. What does the person dislike about his/her work?

4. Who else does the person know who does similar kinds of work or uses similar skills?

5. What can the person tell you about the employment outlook in his/her occupational field with a particular firm, in a particular locality, or in the nation generally?

In making your initial contact with people, be sure to clarify that you are not interviewing for a job. Instead, you are considering that line of work and simply trying to learn more about it. At the completion of your interview, ask the person for the names of other people who are doing a similar kind of work or using similar skills. Make every effort to get a specific person's name, so that you have someone definite to contact for an additional information interview. Also, ask the person you are interviewing if you may use his/her name in contacting this other individual.

Conduct additional career information interviews, using the process outlined here. Be sure to send a thank-you letter to the person you have seen within one to three days after the interview. For possible future reference, keep a list of all the people you have interviewed or plan to interview. You may even want to keep a special notebook or cards with interview notes on the five questions covered. Include the main things that you learned from each interview. This file will be a rich source of information as you conduct your occupational exploration.

APPENDIX D ENVISIONING PROCESS

DAYDREAMING AND FANTASIZING

Daydreaming and fantasizing are commonly considered undesirable, nonproductive activities. An individual may be criticized for being "just a dreamer," and we worry about people living in a "fantasy world." Such concern is often justified because both daydreaming and fantasizing are destructive when divorced from reality and action. However, dreaming and fantasizing can be effectively used to reduce stress, conquer fears and phobias, or plan careers and lives.[1] Specifically, constructive fantasizing can help people develop their inner resources to find imaginative solutions to problem, to discover ingenious alternatives, and to invent original goals for career/life planning. By preparing and mentally rehearsing for the future, constructive fantasizing also builds confidence. This is the power of suggestion.

The constructive use of fantasy has been variously called guided fantasy, inner imagery, and creative imagining. We refer to productive fantasizing as the envisioning process.

THE LEFT AND RIGHT HEMISPHERES OF THE BRAIN

Recent research has shown that the left and right hemispheres of the human brain perform two completely different functions. In the typical right-handed person, the left hemisphere of the brain is the center of logical thought, language, and mathematical reasoning. The primary functions of the left brain have to do with rational thinking, analytical thought, and intellectual activity such as reading, writing, and classifying. The right hemisphere, in contrast, is the seat of intuition, creativity, holistic thought, and symbolic thinking. It is in the right brain where the power to synthesize, dream, and acquire self-awareness exists. In his book, *The Three Boxes of Life,* Richard Bolles points out that the left side of the brain is the crucial hemisphere for wordsmiths, mathematicians, and scientists. The right side of the brain is crucial for artists, craftspeople, and musicians.[2] Apparently, the left and right brain functions are reversed for left-handed people.[3]

USING THE RIGHT HEMISPHERE

While the left hemisphere may work best under pressure, the right operates best in a state of relaxation. To facilitate right-hemisphere use, you need conditions that best enable you to relax while remaining mentally alert. Right-hemisphere functioning is not so much a thinking process as it is a fantasizing process. Right-hemisphere information is experienced as spontaneous awareness or intuition rather than as deliberate or concentrated thoughts. Your right-hemisphere insights are more likely to be images and other sensations than ideas.

---

[1] James Morgan and Thomas Skovalt, "Using Inner Experience: Fantasy and Daydreams in Career Counseling," *Journal of Counseling Psychology* 24 (1977): 391–397.

[2] Richard N. Bolles, *The Three Boxes of Life* (Berkeley, CA: Ten Speed Press, 1978) 96.

[3] For further information on the two hemispheres of the brain, read Robert E. Ornstein, *The Psychology of Consciousness* (New York: Viking Press, 1972).

Before starting an envisioning process, define your task or problem that would benefit from right-hemisphere insight or resolution. Using the left hemisphere of your brain to define your concern opens the way for a spontaneously acquired right-hemisphere response. This spontaneous insight is the breakthrough that people often have after they have been struggling over some issue or problem for considerable time without coming to a logical resolution. When you have struggled with some problem until you were about ready to give up, perhaps you then put aside the task. After taking a nap, going for a walk, or engaging in some other low-key activity, did the solution ever suddenly pop into your mind? If so, you have experienced how the right and left hemispheres of the brain function together. This phenomenon is often reported by people who have achieved sudden creative breakthroughs when they shifted from intensive mental concentration to a relaxed state. How or why this happens is a mystery.

Once the creative breakthrough has been achieved, it needs then to be translated into language by the left hemisphere so it will be fully usable and communicable. Einstein is said to have intuitively achieved right-hemisphere understanding of his famous theory of relativity before he was able to figure it out logically or communicate it to others.

THE ENVISIONING PROCESS

When using the envisioning process, we suggest you follow these steps:

1. Make arrangements to be quiet and completely uninterrupted for twenty minutes to one hour. That may mean turning down your phone, not answering the doorbell, and ensuring that someone does not walk in on you during the process.

2. Verbalize, write, or ponder (left-hemisphere processes) what you would like to accomplish with the right-hemisphere intuitive process.

3. Sit in a straight back chair or lie on your back on a carpeted floor.

   a. If you sit in a chair, sit erect with your back straight, your feet flat on the floor, head facing straight forward, and shoulders level and relaxed. Sitting this way helps reduce muscle tension and facilitates a general state of relaxation.

   b. If you recline on the floor, lie flat on your back with your feet spread slightly apart and your arms flat on the floor, palms up, about six to twelve inches away from your sides.

4. Close your eyes. While remaining awake:

   a. Relax the muscles between your eyes, and experience the flow of energy released from the previously tensed muscles.

   b. Relax the muscles in your jaw and chin while letting your mouth drop slightly open.

   c. Continue relaxing your body, one part at a time, by concentrating on and then loosening your tensed muscles, letting any tension flow out of your body.

   d. Take deep and even breaths, and consciously relax your body, starting with your toes and feet and working progressively upwards to your head.

   Note: As you relax, you may notice a flowing sensation throughout your body. That is caused by the energy released from tightly held muscles that are now relaxed.

5. In this relaxed state, just let your mind go. Do not consciously think or try to force your thoughts; just let them come freely and spontaneously.

   a. Do not try to figure out the meaning of anything you may be experiencing while in a relaxed state. To do so may result in switching from right- to left-hemisphere functioning of your brain.

   b. Remain relaxed and detached from your thoughts and mental imagery. Just let happen what will, and be an observer of your mental processes as if you were viewing a movie in your mind.

6. As you are nearing the end of the process, decide how you want to feel when you finish the process, and then allow yourself to feel that way.

7. When you are finished, come out of your relaxed state gradually. It can be a bit of a shock to your system if you bolt out of a relaxed condition (or are jolted out) too quickly. Begin by moving your feet and/or hands about slowly, recalling your external surroundings. When you are ready, open your eyes.

8. Give yourself a few minutes of detached inactivity as you return to fully conscious thoughts. Then, before doing anything else, begin recording any insights that you acquired during the envisioning process. Do this immediately, so that you will not forget and so that you translate your envisioned insights into language.

   a. Write down what happened in the process, even if you are not aware of any significant insights you had during the process. Sometimes, the process of writing is necessary to make you aware of new insights acquired from envisioning.

   b. By writing, you are likely to more fully understand the insights you had. You also will produce a written record to assist you in career decision making and planning for the future.

9. You may find it helpful to repeat the same envisioning process over several days, continually building and expanding on previous insights.

10. You may also want to discuss your insights, acquired from envisioning, with an interested listener to develop your understanding further.

APPENDIX E

PERSONALITY AND INTEREST ASSESSMENTS

Note: These are psychological assessment instruments that can be purchased only by certified counselors. Individuals may take them at most agencies that provide career counseling services.

California Psychological Inventory (CPI) (Consulting Psychologists Press, 577 College Ave., Palo Alto, CA 94306). The CPI produces a scored report on 20 separate behavioral scales (e.g., dominance, sociability, empathy).

Campbell Interests and Skills Survey (CISS), by David P. Campbell (National Computer Systems, P.O. Box 1294, Minneapolis, MN 55440). Provides a profile of personal interests, relates them to career choices, and compares them with self-rated skills.

Career Passion Revealer & Skills Profiler by David C. Borchard. (Career Counseling Services, RR#1 Box 158, Shepherdstown, WV 25443, Email:OAKWINDS@intrepid.net). The career passion revealer is an assessment to help adults clarify and define their unique style of passion and to see how they might more fully engage their passion in their career and life. The skills profiler provides a self-rating of the competencies associated with passion-based interests. Comparing the two profiles suggests areas in which to capitalize on one's strengths and those in which to concentrate one's development efforts. For further details visit the Career Passion Site at: http://www.careerpassion.com

Deal Me In Question Cards (Career Systems, Inc.; Tel # 800-283-8839). A card sort exercise to help identify your strongest individual interests and arrange them into four categories (data, people, ideas, things).

Myers-Briggs Type Indicator (MBTI) by Isabelle Briggs Myers and Katherine C. Briggs (Consulting Psychologists Press [CPP], Inc., 3803 East Bayshore Rd., P.O. Box 10096, Palo Alto, CA 94303). Delineates 16 personality types, each with its own way of understanding the world and its own strengths and personal challenges.

Self-Directed Search (SDS) by John L. Holland (Psychological Assessment Resources, Inc. [PAR], P.O. Box 998, Odessa, FL 33556). The SDS produces a three-letter code profiling one's individual interests within six general styles. One's three-letter code is then compared to occupations to look for best matches between personal interests and occupational activities.

Strong Interest Inventory (SII), by E.K. Strong, Jr. and Jo-Ida C. Hansen (Consulting Psychologists Press, Inc. [CPP]). The SII generates a profile of an individual's personality style and identifies occupations that match interests. Special reports are available for identifying leadership and management potentials and for providing feedback on leisure interests.

SKILLS ASSESSMENT

Motivated Skill Card Sort by Richard L. Knowdell (Career Research & Testing, Inc., 2005 Hamilton Ave., San Jose, CA 95125, Tel # 800-888-4945). A quick and easy way to identify the motivated skills that are central to personal and career satisfaction and success. Use the cards to assess your proficiency and motivation in 48 separate skill areas.

Functional Skill Cards (Fontelle Gilbert Seminars for Personal Growth, 6501 Inwood Drive, Springfield, VA 22150). This deck of cards contains 90 skills to be sorted into categories based on personal preferences and self-rated competencies.

The New Quick Job-Hunting Map by Richard N. Bolles (Ten Speed Press, P.O. Box 7123, Berkeley, CA 94707). A thorough assessment activity for identifying transferable skills from your personal experience. The map guides you through processes that help identify, classify, and prioritize your "most preferred skills."

Skill Scan Professional Pack (P.O. Box 587, Orinda, CA 94563, Tel # 510-254-2705). A card sort exercise to identify which of the indicated skills you want to play a major, secondary, and minor role in your future work and then sort favorite skills into categories.

BRAIN DOMINANCE AND THINKING STYLES

Learning-Style Inventory by David A. Kolb (McBer & Company Training Resources Group, 173 Newbury Street, Boston MA 02116, Tel # 617-437-7080). A self-scoring, self-interpreting inventory profiling one's dominant mode of learning in four different styles.

Herrmann Brain Dominance Inventory (HBDI) by Ned Herrmann (Applied Creative Services, 2075 Buffalo Creek Rd., Lake Lure, NC 28746). The HBDI generates a personal brain dominance profile showing your thinking-style preferences in four different modes. This information can be very useful in making career choices designed to enhance personal performance.

VALUES CLARIFICATION

Invest in Your Values by Beverly Berstein and Beverly Kaye (Insight Publications, 2252 Beverly Glen Place, Los Angeles, CA 90077, Tel # 310-474-0959). A prioritization process in which you list your top values from a selection of 35 value choices and use a color code to assess the likelihood of achieving your values in your current situation.

Career Anchors by Edgar H. Schein (Pfeiffer & Company, 8517 Production Avenue, San Diego, CA 92121, Tel # 619-578-5900). A self-assessment activity designed for people who have been working for ten years or more to identify their core career-related values from eight general categories.

The Values Scale by Donald E. Super and Dorothy D. Nevill (Consulting Psychologists Press, Inc. CPP). The values scale measures 21 separate values and provides a profile showing your relative degree of strength in each of these.

Career Values Card Sort, by Richard L. Knowdell (Career Research & Testing, 2005 Hamilton Ave., Suite 250, San Jose, CA 95125.) A simple card sort device for examining your personal values.

Values Cards (Fontelle Gilbert, Seminars for Personal Growth, 6501 Inwood Drive, Springfield, VA 22150). A values sort process that helps prioritize values and relate the impact on (1) interaction with others, and (2) conflicts or satisfactions both inside and outside the workplace.

APPENDIX F
SMALL DISCUSSION GROUPS (TRIOS)

By sharing your individual achievements with two other people, your functional-skills identification can progress far more quickly. Why is this? Most people tend to be too critical about themselves, so they ignore certain talents their achievements reveal. Consequently, it can be very difficult for individuals to identify their own skills completely. However, the process of identifying skills that someone else has used is relatively easy.

Start this process by rounding up two volunteers. Ask friends, classmates, or relatives, making sure that they do not have false preconceived ideas about what your talents are or should be. Your two volunteers might even decide to participate in this process themselves. Once you have selected your group members, decide who will be person A, B, and C. Then follow the remaining steps as outlined.

Step 1: Person A reads a story about one of his or her top satisfying achievements while persons B and C listen closely, noting on paper any functional (transferable) skills that they think were used. If the story is not clear, B and C should interrupt by asking the question, *"What did it take for you to do that?"* The pur-

Slow start for a small discussion group.

pose for asking this question is to encourage the storyteller to describe the particular situation more completely. It is important for the listeners (now B and C) to keep asking this question until they fully understand the situation and are able to identify the functional skills involved.

Step 2: Person A next says what functional skills he/she used to make the achievement happen. Person A names and records these skills *before* hearing what B and C have to add.

Step 3: Now, persons B and C respond to person A's story reading. Person B identifies functional skills that he or she heard in the story. When person B is finished, person C repeats the process. Person A, meanwhile, is writing down all the skills that B and C have mentioned.

Step 4: If desired, repeat this entire process, now giving person B the opportunity to read a story while persons A and C listen. Continue as above. For maximum benefit, repeat this process over a period of time until you have uncovered skills from all five stories you wrote in Exercise 2-B.

Murry couldn't decide which discussion group he wanted to attend.

APPENDIX G
PRIORITIZING PROCESS

In many situations, you need to choose your top preference or preferences from among numerous options. While it's easy to choose with just two options, that task becomes much more difficult as the number of options increases. A quick and easy process to find your top preference and rank the remaining choices is the prioritizing process.[1] In this process, you will be choosing between just two items at a time. This greatly facilitates the process of determining overall preferences from a list of items.

To demonstrate how to use this prioritizing process, consider the following list of sample activities for a Saturday night. We have arbitrarily numbered this list without considering preference at this point.

1. roller skating
2. movies
3. supper club
4. Irish pub
5. sports event

6. popular music concert
7. ballet
8. bowling
9. symphony concert
10. dancing

To determine the two most preferred activities you would like to do on Saturday night, you will prioritize the entire list. We have copied each activity from the list in the *Items* blanks down the left-hand side of the sample prioritizing grid on page 293. Once again, we've recorded them in the random order of the original list.

Each number on the right-hand side of the grid corresponds to the same numbered activity. For example, 1 refers to roller skating, 2 to movies, etc. Starting with items 1 and 2 on the list, ask yourself which of the two—roller skating or attending a movie—you would enjoy doing more this Saturday night. Let's assume you say going to the movies. You would then circle item 2 in the pair $\frac{1}{2}$ on the prioritizing grid (see the sample grid). In this way, you have indicated your preference for item 2 when given a choice between 1 and 2. Continue along the top row of the grid, row A, pairing item 1 in turn with items 3, 4, 5, 6, 7, 8, 9, and 10, circling your preference in each pair. For example, when pairing item 1 with item 5, let's assume you would prefer attending a sports event to roller skating, so you would circle item 5 in the pair $\frac{1}{5}$. Continue this forced choice process in rows B through I. If you have done the process correctly, only one choice will be circled in each pair of items, i.e., $\frac{4}{5}$. Make sure you don't end up with two circled items, i.e., $\frac{4}{5}$.

Once you have completed circling the items on the grid, record in the second column the number of times each item has been circled anywhere on the grid. You will use this total to determine final priority ranking. For example, item 2, circled seven times, will rank ahead of item 3, which was circled only six times. In the event of ties, check the grid to see which item is circled when the two are paired against each other. For in-

---

[1.] From *The Three Boxes of Life and How to Get Out of Them,* by Richard N. Bolles, © copyright 1978, by Richard N. Bolles. Used by special permission. Those desiring a copy of the complete book for further reading may procure it from the publisher, Ten Speed Press, P.O. Box 7123, Berkeley, CA 94707.

stance, items 1 and 6 are tied, both having been circled three times. To determine your preference ranking, you merely need to look at the grid to see which item you preferred in your initial assessment. If you look at row A on the sample grid, you can see that item 1 was chosen over item 6. Therefore, item 1, roller skating, wins out over item 6, attending a popular music concert. Similarly, the tie between item 4 and item 7 is resolved in favor of item 4. When you have finished counting the circled numbers, you can see from the sample grid that the first choice for Saturday night is to go to a symphony concert and second choice is to go to a sports event. The final prioritized list then looks like this:

First choice:	symphony concert
Second choice:	sports event
Third choice:	movies
Fourth choice:	supper club
Fifth choice:	Irish pub
Sixth choice:	ballet
Seventh choice:	roller skating
Eighth choice:	popular music concert
Ninth choice:	bowling
Tenth choice:	dancing

This prioritizing process will be used many times throughout the book. You will be using it to prioritize your preferred transferable skills, achievements, self-management skills, values, and people preferences.

This process is an extremely helpful decision-making tool in any situation where you have to make difficult choices from among competing alternatives.

Prioritizing Grid[1] — Sample

Items	Number of Times Circled	Final Prioritized Order
1. roller skating	III	7
2. movies	IIII II	3
3. supper club	IIII I	4
4. Irish pub	IIII	5
5. sports event	IIII III	2
6. popular music concert	III	8
7. ballet	IIII	6
8. bowling	I	9
9. symphony	IIII IIII	1
10. dancing	0	10

Grid

Row									
A	②/1	③/1	④/1	⑤/1	1/6(circled)	1/7(circled)	1/8(circled)	⑨/1	1/10(circled)
B	②/2	2/3(circled)	②/2	⑤/2	②/2	⑦/2	②/2	⑨/2	2/10(circled)
C		③/3	③/3	⑤/3	③/3	③/3	③/3	⑨/3	3/10(circled)
D			④/4	⑤/4	④/4	④/4	④/4	⑨/4	4/10(circled)
E				⑤/5	⑤/5	⑤/5	⑤/5	⑨/5	5/10(circled)
F					⑥/6	⑦/6	⑥/6	⑨/6	6/10(circled)
G						⑦/7	⑦/7	⑨/7	7/10(circled)
H							⑧/8	⑨/8	8/10(circled)
I								⑨/9	9/10

[1] Adapted from *The Three Boxes of Life and How to Get Out of Them*, by Richard N. Bolles, © copyright 1978, by Richard N. Bolles. Used by special permission. Those desiring a copy of the complete book for further reading may procure it from the publisher, Ten Speed Press, P.O. Box 7123, Berkeley, CA 94707.

Prioritizing Grid[1]

Grid

Row									
A	$\frac{1}{2}$	$\frac{1}{3}$	$\frac{1}{4}$	$\frac{1}{5}$	$\frac{1}{6}$	$\frac{1}{7}$	$\frac{1}{8}$	$\frac{1}{9}$	$\frac{1}{10}$
B		$\frac{2}{3}$	$\frac{2}{4}$	$\frac{2}{5}$	$\frac{2}{6}$	$\frac{2}{7}$	$\frac{2}{8}$	$\frac{2}{9}$	$\frac{2}{10}$
C			$\frac{3}{4}$	$\frac{3}{5}$	$\frac{3}{6}$	$\frac{3}{7}$	$\frac{3}{8}$	$\frac{3}{9}$	$\frac{3}{10}$
D				$\frac{4}{5}$	$\frac{4}{6}$	$\frac{4}{7}$	$\frac{4}{8}$	$\frac{4}{9}$	$\frac{4}{10}$
E					$\frac{5}{6}$	$\frac{5}{7}$	$\frac{5}{8}$	$\frac{5}{9}$	$\frac{5}{10}$
F						$\frac{6}{7}$	$\frac{6}{8}$	$\frac{6}{9}$	$\frac{6}{10}$
G							$\frac{7}{8}$	$\frac{7}{9}$	$\frac{7}{10}$
H								$\frac{8}{9}$	$\frac{8}{10}$
I									$\frac{9}{10}$

Items   *Number of Times Circled*   *Final Prioritized Order*

1. _____
2. _____
3. _____
4. _____
5. _____
6. _____
7. _____
8. _____
9. _____
10. _____

[1] Adapted from *The Three Boxes of Life and How to Get Out of Them*, by Richard N. Bolles, © copyright 1978, by Richard N. Bolles. Used by special permission. Those desiring a copy of the complete book for further reading may procure it from the publisher, Ten Speed Press, P.O. Box 7123, Berkeley, CA 94707.

Prioritizing Grid[1]

Row	Grid									Final Prioritized Order	Number of Times Circled	Items
A	1/2	1/3	1/4	1/5	1/6	1/7	1/8	1/9	1/10	_____	_____	1. _____
B	2/3	2/4	2/5	2/6	2/7	2/8	2/9	2/10		_____	_____	2. _____
C	3/4	3/5	3/6	3/7	3/8	3/9	3/10			_____	_____	3. _____
D	4/5	4/6	4/7	4/8	4/9	4/10				_____	_____	4. _____
E	5/6	5/7	5/8	5/9	5/10					_____	_____	5. _____
F	6/7	6/8	6/9	6/10						_____	_____	6. _____
G	7/8	7/9	7/10							_____	_____	7. _____
H	8/9	8/10								_____	_____	8. _____
I	9/10									_____	_____	9. _____
										_____	_____	10. _____

[1] Adapted from *The Three Boxes of Life and How to Get Out of Them*, by Richard N. Bolles, © copyright 1978, by Richard N. Bolles. Used by special permission. Those desiring a copy of the complete book for further reading may procure it from the publisher, Ten Speed Press, P.O. Box 7123, Berkeley, CA 94707.

Prioritizing Grid[1]

Items	Number of Times Circled	Final Prioritized Order	Grid	Row
1.			$\frac{1}{2}$ $\frac{1}{3}$ $\frac{1}{4}$ $\frac{1}{5}$ $\frac{1}{6}$ $\frac{1}{7}$ $\frac{1}{8}$ $\frac{1}{9}$ $\frac{1}{10}$	A
2.			$\frac{2}{3}$ $\frac{2}{4}$ $\frac{2}{5}$ $\frac{2}{6}$ $\frac{2}{7}$ $\frac{2}{8}$ $\frac{2}{9}$ $\frac{2}{10}$	B
3.			$\frac{3}{4}$ $\frac{3}{5}$ $\frac{3}{6}$ $\frac{3}{7}$ $\frac{3}{8}$ $\frac{3}{9}$ $\frac{3}{10}$	C
4.			$\frac{4}{5}$ $\frac{4}{6}$ $\frac{4}{7}$ $\frac{4}{8}$ $\frac{4}{9}$ $\frac{4}{10}$	D
5.			$\frac{5}{6}$ $\frac{5}{7}$ $\frac{5}{8}$ $\frac{5}{9}$ $\frac{5}{10}$	E
6.			$\frac{6}{7}$ $\frac{6}{8}$ $\frac{6}{9}$ $\frac{6}{10}$	F
7.			$\frac{7}{8}$ $\frac{7}{9}$ $\frac{7}{10}$	G
8.			$\frac{8}{9}$ $\frac{8}{10}$	H
9.			$\frac{9}{10}$	I
10.				

[1] Adapted from *The Three Boxes of Life and How to Get Out of Them*, by Richard N. Bolles, © copyright 1978, by Richard N. Bolles. Used by special permission. Those desiring a copy of the complete book for further reading may procure it from the publisher, Ten Speed Press, P.O. Box 7123, Berkeley, CA 94707.

Prioritizing Grid[1]

Row	Grid								
A	1/2	1/3	1/4	1/5	1/6	1/7	1/8	1/9	1/10
B	2/3	2/4	2/5	2/6	2/7	2/8	2/9	2/10	
C	3/4	3/5	3/6	3/7	3/8	3/9	3/10		
D	4/5	4/6	4/7	4/8	4/9	4/10			
E	5/6	5/7	5/8	5/9	5/10				
F	6/7	6/8	6/9	6/10					
G	7/8	7/9	7/10						
H	8/9	8/10							
I	9/10								

Items	Number of Times Circled	Final Prioritized Order
1.		
2.		
3.		
4.		
5.		
6.		
7.		
8.		
9.		
10.		

[1] Adapted from *The Three Boxes of Life and How to Get Out of Them*, by Richard N. Bolles, © copyright 1978, by Richard N. Bolles. Used by special permission. Those desiring a copy of the complete book for further reading may procure it from the publisher, Ten Speed Press, P.O. Box 7123, Berkeley, CA 94707.

Prioritizing Grid[1]

Items	Number of Times Circled	Final Prioritized Order
1.	_____	_____
2.	_____	_____
3.	_____	_____
4.	_____	_____
5.	_____	_____
6.	_____	_____
7.	_____	_____
8.	_____	_____
9.	_____	_____
10.	_____	_____

Grid

Row									
A	1/2	1/3	1/4	1/5	1/6	1/7	1/8	1/9	1/10
B	2/3	2/4	2/5	2/6	2/7	2/8	2/9	2/10	
C	3/4	3/5	3/6	3/7	3/8	3/9	3/10		
D	4/5	4/6	4/7	4/8	4/9	4/10			
E	5/6	5/7	5/8	5/9	5/10				
F	6/7	6/8	6/9	6/10					
G	7/8	7/9	7/10						
H	8/9	8/10							
I	9/10								

[1] Adapted from *The Three Boxes of Life and How to Get Out of Them*, by Richard N. Bolles. © copyright 1978, by Richard N. Bolles. Used by special permission. Those desiring a copy of the complete book for further reading may procure it from the publisher, Ten Speed Press, P.O. Box 7123, Berkeley, CA 94707.

Prioritizing Grid[1]

Items	Number of Times Circled	Final Prioritized Order
1. ___	___	___
2. ___	___	___
3. ___	___	___
4. ___	___	___
5. ___	___	___
6. ___	___	___
7. ___	___	___
8. ___	___	___
9. ___	___	___
10. ___	___	___

Grid

Row	Pairs
A	1/2 1/3 1/4 1/5 1/6 1/7 1/8 1/9 1/10
B	2/3 2/4 2/5 2/6 2/7 2/8 2/9 2/10
C	3/4 3/5 3/6 3/7 3/8 3/9 3/10
D	4/5 4/6 4/7 4/8 4/9 4/10
E	5/6 5/7 5/8 5/9 5/10
F	6/7 6/8 6/9 6/10
G	7/8 7/9 7/10
H	8/9 8/10
I	9/10

[1] Adapted from *The Three Boxes of Life and How to Get Out of Them*, by Richard N. Bolles, © copyright 1978, by Richard N. Bolles. Used by special permission. Those desiring a copy of the complete book for further reading may procure it from the publisher, Ten Speed Press, P.O. Box 7123, Berkeley, CA 94707.

Prioritizing Grid[1]

Items	Number of Times Circled	Final Prioritized Order	Grid									Row
1.	—	—	$\frac{1}{2}$	$\frac{1}{3}$	$\frac{1}{4}$	$\frac{1}{5}$	$\frac{1}{6}$	$\frac{1}{7}$	$\frac{1}{8}$	$\frac{1}{9}$	$\frac{1}{10}$	A
2.	—	—	$\frac{2}{3}$	$\frac{2}{4}$	$\frac{2}{5}$	$\frac{2}{6}$	$\frac{2}{7}$	$\frac{2}{8}$	$\frac{2}{9}$	$\frac{2}{10}$		B
3.	—	—		$\frac{3}{4}$	$\frac{3}{5}$	$\frac{3}{6}$	$\frac{3}{7}$	$\frac{3}{8}$	$\frac{3}{9}$	$\frac{3}{10}$		C
4.	—	—			$\frac{4}{5}$	$\frac{4}{6}$	$\frac{4}{7}$	$\frac{4}{8}$	$\frac{4}{9}$	$\frac{4}{10}$		D
5.	—	—				$\frac{5}{6}$	$\frac{5}{7}$	$\frac{5}{8}$	$\frac{5}{9}$	$\frac{5}{10}$		E
6.	—	—					$\frac{6}{7}$	$\frac{6}{8}$	$\frac{6}{9}$	$\frac{6}{10}$		F
7.	—	—						$\frac{7}{8}$	$\frac{7}{9}$	$\frac{7}{10}$		G
8.	—	—							$\frac{8}{9}$	$\frac{8}{10}$		H
9.	—	—								$\frac{9}{10}$		I
10.	—	—										

[1] Adapted from *The Three Boxes of Life and How to Get Out of Them*, by Richard N. Bolles, © copyright 1978, by Richard N. Bolles. Used by special permission. Those desiring a copy of the complete book for further reading may procure it from the publisher, Ten Speed Press, P.O. Box 7123, Berkeley, CA 94707.

Prioritizing Grid[1]

Items	Number of Times Circled	Final Prioritized Order	Row	Grid
1.			A	$\frac{1}{2}$ $\frac{1}{3}$ $\frac{1}{4}$ $\frac{1}{5}$ $\frac{1}{6}$ $\frac{1}{7}$ $\frac{1}{8}$ $\frac{1}{9}$ $\frac{1}{10}$
2.			B	$\frac{2}{3}$ $\frac{2}{4}$ $\frac{2}{5}$ $\frac{2}{6}$ $\frac{2}{7}$ $\frac{2}{8}$ $\frac{2}{9}$ $\frac{2}{10}$
3.			C	$\frac{3}{4}$ $\frac{3}{5}$ $\frac{3}{6}$ $\frac{3}{7}$ $\frac{3}{8}$ $\frac{3}{9}$ $\frac{3}{10}$
4.			D	$\frac{4}{5}$ $\frac{4}{6}$ $\frac{4}{7}$ $\frac{4}{8}$ $\frac{4}{9}$ $\frac{4}{10}$
5.			E	$\frac{5}{6}$ $\frac{5}{7}$ $\frac{5}{8}$ $\frac{5}{9}$ $\frac{5}{10}$
6.			F	$\frac{6}{7}$ $\frac{6}{8}$ $\frac{6}{9}$ $\frac{6}{10}$
7.			G	$\frac{7}{8}$ $\frac{7}{9}$ $\frac{7}{10}$
8.			H	$\frac{8}{9}$ $\frac{8}{10}$
9.			I	$\frac{9}{10}$
10.				

[1] Adapted from *The Three Boxes of Life and How to Get Out of Them*, by Richard N. Bolles, © copyright 1978, by Richard N. Bolles. Used by special permission. Those desiring a copy of the complete book for further reading may procure it from the publisher, Ten Speed Press, P.O. Box 7123, Berkeley, CA 94707.

Prioritizing Grid[1]

Items	Number of Times Circled	Final Prioritized Order
1.		
2.		
3.		
4.		
5.		
6.		
7.		
8.		
9.		
10.		

Grid

Row	Grid
A	$\frac{1}{2}\ \frac{1}{3}\ \frac{1}{4}\ \frac{1}{5}\ \frac{1}{6}\ \frac{1}{7}\ \frac{1}{8}\ \frac{1}{9}\ \frac{1}{10}$
B	$\frac{2}{3}\ \frac{2}{4}\ \frac{2}{5}\ \frac{2}{6}\ \frac{2}{7}\ \frac{2}{8}\ \frac{2}{9}\ \frac{2}{10}$
C	$\frac{3}{4}\ \frac{3}{5}\ \frac{3}{6}\ \frac{3}{7}\ \frac{3}{8}\ \frac{3}{9}\ \frac{3}{10}$
D	$\frac{4}{5}\ \frac{4}{6}\ \frac{4}{7}\ \frac{4}{8}\ \frac{4}{9}\ \frac{4}{10}$
E	$\frac{5}{6}\ \frac{5}{7}\ \frac{5}{8}\ \frac{5}{9}\ \frac{5}{10}$
F	$\frac{6}{7}\ \frac{6}{8}\ \frac{6}{9}\ \frac{6}{10}$
G	$\frac{7}{8}\ \frac{7}{9}\ \frac{7}{10}$
H	$\frac{8}{9}\ \frac{8}{10}$
I	$\frac{9}{10}$

[1] Adapted from *The Three Boxes of Life and How to Get Out of Them*, by Richard N. Bolles, © copyright 1978, by Richard N. Bolles. Used by special permission. Those desiring a copy of the complete book for further reading may procure it from the publisher, Ten Speed Press, P.O. Box 7123, Berkeley, CA 94707.

Prioritizing Grid[1]

Items	Number of Times Circled	Final Prioritized Order
1. _____	_____	_____
2. _____	_____	_____
3. _____	_____	_____
4. _____	_____	_____
5. _____	_____	_____
6. _____	_____	_____
7. _____	_____	_____
8. _____	_____	_____
9. _____	_____	_____
10. _____	_____	_____

Grid

Row									
A	$\frac{1}{2}$	$\frac{1}{3}$	$\frac{1}{4}$	$\frac{1}{5}$	$\frac{1}{6}$	$\frac{1}{7}$	$\frac{1}{8}$	$\frac{1}{9}$	$\frac{1}{10}$
B		$\frac{2}{3}$	$\frac{2}{4}$	$\frac{2}{5}$	$\frac{2}{6}$	$\frac{2}{7}$	$\frac{2}{8}$	$\frac{2}{9}$	$\frac{2}{10}$
C			$\frac{3}{4}$	$\frac{3}{5}$	$\frac{3}{6}$	$\frac{3}{7}$	$\frac{3}{8}$	$\frac{3}{9}$	$\frac{3}{10}$
D				$\frac{4}{5}$	$\frac{4}{6}$	$\frac{4}{7}$	$\frac{4}{8}$	$\frac{4}{9}$	$\frac{4}{10}$
E					$\frac{5}{6}$	$\frac{5}{7}$	$\frac{5}{8}$	$\frac{5}{9}$	$\frac{5}{10}$
F						$\frac{6}{7}$	$\frac{6}{8}$	$\frac{6}{9}$	$\frac{6}{10}$
G							$\frac{7}{8}$	$\frac{7}{9}$	$\frac{7}{10}$
H								$\frac{8}{9}$	$\frac{8}{10}$
I									$\frac{9}{10}$

[1] Adapted from *The Three Boxes of Life and How to Get Out of Them*, by Richard N. Bolles. © copyright 1978, by Richard N. Bolles. Used by special permission. Those desiring a copy of the complete book for further reading may procure it from the publisher, Ten Speed Press, P.O. Box 7123, Berkeley, CA 94707.

INDEX

Transferable Skill Assessment
(exercise), 175–176

U

Uncovering Your Hidden Values
(exercise), 149–154
University of Waterloo's Values
Assessment, 149

V

Values
discovering, 149, 151, 156
exercises for, 147–156
v. needs, 144–149, 156

W

What Can I do with this Major?, 128
What Color is Your Parachute?,
236, 258
What's Your Number? (exercise), 90
Working. *See* Job search;
Occupations

Y

Yellow Pages telephone directory,
252
Your Career/Life Decisions of the
Past (exercise), 23–24
Your Career/Life Roles (exercise),
23
Your Life and Work (exercise),
21–22